The author welcomes comments and will answer any questions submitted by readers to theseprophets@gmail.com

These Prophets

A Comprehensive Study in
Biblical Prophecy Interfaced with
International Developments

David Lance Dean

These Prophets

Copyright © 2018 by David Lance Dean. All rights reserved.

No part of this publication may be reproduced, stored in a retrieval system or transmitted in any way by any means, electronic, mechanical, photocopy, recording or otherwise without the prior permission of the author except as provided by USA copyright law.

The opinions expressed by the author are not necessarily those of URLink Print and Media.

1603 Capitol Ave., Suite 310 Cheyenne, Wyoming USA 82001
1-888-980-6523 | admin@urlinkpublishing.com

URLink Print and Media is committed to excellence in the publishing industry.

Book design copyright © 2018 by URLink Print and Media. All rights reserved.

Published in the United States of America
ISBN 978-1-64367-036-2 (Paperback)
ISBN 978-1-64367-037-9 (Digital)

Spirituality
14.09.12

Introduction and Foreword

Oftentimes book readers do not read the introduction to books but rather move forward immediately into the books contents. The author feels strongly that in the case of THESE PROPHETS you take the time to read and consider this brief forward to the content. The reason being is at least twofold. First, the interpretation of the Scripture is not always readily discerned and that applies with an even greater emphasis when considering biblical prophecy which contains deep meaning and also including texts which in some sense are mysteries. These mysteries were written with the intentions of the author, the Holy Spirit which will require an enlightenment provided by the Holy Spirit. Secondly, the truths revealed in the following chapters have required a life time of study and will not be found in most commentaries which at best are incomplete and many times are inaccurate. Also, you need to recognize the use of metaphorical language.

The truths of the Bible are revealed to us by the principle of precept upon precept and line upon line, here a little and there a little as we are instructed in the twenty-eighth chapter of Isiah. I have made an effort to order the chapters in such a way that you can build upon a foundation as you move forward in the book. I would recommend that you read the text with a Bible nearby so if you need to gain the benefit of a larger context you may refer to the appropriate passage and gain the benefits of that larger context. I have used the King James Version for all quotations because that is the version which I was nurtured in and it has a familiarity to me.

I have found it to be almost always accurate particularly if in your study you use a concordance for word studies and clarification of word meanings from the original languages. I have provided much commentary to verify an accurate interpretation to the scriptures which are cited throughout.

In your reading of the text I urge to take it slowly for the many truths which are presented contain certain complexities that require your thoughtful consideration and likely you will need to open your Bible in some cases to gather in the full content and expression of certain difficult passages. I commend the examination of the content into your careful and thoughtful scrutiny. My prayer is that you will be blessed and enlightened.

Bound by the liberty of his eternal mercy.

David Lance Dean

Laying Some Necessary Foundations with Daniel

Daniel lays the prophetic foundations, which carries us through history from his day until the end of the age.

Daniel was a special messenger who gained favor with the Lord because he loved, he believed AND OBEYED HIM COMPLETELY, although he spent the majority of his life as a captive in Babylon.

Daniel's faith was thoroughly tried and he was found faithful (tested in the den of lions) because he would not defile himself or turn from the tenets of the law.

The captivity can only be understood in terms of judgment executed on the people of God because of their departure from the truth i.e. sin. Daniel's personal experience in captivity had to do with the sins of his people.

Understanding the captivities of Israel and Judah provide basic foundations for discerning the meaning of future judgments yet to come upon the people of God *"because they received not the love of the truth that they might be saved"*. II Thes. 2:10.

All of the examples and experience of the covenant people of God under the Old Testament economy are for instruction that we may understand his precepts, judgments and righteousness.

Daniel was given extreme wisdom and understanding to interpret dreams and visions.

The first unveiling of his wisdom came with the interpretation of Nebuchadnezzar's dream. This dream unveils an overview of God's plan for the world through to the end and the final judgment.

God's wisdom was to first provide us through Daniel with an overview before filling in the details so we can view the whole spectrum in outline and then make application of more specific details as they relate to the end o the age.

We need to start our prophetic journey with Daniel as he interprets Nebuchadnezzar's dream. I would suggest that your reading experience would be enhanced as you approach the various topical sections to follow by having a Bible available for reference and comparison. The Scripture quotations are from the King James Version.

Contents

Chapter 1: Nebuchadnezzar's Dream 1
Chapter 2: Daniel's Dream..5
Chapter 3: The Beginning Of Sorrows................................13
Chapter 4: The Great Tribulation: John's Revelations.............18
Chapter 5: Measuring The Temple.....................................24
Chapter 6: Measuring The Temple: The Woman and
 the Man-Child 32
Chapter 7: To Him Who Overcomes 38
Chapter 8: The Little Horn 46
Chapter 9: Daniel's Seventy Weeks....................................52
Chapter 10: Who Then Is Israel?...60
Chapter 11: Free Masonary, The Order of the Illuminatti
 and The Revelation of Mystery Babylon 67
Chapter 12: Beholding Heaven's Throne..............................80
Chapter 13: Daniel's Final Vision-Tribulation: Daniel's Vision.....86
Chapter 14: Shaking Of The Heavens And The Earth 93
Chapter 15: The Gathering..97
Chapter 16: The Seventh Seal (First Four Trumpets):
 The Day of the Lamb's Wrath 101
Chapter 17: Woe, Woe . . . And Woe 105
Chapter 18: The Little Book Open....................................114
Chapter 19: The Abomination Of Desolation.....................119
Chapter 20: The Church In The Wilderness......................126
Chapter 21: The Zionism Deception 133
Chapter 22: Understanding The Beast 144

Chapter 23: Mark Of The Beast..153
Chapter 24: The Lamb On Mount Zion..................................156
Chapter 25: The Seven Last Plagues
            (Six Leading To The Seventh)................................162
Chapter 26: Armageddon 166
Chapter 27: The Seventh Trumpet And Pouring Out Of
            The Seventh Vial…...169
Chapter 28: The First Resurrection And The Second Death 176
Chapter 29: The Book Of Life..181
Chapter 30: Gog And Magog 185
Chapter 31: The New Heavens And The New Earth 189
Chapter 32: A Kingdom Of Priests 194

Epilogue..203

Chapter One

NEBUCHADNEZZAR'S DREAM

A good place to reasonably begin this search for understanding of the prophetic record is in the second chapter of Daniel. At this point we have met and seen that Daniel was a young man carried away into the Babylonian captivity. We find him to be full of faith, undefiled and with an unwavering devotion to God. These qualities of character were the reason he was chosen to have revealed to him these truths that form the foundations of prophetic understanding through the rest of the Old Testament and on to the very end of the age.

The king of Babylon who Daniel was in subjection to had a dream. It was a dream, which although it greatly troubled him, he could not recall to his mind either its content or meaning. Because he was troubled in his spirit he called for the magicians, sorcerers, astrologers and Chaldeans who were deemed to possess the secrets of wisdom and would be able to explain to him the content as well as the interpretation. They were unable to do so and protested that if he could not provide the content of the dream it was an impossible thing he was asking of them and expecting of them to provide the interpretation. He persisted in his demands and past a sentence of death upon them and all of the wise men of the realm for their failure to satisfy his demands. Daniel was called upon and receiving this decree from the king Daniel came forth blessing and extolling the God of heaven to whom he ascribed to be the source of all true wisdom and understanding and declared to the king that his God was able to reveal the king's dream to Daniel as well as the interpretation. He also entered a plea with the king to have mercy on those who were unable to give an answer. He made his declaration that there is a God in heaven who reveals secrets. *"…he giveth wisdom to the wise and knowledge to them of understanding."* (Daniel 2:21 in part).

"Thou O king sawest and behold a great image" (Daniel 2:31). You beheld its excellent brightness that stood before you, and the image was very terrible. The image was that of a man and it began with a great head of fine gold. The breasts and arms of the image were of silver, the belly and thighs were or brass, and his legs of iron and his feet partly of iron but mingled with miry clay. And then you beheld it until a stone was cut out without hands, and it smote the feet of the image which was partly iron and partly of clay, and brake them in pieces. Then was the iron, the clay, the brass, the silver and the gold, broken in pieces altogether and became as the chaff of the summer threshing floor, and the wind carried them away that there was no place found for them. And then the stone that smote the image became a great mountain and filled the whole earth. This then is the image that was seen and this is what happened to the image. What then is the interpretation of the dream and the meaning of the image in all of its parts and what is the significance of what ultimately befell the image?

"Thou O king are a king of kings and the God of heaven has given you a kingdom, power, strength and glory." (Daniel 2:37). Daniel tells us that he kingdom of Babylon under its potentate was that head of gold. The image and the interpretation of the parts become a representation of the kingdoms of this world i.e. those significant kingdoms and empires, which were structured by men and allowed by God to have dominion and to rule in this earthly realm. And then afterward shall raise a kingdom inferior to you, and then a third kingdom, which will bear rule over the whole earth.

Before explaining the fourth kingdom necessarily in some detail we will come to understand in the later dreams and visions of Daniel that the second kingdom was that which we know both historically and biblically to be the Medio-Persian Empire. It was a two headed coalition of the Medes and Persians which overthrew the Babylonian empire at the end of a seventy-year period of judgment upon Judah for her sins and departure from God. The Medes and Persians prevailed for a period of about two hundred years holding dominion and bearing power and rule. Under their dominion there came a release for a remnant of the people of the Lord, as indeed some were allowed to return to Jerusalem and provision was made for them to rebuild the temple, the wall, and the city. We will cover these events more thoroughly in a later chapter.

The third kingdom represented and described as the belly and thighs of brass was that vast empire established by the Macedonian, Alexander the Great, tutored by the philosopher Aristotle, and destined to establish and spread Greek culture, he gathered a great army and swept from west to east conquering all that was before him. In a short span of time in about 332 B.C. E. he became a world ruler. He was a great warrior and at a very young age, while still in his twenties he conquered all of the then known civilized world, and then not long after his conquest he died, but not in battle at the young age of thirty-two. Likewise, more will be added concerning the conquest and significance of Alexander in a later chapter as we examine the further dreams and visions of Daniel.

The fourth kingdom represented by the legs of iron and running down to the feet and toes partly of iron and partly of miry clay are of the utmost significance for our present understanding because these images take us to the end of the age and the return and judgment of Jesus Christ upon the kingdoms of this world. The legs are lengthy and made of iron. They represent the Roman Empire, later become known as the Holy Roman Empire in which there was a dividing but also a continuance being dominated by the Roman Catholic Church. The beginning of conquest by the Romans began to manifest power about forty-seven B.C.E., forming itself eventually into a Republic and ultimately into a vast and great empire. We know the Roman empire prevailed over the world for many centuries, was ultimately divided but continued to exercise power and influence into the later periods of western civilization, and we see that this influence is recognized down to the feet of the image which retains part of the imagery of iron, and then introduced is the miry clay. The scriptural description is that it is partly strong and partly divided. Notably the final expression of empire is world government and the plan for its establishment is now well advanced bringing the nations of the world together into an evil coalition, which can be likened, in many ways to the tower of Babel. This is an orchestration of the utmost evil having as its author Lucifer himself. Its form will take a dividing into ten regional governments as is symbolized by the ten toes of the image. We will have much more to say about this New World Order, its aspirants, framers, government and powerful world dominion in later considerations as we look in depth into the Revelation in chapters 13, 17 and 18. For now we must conclude the description and interpretation of the image in Nebuchadnezzar's dream, which Daniel perceived and described to the king of Babylon.

The final imagery of the dream is a stone which was cut out without hands which smote the image upon his feet which were of iron and miry clay and brake them in pieces, and then all of the materials and composition of the image were broken in pieces together and became as the chaff of the summer threshing floor and the wind carried them away and there was no place found for them. Then the stone, which smote the image, became a great mountain and filled the whole earth. Clearly we see and understand that in the days of those kings shall the Lord Jesus Christ return in power and great glory bringing judgment upon the kingdoms of this world and bringing them into utter destruction. Then shall it be said the kingdoms of this world and this present earth shall be passed from existence and become the everlasting kingdom of our God and of his Christ and this kingdom will endure forever. *". .... the dream is certain and the interpretation thereof is sure."* (Daniel 2:45 in part).

Chapter Two

DANIEL'S DREAM

We move now from the interpretation of the dream of Nebuchadnezzar King or Babylon to Daniel's own dream. The text is the seventh chapter of Daniel.

In the first year of Belshazzar King of Babylon while he remained in the captivity, the Lord gave Daniel a dream and visions in his head. Daniel saw in his dream four beasts come up from the sea, and they were each different, each one was diverse from the others.

The first beast was by description as being like a lion and having eagle's wings, and Daniel beheld until the wings were plucked, and it was lifted up from the earth and made to stand upon its feet as a man and a man's heart was given to it. (Comp. Daniel 7:1-4). In the symbolism of this first beast we see two significant likenesses in the beginning. Like a lion portrays the expression of power and dominion, and the eagle's wings express that which is very high and lofty. This again is a metaphorical picture of the kingdom of Babylon and its original King Nebuchadnezzar. We see in the early chapters of Daniel that the king was very taken with the image in his dream and he set up his own great image to be worshipped. He put on an elaborate ceremony and made overtures to his own greatness, even to the extent of placing a sentence of death upon those who would refuse to worship the image. A testimony of God's power was given the king when he cast the three Hebrews into the great furnace of fire and they emerged unscathed. We see in the two following chapters something of a great spiritual awakening takes place in the life of the king when God deals with him and brings him very low to acknowledge and worship the God of heaven. I believe we have here in the symbolism an expression of this transforming experience. Daniel beheld until the wings were plucked and it was lifted up from the earth and a man's heart was given unto it. I believe that is what is being portrayed is the experience of Nebuchadnezzar as the King of Babylon; first very pompous and lifted up in his own glory, and then something very different after he was humbled and turned by experiencing the hand of God upon him. He became one who glorified the God of heaven. My conclusion is that the first beast in Daniel's dream is Babylon personified by its king.

"And behold another beast, a second like unto a bear and it raised up itself on one side, and it had three ribs in the mouth of it between the teeth of it: and they said unto it arise and devour much flesh." (Daniel 7:5). The description of the bear and that which was done leads us to behold the overthrowing empire of the Medes and Persians. We know that there were two distinct peoples in coalition forming the Medio- Persian Empire—the Medes and the Persians. We see the bear lifting itself up on one side of it. Historically Cyrus the Mede came first to power *"lifting up itself on one side"* at the overthrow of the Babylonians. Many of the later kings were Persians. Earlier in the histories of the relations between these peoples the Medes were dominant. Later the Persians and thus Persian kings came to dominate. They established a very vast empire encompassing a landmass from Greece on the West to India on the East, and being divided into 120 provinces. This great bear consumed much flesh having the three rib bones remaining in his mouth. These three would figuratively represent the empires enveloping the region. These former great world empires included the Babylonians, as well as the remnants of the Assyrians and Egyptians. We see from the Scriptures that at the end of the captivity period that God moved in the hearts of more than one of the kings to bring about a release and allow the return of a remnant of Jews to rebuild both the temple and the city of Jerusalem. This history is fascinating and significant spiritually but is not in the mainstream of our subject matter so we

will not make further comment concerning these developments. The empire of the Medes and Persians survived also for approximately two hundred years.

"And after this I beheld, and lo another, like a leopard, which had upon the back of it four wings of a foul; the beast had four heads; and dominion was given unto it." (Daniel 7:6). We are now looking at the kingdom of Alexander the Great. Alexander came from the western region of Greece and Macedonia with a great army and with his ambition to conquer the world which he proceeded to do in a very few years. His victories and subsequent dominion from his homeland all the way to India is probably the most notable conquest in history having been accomplished in about twelve years. The significance of his dominion is highlighted by the fact that he brought with him the Greek culture, language and influence, which had a wide effect on the peoples, and territory he conquered. The philosopher Aristotle who had a profound effect on his thinking mentored him and he embraced that cultural philosophy and influence which came to be known as Hellenism. The establishment of his vast influence provided a backdrop for the entry of the Messiah into the world and the ultimate spreading of the gospel assisted by the wide acceptance of the Greek language. We see that Greek became accepted as a quasi-universal language.

We would note in the symbolism that the four wings on the leopard speak of the swift stealth of the leopard in gaining the conquest between 336 B.C.E. and 325 B.C.E. The four heads represent the four generals assisting him in victory and among whom the kingdom was divided after his death. There will be more to say on the subject of these divisions later in our prophetic search.

After this in the night visions a fourth great beast a fourth great beast dreadful and terrible and strong exceedingly, and it had great iron teeth, it devoured and brake in pieces, and it stamped the residue with his feet, and it was diverse from all of the beasts that went before it, and it had ten horns. I considered the horns there was another little horn, which came up among them and before whom three of the first horns were plucked up by the roots and behold in this horn were eyes as the eyes of a man and a mouth speaking great things. " (Daniel 7:7-8).Let us look at the interpretation of this fourth beast as it has been revealed thus far. We remember from Nebuchadnezzar's image seen in his dream and interpreted by Daniel that the image came down to the feet and ten toes partly of iron and partly of miry clay. We saw the ten toes on the feet in the image with the iron and miry clay mingled together.

What we have seen at this point are these four beasts as Daniel has revealed his dream and has set it down in the scriptures. The manifestation of the fourth beast is before us prophetically. It now becomes extremely important for those who would name the Lord to gain wisdom and understanding of every aspect of the prophetic record. There exists a great delusion in the realm of the evangelical Christian influence, which has led to significant false and misleading doctrinal interpretations concerning the unfolding of end time prophetic events. My motive here is not to be critical of other believers as my early roots in the faith were in association with those we would identify as evangelicals. However, as we are approaching the soon to come final fulfillment of the scriptures, the return of the Lord in judgment, and the establishment his kingdom in the new heavens and new earth. These issues of false and misleading doctrines must be exposed, and the truth must be made available to all amongst the people of God who have an ear to hear. I hope that none will take offence and that the hearts of all who have engaged themselves with reading this prophetic discourse will be opened as we carefully consider the exposition of these truths as we go forward which will be vitally important to understand in these perilous days which are coming upon us. I make this caveat at this point in my writings because much of what lies ahead will be in at least in some sense "new ground" for many believers, and I seek not to offend, but to carefully expound, explain, and support each declaration and conclusion with the Word of God to unveil the truth. What I am asking in a word is hear me out.

In order to begin to understand this fourth beast in Daniel's dream who is great and terrible and that was diverse from all that had gone before it we must look upon the current existing world scene as a whole, which is in a word **internationalism.** For many years and even decades we have heard much theological discussion about the "Revived Roman Empire", the European Union, and the rebirth of Israel as a nation. I think in each instance of these there is much of that which has been preached and taught about the significance of the foregoing has been inaccurate and most certainly premature, and has lead to theological confusion in the Lord's people in so far as the broad subject matter of eschatology (the study of end time prophetic events) is concerned. As the first three kingdoms identified in Daniel's dream dominated the entire civilized world in the time of their dominion, we will likewise only understand the power and influence of this final great beast as we recognize that it shall dominate the entire world. This final beast will be a universal world government bringing the entire world under the influence of the powers of darkness. Consider in this context the United Nations headquartered in New York. There will ultimately be a unification leading to the worship of the devil through his chief agent, the Antichrist, also identified as the son of perdition. The devil has aspired from his fall to be worshipped as a god. He has declared that he will ascend into heaven, and exalt his throne above the stars of God. His ultimate objective is to be as the most High.(See Isaiah 14:13-14). In execution of his plan to attain to his evil aspirations he must bring into spiritual captivity and bring under his control the peoples and tongues and nations of the whole world *"and all of the world wondered after the beast"* (Rev. 13:3).

The United Nations has been established as the framework for world government and those who serve the powers of darkness are rapidly implementing this international agenda. They have planned and will put into place a New World Order. This is the fourth beast of Daniel's dream. We see already in place the World Trade Organization (WTO), International Monetary Fund (IMF), the World Health Organization, World Court, and many other lesser institutions which have been given one goal and that to being to unify and control the world under a single governing world system in one organized body. The sovereignty of nations is to be destroyed and the new order will consist of the division of the world into ten regions each having a regional government. This is represented by the ten toes envisioned in Nebuchadnezzar's dream. The prototype is the

European Union which is basically a regional government. These are also the ten horns of Daniel's dream. The European Union is but the first of those regions with nine others to follow. The United States will be enveloped into the North American Union with a loss of national sovereignty and the Constitutional guarantees of individual liberties and unalienable rights. This union is the well planned and soon to be implemented as a consolidation of Canada, Mexico and the United States. There are further plans and foundations well laid for the African Union, the South American Union, and all of the others bringing the total to ten, partly strong and partly broken *"as iron mingled with miry clay"*. We will be adding to these precepts as we move forward in unfolding the prophesies of Daniel and John revealing the soon to be realized through wars and conflicts a one world government.

Continuing then with Daniel's dream we come to understand that the beast has these ten horns, which are the counterpart of the ten toes on the image in Nebuchadnezzar's dream. We see that the horns represent a kingdom or a political entity possessing certain powers and control. So even as Daniel considered the ten horns there came up among them another little horn by which three of the original ten horns were plucked up, *"and in this horn were eyes like the eyes of a man, and a mouth speaking great things"*. (Daniel 7:8) It would be premature at this juncture in our considerations to identify this horn as additional foundations need to be laid, but some may be able to glean even now the possible identity of the one having a mouth and speaking great things. Understand that these changes and actions are in the context of the fourth beast having been established, and a full expression of world dominion is in place. The return of the Lord in his final judgment of the world is into the context of this world empire or world government.

Now let us follow what Daniel says further from his dream about the fourth beast whose teeth were of iron, which devoured, brake in pieces, and stamped the residue with his feet. Of the ten horns that were in his head, and of the other which came up, and before whom three fell, even of that horn that had eyes and spike very great things. As Daniel beheld, the same horn made war with the saints, and prevailed against them. This fourth beast shall be the fourth kingdom upon earth, which shall devour the whole earth, and shall tread it down, and break it in pieces. And the ten horns out of this kingdom are ten kings that shall arise, and another shall rise after them, and he shall be diverse from the first and subdue three kings. And he shall speak great things. Out of the little horn, which comes up after; we identify the emerging Antichrist who will prevail over the saints in persecution.

These events and days of martyrdom and persecution to be endured by the saints are in the context of a three and one-half year period which we can fully identify as the great tribulation which leads directly up to the time of the Lord's return, the resurrection of the saints, and the judgments which follow constitute the Day of the Lord or otherwise spoken of as the day of the Lamb's wrath. Let us follow what Daniel has to say about it." *I saw in the night vision, and behold, one like the Son of Man came with the clouds of heaven, and came to the Ancient of Days and they brought him near before him. And there was given him dominion, and glory and a kingdom, and glory and that all people, and nations, and languages should serve him: his dominion is an everlasting dominion, and his kingdom which shall not pass away, and that which shall not be destroyed,* (Daniel 7:13-14). *"I beheld and the same horn made war with the saints, and prevailed against them; until the Ancient of Days came, and judgment was given to the saints of the Most High, and the time came when the saints possessed the kingdom"* (Daniel 7:21-22). *"And the ten horns out of the kingdom are ten kings that shall arise: and another sll arise after them: and he shall be diverse from the first, and he shall subdue three kings. And he shall speak great things against the most High, and shall wear out the saints of the most High, and think to change times and laws. And they (the saints) shall be given into his hands until a time, times and the dividing of time. "* (3 ½ years). (Daniel 7:24-25). The emerging Antichrist will seek to destroy any who have the testimony of Jesus Christ.

"But the judgment shall sit, and they (the saints) will take away his dominion to consume and destroy it unto the end. And the kingdom, and the dominion, and the greatness of the kingdom under the whole heaven, shall be given unto he people of the saints of the Most High,

whose kingdom is an everlasting kingdom, and all dominions shall serve and obey him" (Daniel 7:26). Daniel's dream is complete having taken us from the empire known as Babylon through succeeding dominions to the very end of the age, the kingdom of Antichrist, the resurrection of the saints at the end if the tribulation period, and finally the judgment of that great Day of the Lord. Those who have been found faithful to the King of Kings shall then inherit an everlasting kingdom. It is fully understood that a theological conflict exists among believers concerning the time of the resurrection of the saints, the duration of the tribulation, and who may be subjected to the war waged by the evil one in which the Scripture clearly tells us that he prevails. It is clear that Daniel's dream does not include or reveal a "rapture" of the saints prior to this time of persecution and trouble. We have yet to identify the little horn more definitively.

Chapter Three

THE BEGINNING OF SORROWS

Daniel has provided us with an overview of world history. First, by his wisdom in interpreting Nebuchadnezzar's dream, and then by confirmation of these revealed worldly kingdoms and empires through his own dream as we have seen in Daniel chapter seven. While keeping in view the larger picture of his revelations, we will need to move into a much more detailed understanding of events, signs and seasons as we approach the time of the consummation of all things relative to the unfolding of the prophesied history of this present age. The words of the Lord himself have given us many of the more significant details as he taught his disciples on the Mount of Olives. The theologians have called this the Olivet discourse as recorded in the three synoptic gospels of Mathew (chapter 24), Luke (chapter 21) and Mark (chapter 13). Let us now take some time to examine a portion of is teaching in response to the inquiry of the disciples for he is the greatest of the Prophets knowing the beginning as well as the end of all things.

Certain definite conditions and events are revealed to us by him in a general way leading us up to the *abomination of desolation* revealed by Daniel as found in chapter twelve at verses ten and eleven of his prophesies, and which the Lord has identified as the key to understanding the onset or beginning of the *great tribulation* which we will examine in detail in later portions of our study. Many different teachers give commentary on end time events, but mostly missing this key, which the Lord has instructed us to watch for and be ready to understand. This is the *abomination of desolation*. *"When ye therefore shall see the abomination of desolation, spoken of by Daniel the prophet, stand in the holy place, whoso readeth let him understand for then shall be great tribulation, such as was not since the beginning of the world to this time, no, or ever shall be."* (Matthew 24:15 and following through the context to Matthew 24:21). Details of the meaning of *the abomination of desolation* will be covered in a later portion of this study, but for now we want to cover a preparation for understanding leading us up to the end of this age under the considerations of *the beginning of sorrows*.

"*And they asked Him, saying Master, but when shall these things be? And what sign shall there be when these things shall come to pass? Take heed that ye be not deceived: for many shall come in my name, saying I am Christ: and the time draweth near: go ye not after them*". (Luke 21:7-8). "*But when ye shall hear of wars and commotions, be not terrified: for these things must first come to pass: but the end is not by and by*". (Luke 21:9). "*And ye shall hear of wars and rumors of wars: see that ye be not troubled: for these things must come to pass, for nation shall rise against nation, and kingdom against kingdom: and there shall be famines, and pestilences, and earthquakes, in divers places. All these are the beginning of sorrows.*" (Matthew 24:6-8.).

Many who would give commentary on the foregoing events would identify them as the definite signs to be observed as those which precede the coming of Christ. Others would say that there are no specific signs, but that his return for the Church is an immanent event, which could happen any day. The later group would place the foregoing into the context of the tribulation, which they say will not affect the Church for they will be "ruptured" prior to the tribulation. Both of these theological positions are in error for the Lord is giving us instruction for understanding, and while some of these happenings as they intensify may be very significant, indicating that the end is approaching, they in and of themselves are not to be observed as the signs of his return.

The working of the Holy Spirit within the people of God is *always* to bring them along a spiritual pathway leading to their purification. This will always be through a process of trial and individually designed affliction undertaken as a discipline to be personally experienced and applied to the hearts of each according to their need. *"Wherein ye greatly rejoice, though now for a season, if need be, ye are in heaviness through manifold temptations: that the trial of your faith, being much more precious than gold that perisheth, though it be tried with fire, might be found unto praise and honor and at the appearing of Jesus Christ."* (I Peter 1:6-7), and again, *"Beloved, think it not strange concerning the fiery trial which is to try you, as though some strange thing happened unto you. But rejoice, inasmuch as ye are partakers of Christ's sufferings, when his lorry shall be revealed, ye may be glad also with exceeding joy."*. (I Peter 5:12-13). For the sake of purification the Church must endure sufferings. Those who would suffer both individual afflictions and/or persecution, as a necessary prerequisite to be perfected in personal holiness will increasingly understand this principle. This process will be intensified in time as we approach the end of the age both before the tribulation period and after it has begun. Consider the words of Daniel as touching this reality. *"Then I heard one saint speaking, and another saint said unto that certain saint which spake, How long shall be the vision concerning the daily sacrifice, and the transgression of desolation, to give both the sanctuary and the host to be trodden under foot? And he said unto me, unto two thousand and three hundred days"* (six years and five months) *then shall the sanctuary be cleansed"* Daniel 8:13-14). We must understand that under the new and everlasting covenant that the sanctuary of the Lord is within the spirits of his people. So we see a period, which exceeds and leads up to, and including the tribulation that the Lord is striving with His people to bring forth purity. This period *is not* the seven years of tribulation as held by dispensational theologians, which we will cover in detail in later sections of this study. We would move then to that point immediately before the beginning of the tribulation period as given to us by the apostle John in his vision recorded at Revelation 12. Quoting a relevant portion: *"And his tail* (the dragon i.e. Satan) *drew the third part of the stars of heaven* (the saints) *to the earth and the dragon stood before the woman* (the church) *which was ready to be delivered, for to devour the child as soon as it was born. And the woman brought forth a man-child, which was to rule all nations with a rod of iron; and her child was caught up unto God and to his throne".* (Revelation 12:4-5).

We will elaborate on the details and further spiritual principles involved in this portion under a separate treatment: Measuring the Temple- the Woman and the Man-child. The point we are making here is that the woman is in the travail that leads to a birthing even at the very outset of the tribulation and the work of purification has already resulted in a company of saints (the man- child) being "caught up "to the throne prior to the tribulation period which we will later see to be three and one-half years. This is something entirely different from what is taught under dispensational theology as will be proven as we advance our study of the whole counsel of God on these issues. Again we see the woman in travail pursuant to the experience of a time of trial and travail leading ultimately to perfection. She (the Church) is metaphorically experiencing the pangs of labor leading to bringing forth a spiritually exercised people in her midst that have been wholly responsive to the dealings and workings of the Holy Spirit in their lives. This preparation is referred to by our Lord within the context of the beginning of sorrows, and it will bring forth the fruits of the Spirit to all who are watchful, take heed, and are preparing their hearts to be ready for his kingdom.

As we go forward in study we will deal more directly with the remainder of the Church in the tribulation, and the further purification leading to the final preparation of his bride and the gathering of all of the saints after a time of great tribulation. The world at large will undoubtedly experience and have great awareness of this period of sorrows, as it will be affecting the inhabitants of the earth; just as they will most certainly experience all of the great troubles of the tribulation. But only those who can be exercised by the Holy Spirit will have an understanding of the times and seasons. *"So likewise ye, when ye shall see all of these things know that it is near, even at the doors. Verily I say unto you, this generation shall not pass, till all of things be fulfillfiled,"* (Mathew 24:33-34). Again it is necessary to state that those events, signs, and troubles preceding the *abomination of desolation* provide indications of the approaching end of the age but other factors are involved as will be seen as we go forward with our study. *These things* will tell us that the time is drawing near but the manifestation of the *abomination of desolation* is the sign which the Lord has given as indicating that the time of great tribulation is about to begin. The admonition to the Church is to be watchful, waiting in anticipation, and seeking to know the truth to avoid deception while they are at the same tine being perfected in love so that each one may be ready. Compare Mathew 24:29-31 as well as the corresponding portions of Mark 13 and Luke 21 which are things spoken by Jesus Christ and are important preparatory texts to gain an understanding of as a preparation to the details provided by the prophets, which will be the focus of this continuing study.

Chapter Four

THE GREAT TRIBULATION

John's Revelations

Daniel's dream and his interpretation of Nebuchadnezzar's dream have laid some important foundations for further investigation. We saw clearly that this great and terrible beast, which is the fourth kingdom, shall devour the whole world, shall tread it down, and break it in pieces. We have also seen that out of this kingdom will come one who will prevail over the earth, and who will make war with the saints, and indeed will prevail over them. We see further from Daniel's dream that these things will be accomplished in a time, times, and the dividing of time. This is understood and supported by other scriptures to be one thousand two hundred and three score days or three and one-half years. This is the great tribulation.

We fast forward to the book of Revelation to see those things, which were revealed to the prophet John to gain further insights about this time of terrible trouble on the earth. At the outset I would point out that there are four chapters in the Book of Revelation which deal directly with various details of those events and conditions which make up this relatively short period of time at the end of the history of the world as we know it, i.e. great tribulation. Those chapters are chapter six, chapter eleven in part, chapter twelve, and chapter thirteen.

Each of these chapters provides details and perspective concerning the tribulation period. Contrary to the belief of many expositors the accounts given in Revelation are not precisely in chronological order. I would add that chapters seventeen and eighteen provide certain descriptive details of Mystery Babylon and her judgment. Mystery Babylon is a special topic, which will require detailed consideration before we finish our study. At this point we would just point out that Mystery Babylon has a special relationship to the world system prior to and continuing into the tribulation period.

"And I stood upon the sand of the sea, and I saw a beast rise up out of the sea, having seven heads and ten horns, and upon his horns ten crowns, and upon his heads the name of blasphemy. And the beast, which I saw, was like unto a leopard, his feet were as the feet of a bear, and his mouth was as a lion; and the dragon gave him his power, and his seat and great authority." (Rev. 13:1-2). *"All of the world wondered after the beast and they worshipped the dragon who gave power unto the beast, and they worshipped the beast..(.* Vs.4). *... power was given unto him to continue forty and two months."* (Vs.5).

This period of great tribulation is confined to a period of forty two months, three and one-half years or said another way, time, times and a half of time. During these days of trouble the fourth beast of Daniel's dream will emerge in full manifestation empowered by the dragon, i.e. Satan himself. Please take careful note that this time of great tribulation is not a seven-year period as is generally held by most evangelical denominations. Their doctrine is based on an erroneous interpretation of Daniel's seventy weeks found at the end of Daniel chapter 9. We will look very closely at that scripture latter in our considerations for the purpose of clarifying some crucial corrections of that doctrine. We have introduced our investigation of the great tribulation with the first few verses of Revelation chapter 13 where we see this beast has emerged. Please note that the ten horns of the beast answer to the toes of Nebuchadnezzar's image, and the original ten horns of Daniels's dream. Notably an additional "little horn" will arise and subdue three of the original ten horns.

It is of great importance to have a complete understanding of the events of this period, which immediately precedes the return of the Lord, the resurrection and the following judgment of that great day of the Lamb's wrath. We will begin with chapter six of John's revelation. Introducing this chapter we see in chapter five that *"the lion of the tribe of Judah, the root of David has prevailed to open the book"* (Rev.5: 5). This is, of course, is our Lord Jesus Christ who has been found worthy to open the seven seals of the book. The book as we have seen is sealed and as it is opened reveals in metaphor all of the events and judgments which are to occur at the end of this age. We must always make distinction between the tribulation and the Day of the Lamb's Wrath. The first six seals are opened within the context of chapter six and this entire chapter is dealing with happenings on the earth, which have been released by the Lord, and each seal has a distinct application to occurrences and conditions, which will prevail during the period. It is worth taking note that the account in chapter six does not say that the exact period of three and one-half years are in view. These events could begin in seed form somewhat earlier in preparation for the times, time and dividing of time, but we do know from the content of the chapter and the opening of the sixth seal at the end of the chapter that the events are those events confirmed elsewhere in Scripture as belonging to this period of tribulation. Let us begin with the first seal.

"And I saw when the Lamb opened one of the seals......and I saw and behold a white horse and he that sat upon him had a bow and a crown wgiven unto him, and he went forth conquering and to conquer". (Rev 6:2). This is not the Lord as He does appear on a white horse leading a great army in chapter nineteen. But that context is in the Day of the Lord. We know this because He is yet in heaven opening these seals and nothing for his coming has been prepared at this time or juncture. I think that it is not speculation to say that the one riding the horse in this symbolism is the Antichrist. He is going forth to conquer and this white horse is a counterfeit as he will manifest himself with great deception and he will be exalting himself and declaring great things. The peoples of the world will believe that he is their savior, falling down and worshipping him and worshipping the devil that has sent him forth. We will later explore more details of his conquest and his crowning, and his short-lived kingdom.

"And when he had opened the second seal, I heard the second beast say, come and see. And there went out another horse which was red and power was given him to take peace from the earth and they shall kill one another, and there was given him a great sword." (Rev.6:3-4). Red is the color of blood and much warfare and much shedding of blood creating great difficulties and trouble on the earth will mark this period.

"And when he had opened the third seal and I heard the third beast say, come and see. And I beheld and lo a black horse and he that sat upon him had a pair of balances in his hand, and I heard a voice say in the midst of the four beasts say, "*A measure of wheat for a penny, and three measures of barley for a penny, and see thou hurt not the oil and the wine."* (Rev 6:6). We see the third horse is the black horse of death by famine. This careful measuring of the food is speaking of its value and scarcity for the great tribulation will bring a time of great famine in many parts of the earth if not universally and multitudes will die of starvation.

"And I looked and beheld a pale horse and the name of him that sat upon him was Death and Hell followed him, and power was given him over a fourth part of the earth to kill with the sword, with hunger, with death and the beasts of the earth." (Rev 6:8). So we conclude the four horses with the issues of death and hell, which will include pestilence, disease, and natural disturbances which will place the earth in a state of travail, commotion and death such as has never been seen before.

Looking at the fifth seal we see the very wide spread and complete persecution of the saints, for we see when the fifth seal has been opened the souls of them that were slain for the word of God and for the testimony that they held. And they cried with aloud voice, *"how long O Lord, holy and true does thou not judge our blood on them who dwell on the earth? And white robes were given unto every one of them, that they should rest a little while until their fellow servants and their brethren should be killed as they were should be fulfilled.* "(Rev.6: 11). This flies in the face of those who hold the "rapture" to be pre-tribulational including the gathering up all of the church. In their view God has turned back to deal with his "chosen" people, i.e. the Jews for the seven-year period they identify as the tribulation. The scriptures never speak if the tribulation as a seven year period but rather it is always three and one-half years as both prophets, Daniel and John have confirmed in several places.

As we continue to pursue the truths revealed by these two prophets we will prove by their testimony beyond any question not only the fallacy of the pre-tribulational rapture doctrine of all believers of the "church age" but many other errors and deceptions which have blinded the minds of those naming the Lord. The vast majority of the evangelical community has based their interpretations of Scripture on a system of theology known as dispensationalism, which divides time into seven dispensations or economies. They believe that the seven year tribulation is the seventieth week of Daniel's prophesy happening after a "gap" of some two thousand years during which God is calling out the church, and when it is complete he will come to gather them in resurrection (rapture they have called it). Now in their view it is that the tribulation period is primarily for the conversion of the Jews, even all of them. We will only be able to unravel the truth by establishing precept upon precept revealing what the scriptures teach.

When the Lamb opens the sixth seal we behold a great earthquake and the sun becoming dark as sack cloth and the moon as blood, and the stars falling form the heavens, and the heavens rolling together as a scroll..(Rev 6:12-14). This is the signal of the return of the Lord for his own and those on the earth remaining recognize that the great day of his wrath is come. (Rev 6:17). His coming is after the tribulation as our Lord instructs his disciples; "*Immediately <u>after the tribulation of those days</u> shall the sun be darkened, and the moon shall not give her light, and the stars shall fall from heaven.... then shall appear the Son of Man in heaven.... and then shall they see the Son of Man coming in the clouds with great glory.... and with His angels, and they shall gather together His elect from the four winds and from the four corners of the earth.*" (Mathew 24:29-31) as taught by his own words. This account is given very similarly at I Thes. 4: 14-17. This is the resurrection and the gathering of the saints... **After the tribulation.**

These Prophets

As we have stated there are other portions of the Revelation and the visions of Daniel which add further details and other perspective to this period of great tribulation. We will endeavor to cover those important prophetic insights but we will do so under separate topics and aspects of emphasis. Daniel's coordinating views of John's revelations will require a complete chapter later in our study.

Chapter Five

Measuring The Temple

As we have already seen there will be some very difficult trial and persecution including large scale martyrdom which will come upon the saints under the violent and powerful oppression of this fourth great beast.

We have taken note of the opening of the firth seal as revealed in chapter six, as is also confirmed by Daniels' dream wherein he saw that the saints will be given into his hands for a time, times, and the dividing of time (3 ½ years). This reality will be confirmed again in this present review of Revelation 11:1-12 as well as other related Scriptures in Daniel.

Before we begin to make comment on the content of the Revelation passage it is important that the reader understand that John's revelation is fundamentally the revelation of God's Son in multiple aspects of his ordering and involvement in all that surrounds the events, which will consummate this age.

A second very important point is that if one is to come to understand the truths revealed here it will be absolutely necessary to recognize the use of metaphor and symbolism which characterizes the entire book. You will not truly understand the meaning of any passage unless you can discern the usage of the metaphor, symbolism or example and make a proper application in the context of its usage and the corresponding accord it has with the established spiritual principles, which are consistent through the word of God. Revelation chapter 11 in the first twelve versus which we are now going to explore provides us with an excellent opportunity to see this rule or principle of interpretation in operation.

Let us examine the text. Verse 1: *"There was given me a reed like unto a rod, and the angel stood"* (*the* Angel [messenger] is the one which is identified in the early verses of chapter 10). It will be important to understand that this messenger sent to John is the Lord and the message is from him throughout the book. Regardless of how much or how little exposure you may have had to the Revelation I do not expect you to immediately grasp this truth. It will likely require further evidence and exposition. At this point I only ask you to see that an Angel (messenger) has given John a reed like unto a rod and have some instructions for John. *"Rise and measure the temple of God and the altar, and them that worship therein. But the court which is without the temple leave out, and measure it not for it is given to the Gentiles and the holy city shall they trod under foot for forty and two months"* (Rev11: 1-2). This is written with the use of metaphor as example, but if we open our hearts to the Holy Spirit we can understand it, as well as that which is to follow. First of all we must recognize that the author is not referring to a physical temple. We are here operating under the new covenant and under the tenets of that covenant the temple of God is not ta building, but rather the people of God. *"What? Know you not that you are the temple of God and the Holy Ghost which is in you, which you have of God, and you are not your own? For you are bought with a price, therefore glorify God in your body and in your spirit which are God's".* (I Cor. 6:19). Now the question for each one to answer is this, are you worshipping God in the Spirit and in truth as our Lord admonished the woman at the well in John chapter 4? Do we doubt that the Spirit of God who dwells in us can take measure of our true relationship with him? So we see that there is a measuring taking place which is separating between those who are the people of God and who are in truth worshipping him inwardly in His temple (in the heart by the spirit), and those who are merely lingering in the outer court. We are told that those in the outer court are not here being measured but are given to the Gentiles and that the holy city shall they trod under foot for forty and two months. Is this forty and two month period not the great tribulation, and have we not been previously told by Daniel as he perceived in his dream that the people of God would be trodden down by this fourth beast and the last form of world government? Did not Daniel clearly tell us that the beast would make war with the saints and that he would prevail against them? So we conclude that the church as a whole will go through this time of trouble for the very purpose of God in allowing these things to come about is, at least in part for the purpose of purifying the saints and establishing them with an undivided heart before the Lord. We will later confirm this premise from a portion of Daniel chapter eleven but for now we must press forward with the text.

We see that power will be given unto his two witnesses and that they will prophesy one thousand two hundred and three score days *clothed in sackcloth*_(3 ½ years). Who are the two witnesses? Many would say Elijah and Enoch . . . or Moses and Elijah. Is there one verse of Scripture to confirm these interpretations or is this just convenient and unsupported theological speculation? To understand this we must grasp an understanding of the concept of two witnesses for God has told us in the book of Deuteronomy that in the mouth of two or three witnesses every word will be established. God has put His Holy Spirit inside of us. Our power and ennoblement in all that we do requires that we are walking and talking in accord with the Holy Spirit i.e. we need the Spirit's anointing or all that we do is of no avail. When people truly humble themselves before the Lord (put on the garments of sackcloth speaking metaphorically as in this text), He truly gives wisdom and understanding so that w may know these things, which are true and speak them in power because the Spirit himself is saying Amen to the utterance of that which has been spoken. As the tribulation begins many of God's people will be enlightened and they will know of a certainty that the time of the end has come. Do we not see in Matthew's account that the gospel of the kingdom will be preached in all of the earth and then shall the end come? What is the sign that these saints will see that will awaken them to this hour of trouble? *"When you shall therefore see the abomination of desolation spoken of by Daniel* *the prophet standing in the holy place then shall you understand*" (see Mathew 24:15f). Now they are humbled, now they are enlightened, and in this they are empowered to speak words of truth to all that will hear. This testimony will continue throughout the world during the duration of the forty and two month period. This is the meaning of the two witnesses, a people empowered by and speaking the word of the Lord by the Holy Spirit. *"These are the two olive trees and the two candlesticks standing before the God of the earth"* This citation of scripture is taken from Zechariah 4: 14. You may want to explore this chapter and context, but the meaning of the metaphors are therein stated that these are the golden pipes that empty the golden oil (the Holy Spirit) resulting in the light of the candlesticks.

It is clearly set forth in chapter one of Revelation that the seven churches of Asia are the seven golden candlesticks. (See Rev 1:20). Your understanding of these metaphors will be quickened if you are familiar with, or can review the purpose of the seven piped golden lamp stand that stood in the holy place to give light for the ministry under the old covenant both in the tabernacle and in the temple. The priest had a responsibility to keep the light ever burning for it was the light of the testimony. The fuel was olive oil, symbolic of the Holy Spirit. Are you now able to see that the power of the two witnesses is the church (candlesticks), but of necessity the light can only shine forth as the Spirit of God (olive oil) flows through the vessel?

Manifesting the power of the Holy Spirit we will now examine the effects of the ministry on others as well as the resultant consequences for them. *"If any man will hurt them fire proceeds out of their mouth, and devours their enemies, and if any man hurt them he must in this manner be killed."* (Rev 11:5). Again, we will need to understand not only the metaphorical language, but the purpose of their ministry. We must go to the word of the Lord from Jeremiah the prophet to help us to understand. Remember that Jeremiah was speaking to a people at the outset and in the early portion of the Babylonian captivity who were coming under the judgment of God for their sin and departure from his precepts as expressed in the law. The Lord was using the prophet Jeremiah as his vessel to speak to them, and it is always to convict them unto repentance. Wherefore, thus smith the Lord . . .

"Because you speak this word, behold I will make my words in your mouth fire, and the people wood and it shall devour them" (Jeremiah 5:14). Did Jeremiah breathe literal fire? No. Will fire proceed from the mouths of the witnesses in the context of their testimony? No. It clearly is a metaphor. When the word of the Lord is spoken in the power of the Holy Spirit it has the power of condemnation and death to those who would resist it. Those who would hurt the testifiers are the enemies of God. Fire as it is used metaphorically in Scripture is to speak of God's destroying judgments.

They shall also have power to shut up heaven that it rain not in the days of their prophecy. Shadows of the great prophet Elijah: *"As the Lord God of Israel lives before whom I stand there shall not be dew or rain but according to my words."* (I Kings 17:1f). The absence of rain was the withdrawal of God's blessing for the Israelites as living was dependent on the harvest of their crops, which was in turn dependent upon the rain in its seasons. Elijah, as was Jeremiah acting as a savant and a prophet to bring the people to repentance. A three and one-half year drought will certainly result in famine. Will it cause the sinful people to repent and turn back to him who are the source of their life? This is the issue being imposed on the hearers of the words of the two witnesses. Their words, if received, contain spiritual life and blessing to those who will receive it as the dew of heaven. This is a metaphor enforced by the ministry of Elijah representing blessing from heaven, which has been placed in their power by the Holy Spirit. While there may likely be drought causing famine during the tribulation we should not conclude that these conditions are being brought upon the world directly by those who are ministering the word of God. The metaphor is simply showing us that the power of God rests with them as they speak his word. Moving on with a further message in metaphor in the text we see that it is stated that they have power to turn water into blood and to smite the earth with all plagues as often as they will. These miracles were associated with Moses and the exodus as he dealt with Pharaoh on the single issue of God's imitative to let his people go from the bondage of Egypt. The same principles are true in the testimony of the witnesses. Their ministry is to bring souls to repentance and miraculously by the power of God and his word to deliver them from captivity and the bondage of sin and enslavement in the world. Understanding that these witnesses are the ministers of God empowered to deliver this message throughout the world in this short period of time. As the Lord himself has said and as has been recorded in Mathew's gospel. *"And this gospel of the kingdom shall be preached in the entire world for a witness unto all nations, <u>and then shall the end come</u>."* (Matthew.24:14).

Being empowered to bring the testimony as these individual witnesses serve the Lord the message cannot be contained in spite of the resistance of the powers of evil. However, when they have finished their testimony, the beast that ascends up out of the bottomless pit shall make war with them, overcome them and kill them. These many witnesses carrying the message of deliverance in Christ to the peoples of the world with the mighty power of the Holy Spirit shall be subjected to the death of martyrs as Satan seeks to destroy everything that testifies of the true and living God from the earth. And their dead bodies shall lie in the street of that great city which spiritually *is* called Sodom and Egypt where our Lord was crucified. And they of the people and kind reds and tongues and nations shall see their dead bodies three days and an half, and they shall not suffer their dead bodies to be put into graves. (See Rev 11: 8-9). Again, we have to see that the revelation is given in metaphorical language and we cannot interpret the words of the verses in a precise or literal sense. We must be able to interpret the spiritual meaning of the metaphorical portion and then discern the application of the remainder of the passage according to the context of the passage as a whole.

You may be familiar with the popular interpretation of this portion, which goes something like this: First, of course, the witnesses are determined to be literally two individuals. These two witnesses most certainly must be Moses and Elijah (some think Elijah and Enoch who never experienced physical death) since the acts and miraculous things ascribed to them are those things performed by these two savants of God. Their prophesying takes place in Jerusalem where also these two dead saints have returned alive to give their testimony. They are killed and lie in the street of Jerusalem and are seen laying there for three and one-half days so the world may observe them on international television and rejoice over their deaths by sending gifts to each other. This interpretation is flawed on several points. First; Jerusalem is not named as the literal location of the martyrdom. Secondly, the word **spiritually** in the context is of utmost significance. It means, *non-physically, figuratively* according to Strong's concordance. So we must interpret the entities of Sodom and Egypt in a spiritual sense. We know that Sodom was a city filled with wickedness, which was destroyed completely by God's wrath in the days of Abraham. We also know that Egypt was an ancient empire from which the Jews made an exodus in the days of Moses. The further statement in the verse is where our Lord was also crucified. Our Lord was crucified in Jerusalem, which was supposed to be the city where God had chosen to put His name, but we know the Jews religion was corrupted in every way and the religious system they claimed to represent was apostate and had fully departed from the laws and precepts of the Old Testament. So it is *non- physical and figuratively speaking* that Sodom and all it represents in wickedness and debauchery, and Egypt in all that it represents of this worlds systems and corruption, and Jerusalem in all of its religious charade and apostasy where these witnesses are killed and come to lie in their martyrs deaths. It all happens in a world system that hates God and His Son Jesus Christ. The city is not literal or physical as their deaths will occur all over the world over the course of the three and one-half years of tribulation when the Devil, the beast and the powers of darkness will seek to obliterate the name of the true and living God from the earth.

One other important point for clarification is that the account in the King James Bible says three and one-half *days. (*Strong's says the word figuratively means a season of time defined more or less clearly by the context). The word translated days here has to do with a season of time identified by the present context of one thousand two hundred and three score days. It should have been translated *years* for it is through the entirety of this period that the martyrs for Christ are killed. Review again the fifth seal of chapter six where we are told that those who cry out to the Lord for revenge upon their murderers that they should rest yet for a little season until their fellow servants and their brethren that should be killed should be fulfilled. We know that there will be great rejoicing at the death of the Lord's faithful servants by those in the world who hate him because these two (the saints and the Holy Spirit) prophets tormented them that lived upon the earth.

But after the appointed time had passed the, *"Spirit of life entered into them and they stood upon their feet"* (see Ezekiel 37: 10-14). And great fear fell upon them that saw them. And they heard a great voice from heaven saying unto them, *"Come up hither, and they ascended into heaven in a cloud and their enemies beheld them"* (Rev 11:12). Compare with: *"For the Lord Himself shall descend from heaven with the voice of the Archangel, and with the trump of God, and the dead in Christ shall rise first; then they which are alive and remain shall be caught up with them in the clouds, to meet the Lord in the air"* (I Thes.4:15-16). This is the resurrection and the gathering of the saints **after the tribulation, not** the pre-tribulation rapture of the church.

We have not finished with the issues relating to measuring the temple but we have dealt only with those in the court without who were not measured, but were given unto the Gentiles to tread them under foot forty and two months. It was necessary to lay all of the background first and to cover the ministry of the two witnesses. There is a break in the text after verse thirteen of chapter eleven. The text here reverts back to complete the narrative of the three woes introduced at the end of chapter nine. It would create confusion at this juncture of our study to try to explain these three woes for they do not fall in the context of the tribulation, but rather in the Day of the Lamb's wrath. We must put that subject on hold until a later time. Our study now moves us necessarily to the twelfth chapter of Revelation so that we may further understand the issues covered in the first twelve verses of chapter eleven, and finish up the importance of the measuring of the temple.

Chapter Six

MEASURING THE TEMPLE

The Woman and the Man-Child

We will need to read the first portion of Revelation chapter twelve to begin to develop the connection between the two witnesses of chapter eleven, and the woman and the man child which come into consideration in chapter twelve. I would even suggest that it might be helpful for you to read the whole of the chapter before we begin to break it down by interpretation.

"*And there appeared a great wonder in heaven; a woman clothed with the sun and with the moon under her feet, and on her head a crown of twelve stars*" (Rev 12:1). Who is this woman? "*And she being with child cried travailing in birth to be delivered*" (Rev.12: 2). "*And there appeared another wonder in heaven, and behold a great red dragon having seven heads and ten horns, and seven crowns upon his heads. And his tail drew the third part of the stars and did cast them to the earth, and the dragon stood before the woman which was ready to be delivered for to devour her child as soon as it was born. And the woman brought forth a man child who was to rule all nations with a rod of iron; and her child was caught up unto God, and to his throne*" (Rev. 12:3-5).

It is now necessary that we identify all of the players introduced in the foregoing early verses of chapter twelve. Most would not have any difficulty in identifying the great red dragon as Satan. We would see further that he has a representation on the earth having seven heads and ten horns. In the early portion of the chapter on the great tribulation we cited the early verses of Revelation chapter thirteen and compared them with the fourth beast of Daniel's dream. We will have much more to say about the beast as we continue with this study. We have yet to identify the woman and the man-child who was caught up to the throne, but before we continue with that revelation I believe it would be worthwhile to state unequivocally who the woman and man-child <u>are not</u>. A common interpretation is that the woman is Mary the mother of Jesus, and the man-child is Jesus Christ. While we know that Mary was the mother of Jesus and he did ultimately go into the heavenly realm in resurrection to reside at the right hand of the throne of God; there are no other facts in the context, which will allow this inaccurate interpretation. First, we would not see a beast having seven heads and ten horns at anytime seeking to devour Jesus at his birth. Secondly, this Book of Revelation is prophetic in its essence revealing future scenes and events.

Nowhere is it recounting history except as the Spirit ministers the word of God to the seven churches in Asia, which is who the revelation is addressed to. We are told at chapter four and verse one, *"I will show you things, which shall be hereafter"*. After the review of the seven churches in Asia the text carries us forward to future events all of which are associated with the end of the age, the tribulation period, and the return of Christ in judgment.

Another common interpretation of this passage is that the woman is Israel. This also is clearly an impossibility as neither the nation of Israel, Mary the mother of Jesus, or the birth of Jesus can be superimposed on the context of this prophetic passage which deals with scenes, visions and events which are yet future. So the woman and the man-child remain a mystery and before they are disclosed let us look at the heavenly vision of a woman clothed with the sun with the moon under her feet and on her head a crown of twelve stars. We are here being presented with another metaphor or picture story and we can again return to the Old Testament to help us to understand the vision being placed before us by the prophet.

In the latter chapters of Genesis there comes to the forefront a very significant servant of God who we know as Joseph. The account of his life is taken up in chapter thirty- seven and continues virtually to the end of Genesis. This gives us a sense of how significant Joseph was in the plan of God as well as his importance as a servant. Joseph being next to the youngest among the twelve sons of Jacob was hated by his brothers and they laid a plan to sell him to a passing band and he was carried away into the land of Egypt. Without spending a lengthy period of time covering his life, we know that after passing through trial and testing he rose to be the prime minister of the empire, and from that place of authority he became an instrument of God to bring deliverance to his family, and also a great blessing to all of Egypt. I hope you know the entirety of the story of this faithful servant of God, as we cannot cover all of these details in this context. We are going to focus on a dream, which Joseph had as a lad. He actually had two dreams, which were complimentary in their content and meaning bringing to him the same message and understanding. The one we want to take a close look at is as follows: (See Gen. 37:9-11) In the dream he beheld the sun and the moon and eleven stars representing his family which made obeisance to him, and he told the dream to his father and to his brethren. And his father rebuked him and said shall I and your mother and your brethren indeed come to bow down ourselves to you in the earth. And his brethren envied him but his father observed the saying. There was recognition amongst the whole family that the dream had a significant meaning, but the brothers who hated him only sought to get rid of him, which is what they did at the earliest opportunity. The dream encompasses all of the people of God living at this early stage of God's moving with Jacob and his family, which became Israel as a man chosen to father the families of God, which became the tribes of Israel because of Jacob's faith and insistence on the blessing. The dream is prophetic because Joseph eventually through the favor of God was taken to the throne at the very right hand of Pharaoh finding favor and being given great authority. He ultimately became the instrument of the deliverance of the rest of his family and they did indeed come to a place of obeisance in the days when the famine came and Joseph had made provision for all. Is this not the fulfillment of Joseph's dream, which the Holy Spirit chose to use in John's vision of the woman and the man-child? This place of honor was based on his faithfulness to his God and we find that when his father dispensed the blessings to his sons at his death that Joseph was found to *"be a fruitful bough . . . his bow abode in strength and his hands were made strong by the mighty God of Jacob . . . , and the blessings of thy father have prevailed above the blessings of thy progenitors unto the utmost bound of the everlasting hills and they shall be on the head of Joseph and on the crown of the head of him who was separate from his brethren."* (Gen. 49:22-26) So we discern from Joseph's life something very special in not only his love and faithfulness for his brethren but something which merited the total blessing of God upon him for he perceived that God had called him and enabled him in a special way and he was faithful in his performance to fulfill God's purpose.

Now how does this all relate to our text in Revelation chapter twelve?

Joseph's dream was prophetic. He understood that it would come to pass and that he had been chosen to fulfill a very important spiritual function in relation to his family and the ultimate destiny of his progeny. The sun, moon and stars in Joseph's dream represent metaphorically the whole household of God i.e. all of the people of God, and Joseph's calling was one of separation and faithful service which carried him to the very throne of Egypt. Joseph's whole life is an example of what God has called us to do in love, in survice and in faithfulness. The woman in the vision is the church, she is clothed with the sun (Son) and she has a crown of twelve stares upon her head. This represents the church as a total number of the people of God metaphorically just as it held that significance in Joseph's dream for we see she is set over against, and is in conflict with the dragon. (Compare Rev. chapter seven).We see her in the midst of travail, conflict and trial. Out from that conflict and travail she is giving birth and when she was ready to be delivered the devil sought to devour her offspring as soon as it was born. She brought forth a man child who was to *"rule all nations with a rod of iron"*, and the man child was caught up to God and to his throne, and the woman fled into the wilderness where she has a place prepared of God that they should feed her there one thousand two hundred and three score days. Our conclusion is that the man-child is a company of people, we know not how many, who are as Joseph was in their character, in their faithfulness and in devotion to their Lord. They are watching and waiting and fully aware. They have not only been washed in the blood of the Lamb but have also been thoroughly purified in the trying of their faith as Joseph had been. They are ready and need not be subjected to the trials or the tribulation for their hearts are already pure and undivided.

Let us read what the Spirit says unto the church at Philadelphia (brotherly love) in chapter three of Revelation. *"I have set before you n open door and no man can shut it. For thou hast a little strength and have kept my word, and have not denied my name"*. (Rev.3:8). *"Because you have kept the word of my patience, I also will keep you from the hour of temptation which is to come upon all of the world to try them that dwell upon the earth"* (Rev.3: 10). They have been measured as the temple and the altar and those who worship therein. (See Rev 11:1). The man-child is a company of faithful saints who were watching and waiting for their Lord and they will not pass through the tribulation, but will be caught up to God and to His throne. The woman, the church as a whole is still alive on the earth and will be subjected to a wilderness experience, great trial and conflict and as we have already seen will experience persecution and martyrdom on a vast scale. Why is this? Let us see what Daniel has to say. *"And they that understand among the people shall instruct many* (the ministry of the two witnesses), *and yet shall they fall by the sword and by flame, and by captivity, and by spoil many days. Now when they shall fall they will be helped with a little help; but many shall cleave to them with flatteries. And some of them of understanding shell fall, to try them. to purge, and to make them white even to the time of the end"*. (Daniel 11:33-35). If you are a born again believer in Jesus Christ your new birth was a miraculous transforming work of God to bring you into covenant relationship with the Father and the Son, but it imitates in you a solemn spiritual mandate to come to know him and walk obediently in the light of the Holy Spirit. We each one must *"work out our own salvation with fear and trembling, for it is God who works in you both to will and to do his good pleasure."* (Phil. 2:12-13). We must see that one of the purposes of the great tribulation is the purifying of the church for we are engaged in a great spiritual conflict with Satan and the powers of darkness, and our victory will be assured if we are found faithful in the trial of affliction. We are also assured that many unbelievers will turn to Christ in the midst of this time of great difficulties. Do we not see from the words of our Lord that *"the gospel of the kingdom will be preached in all of the world for a witness to all nations and then shall the end come."* (Matthew. 24:14).

The intensity of this conflict is graphically illustrated in the next portion of chapter 12. The woman (the church) having fled into the wilderness where she has a place prepared for her of God, the man- child having been caught to the throne is the occasion for great war in haven. Michael and his angels fought against the dragon, and the dragon and his angels fought; *"and prevailed not and neither was there place found any more in heaven. And the great dragon was cast out, that old serpent called the Devil and Satan, which deceived the whole world, was cast out into the earth, and his angels were cast out with him."* (Rev. 12:7-9). A great battle in advancing the kingdom has been wrought. This victory has great significance!! The Devil who has had access to the throne of God over the ages since the fall of man has now been displaced and cast out of heaven. This has been made possible because a company of saints found faithful to the truth have been <u>measured and not found wanting</u>, "and *they overcame him by the blood of the Lamb, and by the word of their testimony, and they loved not their lives unto the death"* (Rev.12:11). And a loud voice in heaven declares, *"Now is come salvation, and strength, and the kingdom of our God, and the power of His Christ, and the accuser of our brethren is cast down who accused them before our God day and night".* (Rev.12: 10). Now it is woe unto the inhibitors of the earth for the Devil has come down unto them, having great wrath and knowing he has but a short time (3 ½ years). *"Now the dragon was wroth with the woman (the church) and went forth to make war with the remnant of her seed who keep the commandments of God and have the testimony of Jesus Christ"* (Rev.12: 17).

Chapter Seven

To Him Who Overcomes . . .

> "*And they overcame him by the blood of the Lamb, and by the word of their testimony, and they loved not their lives unto the death*" (Rev.12: 11).

This is as clear as it gets. The Lord called us into a covenant of unwavering commitment and faithfulness. There stands against every believer in Christ a threefold adversary to resist and hinder from a full and victorious spiritual life. We must each overcome the world, the flesh and the devil. It becomes appropriate at this point after having seen the marvelous spiritual victory wrought by the man-child in chapter twelve that we should take a very close look at the admonitions of the Lord to the seven churches in Asia. These admonitions and exhortations are found in the second and third chapters of Revelation and stand as universal instruction and warning to all of the church throughout the age, and having some very specific application for believers living at the time of the end. The teaching that the seven churches represent historical periods of the church from beginning to end and that each church represents a period in the history of the church is rejected by this writer as not having any validity as well as any support either in the context of the letters or any other Scripture.

THESE PROPHETS

It is necessary to cover some important points established in the early record of the book and cover spiritual principles needing to be understood before looking more closely at the letters addressed to each individual church. I think it will be very helpful to establish some revealed truths at the very outset of the book. Let us set forth first the initial three verses of chapter one. *"The Revelation of Jesus Christ which God gave unto him to show unto his servants' things which must shortly come to pass; and he sent and signified by his Angel unto his servant John: who bare record of the word of God and the testimony of Jesus Christ; and of all things which he saw."* There are issues and points of truth, which are critical to understand in these opening verses. First of all, we see that God held the Revelation as the Father, and the Revelation *is of Jesus Christ*. We will see this reality of the Son being everywhere revealed as we search the Scriptures. The revelation is given so that his servants may know these things, which must shortly come to pass. In short, it is intended that we understand the content of this final record of Scripture. *"And He sent and signified it by his Angel (messenger) unto his servant John."* The word angel here must be understood according to the meaning of the word, which means a messenger, or to send a message. It does not have a stereotyped meaning as an angelic being which would be our tendency to assume. The message from God was not transmitted through Jesus Christ and then to an angel. The new covenant order of revelation is that the word of Jesus Christ being *the messenger i.e. Angel* bringing the message to his servant John. The only intercessory agent is the Holy Spirit in conveying the message to our spirit. The usage of the word angel appears multiple times in the book and as we will see it rarely refers to an angelic being, but rather to the messenger. God's messenger in the first instance is Christ and likewise secondarily the word angel will find many applications to the Holy Spirit as we unfold the messages in the various subsequent texts of Scripture. Again, how does God transmit truth to his people? The word of the Lord is from Jesus Christ and the Holy Spirit us the vehicle of ministering the truth into our hearts just as we saw that principle operative with the two witnesses. You must escape the tendency to stereotype the word angel and interpret it as referring to an angelic being, as this will be a critical key to your ability to understand. Another truth which will play an important role as we move forward is that the message involves the seven Spirits of God which we will come to understand to be the Holy Spirit "sevened" i.e. that is to say in fullness or completeness. Those seven Spirits are under the direction of the Son of God as the Father gives the Revelation to the Son. (See Rev.1: 4).

We will not do a verse-by-verse study of the whole first chapter, but we must lay some essential foundations before moving on. The awesome overwhelming reality of the first chapter is that the Son of God is revealed to John and this revelation is in the context of the symbolism of the seven golden candlesticks, which are representations of not only the seven churches in Asia but ultimately the universal church through the age even to the end. Did we not see this same symbolism of the candlesticks as being the "light of the testimony" with the two witnesses of chapter 11? Please take note of the descriptive qualities and the revealed appearance of the Lord in verses 14 through 16 as they are repeated elsewhere; both in Daniel chapter 10 and in Revelation chapter 10 as confirmations of his identity. Now John is instructed to write the things, which he has seen, and the things, which are, and the things, which shall be hereafter. Note this threefold designation of chronology for it is of importance. John then is given another key relative to what he has seen thus far. The mystery of the seven stars, which he saw in the Lord's right hand, and that of the seven golden candlesticks. The seven stars are the angels (messengers) of the seven churches and the candlesticks are the churches themselves. Take note that in the vision the Lord holds the seven golden candlesticks in his right hand. This is symbolically expressing his possession, power, and control over them. Also, it must be seen that the seven stars are the angels (messengers) to the seven churches. By way of understanding the seven Spirits of God, which are before his throne in verse four of the first chapter; we say again that we see a portrayal or a representation of the fullness of the Holy Spirit. The seven stars, angels (messengers) are the means of conveyance of the messages to the church, i.e. we only understand as the Holy Spirit ministers to us so *"he that hath an ear to hear let him hear what the Spirit says to the churches"*, repeated seven times. This admonition is uttered over again seven times in the text of chapters two and three. The identity of the symbolism of the stars as representing the seven Spirits of God is confirmed at Rev. 3:1. Also urn in your Bible to Rev. 4:5 and Rev. 5:6 and I believe that by comparing the three verses cited that you will be able to see that this is an accurate interpretation. One of the standard interpretations of the stars or angels is that they are the pastors of the seven churches. This can only be the figment of a fertile imagination, which has no support in the text.

After laying these foundational truths we can move on now to the things which are, i.e. the messages to the churches (i.e. the church). Unto the angel (messenger) of the church at Ephesus; *"these things says He that holds the seven stars in His right hand."* There is a message to the church at Ephesus. It is clear that the message originates and comes form the Lord (as the one holding the seven stars in his right hand). It must be conveyed to the church by the Holy Spirit, otherwise it is only words written on a scroll. This is the pattern of revelation to the churches, and is always the pattern of conveying the Word of the Lord to his people. We read these words on the pages of the Scripture. We do not have the benefit of the visions that John saw. But by the Spirit of God in us we can see and understand the words John has written down. Without the Spirit's ministry we are spiritually blind, we will not understand the message, and we will not rightly interpret the Scripture. Many good things are attributed to the church at Ephesus, but the Lord states He has somewhat against them in that they have left their first love. There is therefore a need of repentance and turning back again. You shall love the Lord your God with all of your heart, soul, mind and strength, and if he is not now your first love He must become that for that is a condition of overcoming. *"He that has ears to hear let him hear what the Spirit says to the church.* **To him that overcomes** *will I give to eat of the tree of life, which is in the midst of the paradise of God."* (Rev.2:7).

To the church as Smyrna says He that is the first and the last, which was dead, and now is alive and by the Holy Spirit says to write. Again some words of encouragement come to them concerning their works, their trials, and their poverty. But a problem does exist in their midst concerning those that say they are Jews and are not (see Romans 2:28-29 identifying who really is a Jew in the clear statement of Scripture). A mixture is present in their midst. Tribulation will sort out those who are true and faithful from the false professors." *He that has ears to hear let him hear what the Spirit says to the church.* **<u>To him that overcomes</u>** *he shall not be hurt of the second death.*" (Rev.2:11). As the first death is a separation of the soul and spirit from he body hence causing the body to die even so the second death is a separation of the spirit from the Lord resulting effectively in the death of the soul, that is to say it's separation from the presence of the Lord as the source of life (not it's total destruction from existence). These are deep things that are to be understood and things that we will consider later under the topic of judgment at the great white throne, i.e., The Book of Life in chapter 29.

The Lord as He that has the sharp sword with two edges says by the Spirit to the church at Pergamos. There are those there who are faithful holding fast His name and displaying their good works of faith. Dwelling in a place where Satan has a seat. He does have somewhat against them. There are those there who hold the doctrine of Balaam who taught Balac to cast a stumbling block before the children of Israel and teaching them to eat things sacrificed to idols and to commit fornication. The doctrine of Balaam is expressed by those presuming to serve God, but doing so for personal advantage i.e. either to be promoted or for monetary or financial reward. Its spiritual effect in the people will be to feed them something unclean i.e. to eat (take within themselves) things sacrificed unto idols and to defile their separation by committing spiritual fornication and defilement from a state of purity. Also it results in the embracing of the doctrine of the Nicolaitans. This literally means "victorious over the people" (see Strong's Concordance) It is placing a man in a place of preeminence over the people. Much more could be said about these maladies, which occur in the church. The admonition is to repentance lest the Lord come and fight against them with the sword of his mouth. But it is again; let us hear what the Spirit says unto the church. The word is" **<u>to him who overcomes</u>** *who will be* *given to eat of the hidden manna, and will give him a white stone."* (a good vote). (Rev.2:17).

The Son of God who has eyes like a flame of fire admonishes those at Thyatira by the Spirit. Acknowledging their service, patience and works and yet having a few things against them, such as allowing spiritual whoredom in prophecy and teaching to seduce the people as typified by Jezebel (the wicked wife if Ahab king of Israel), it having the same spiritual effect on the people as the acts of Balaam. She becomes an arch type of unclean union and those who engage her in spiritual adultery will suffer great tribulation unless they truly repent of their deeds. Her offspring are the children of death. He who has the eyes like a flame of fire sees into the heart and discerns all motives. As many as have not this doctrine he promises no further burden, so they are to hold fast till he comes, and" ***to him that overcomes*** *will he give power over the nations to rule them with a rod of iron, and they will also be given the morning star." (Rev. 2:27-28)*(Christ- see Rev. 22:16). As one who would or could prevail as an overcomer your authority would be to rule over the nations; your inheritance is Christ.

To Sardis the Lord who has the seven Spirits of God (seven stars) He says you have a name that you live, but you are dead. Be watchful and strengthen those things that remain, that are even ready to die. Remember the things you have received and heard and hold fast and **repent.** The further admonition is to watch for he comes as a thief. What will be our state when he is revealed? There are a few are Sardis who has not defiled their garments and they will walk with Him in white for they are worthy. *"**To him who overcomes** will be clothed in white raiment (righteousness), and I will <u>not blot out their name</u> out of the book of life, but I will confess them before the Father, and before his angels* (angelic beings). *"He that has an ear to hear let him hear what the Spirit says unto the churches."* (Rev.3:5-6).

And to the angel (messenger-Holy Spirit) of the church at Philadelphia (brotherly love), says he that is holy, he that is true, he that has the key of David, he that opens and no man can shut; he that shuts and no man can open. He has placed an open door before us brethren that no man can shut and having a little strength, and if we have been those who have kept his word (see Rev 1:3), and not defiled his name. If it be thus with us in these very last days and he can say to us *"you have kept the word of my patience"*, he will even say to us "***I will keep you from the hour of temptation*** *which shall come upon all of the world (great tribulation) to try them that dwell upon the earth. Behold, I come quickly. Hold fast which you have that no man take your crown".* (Rev. 3:10-11). One clear application of these verses to the church at Philadelphia will have application to the man-child revealed to us in chapter twelve who overcame and ascended to the throne. The Lord has no words of correction or need of repentance to those who dwell in the reality of the church of brotherly love. "***To him who overcomes*** *will he make a pillar in the temple of God, and he shall go nor more out and I will write upon him the name of my God, and the name of the city of my God which is New Jerusalem, and my new name,"* (Rev.3:12).

Truly in these days of the consummation of the age . . . *"he that has an ear to ear let him hear what the Spirit is saying* unto the church. And finally to the church of the Laodicea's says the Amen, he who is the faithful and true witness, the beginning of the creation of God who is speaking by the Holy Spirit. Knowing their works he says they are neither cold not hot but lukewarm. Wishing them to be one or the other he says I will spew you out of my mouth. The apostate assemblies say in their hearts that they are rich and increased in goods and have need of nothing and are blinded to the fact that they are poor and blind and naked. Counsel to them is to buy gold tried in the fire that they may be spiritually enriched and white raiment to cover their nakedness. Anoint your eyes with eye salve that you may see. Those who he loves he rebukes and chastens to the end that they may **repent**. He is standing at the door of hearts knocking that we may open the door and allow him to come in that he may fellowship with us and that we may be among those worshipping in the temple and at the alter and not wandering around in the outer court. "***To Him that overcomes*** *will he grant to sit down with him in his throne even as he has set down in his Father's throne. he that has an ear to hear let him hear what the Spirit is saying to the church."* (Rev. 3:21-22).

We have briefly reviewed the exhortations and admonitions of the Lord to his people having application to all who truly have come into life by a new birth. That new birth is just our beginning. We must ever press toward the mark for the high calling of God in Christ Jesus. Clearly if we are seeing what the Spirit is saying to the church we will understand that our inheritance in the kingdom of God is conditional and contingent upon being found faithful and cleansed of all defilement while walking in the power of worship in the Holy Spirit.

Chapter Eight

THE LITTLE HORN

Having now surveyed the early chapters of Revelation where we have dealt with the church, its relationship to the revelation of Christ in and through the Holy Spirit, and the need for individual believers to be steadfast and faithful unto the end, that they may overcome; we are now ready to turn back to the prophesies of Daniel to fill in more pieces of the prophetic puzzle. The hope is that each one who reads will be gripped by the Holy Spirit and the search for truth as God has intended *"to show unto His servants these things which must shortly come to pass."* (Rev. 1:1).

In Daniel chapter eight we will explore a second vision, which Daniel had in the third year of Belshazzar who was the last king of Babylon. We know this from Daniel chapter five where he is confronted with *"the hand writing on the wall"* which spelled the demise of the Babylonian empire. (See Dan.5: 25-31). The fall of the empire was approaching and this event known to the Lord sets the stage for that which is to follow in Daniel's second vision. As he stood before the river Ulai he saw in the vision a ram standing before the river having two horns, and the two horns were high; but one was higher than the other, and the higher one came up last. He saw the ram pushing westward and northward and southward; so that none could stand before it nor be delivered from it. And the ram did according to its will and became great. This portrays the Medio-Persian Empire, which overwhelmed all of the Babylonian power and control, displacing it as a world dominant power. The Median kings were first prominent and then to be followed by the Persians who were later dominant (the higher horn which came up last). The vast Medio-Persian Empire prevailed for about two hundred years, and in that context many of the Jews were allowed to return to Jerusalem and rebuild the temple, the wall and the city. These facts are very significant but not in the center of our current considerations so we will not spend time considering those events here.

Next in Daniel's vision he sees a he goat coming from the West on the face of the whole earth, and this he goat had a notable horn between his eyes. The he goat came upon the ram, which had the two horns and ran into him with fury and power. He was moved with choler and smote the ram and broke the two horns, and there was no power in the ram to stand against him. The he goat cast down the ram and stamped upon him and there was no power to deliver the ram out of his hand. The he goat waxed very great and took dominion, and when his power had been established the great horn was broken, and in place of it came four notable ones towards the four winds of heaven. The vision has now revealed to us that which Daniel foresaw of the world conquest of Alexander the Great coming from the West with his large Macedonian army intermingled with Greeks and overwhelming completely in a period of a few years the established dominion of the Medes and Persians. When Alexander died at a young age the realm of his dominion, which had been established, was divided among the four of his generals. Alexander, although Macedonian, was given to and very strongly influenced philosophically and culturally by the Greeks. He was mentored and taught by the Greek philosopher Aristotle who in turn was a student of the philosopher Plato. Alexander's influence was philosophically Grecian which came to be known and spread abroad as Hellenism. The Greek culture and language became pervasive and laid a universal seed bed for the spreading of the gospel of Jesus Christ 350 years later. Even though the Roman Empire was well established by the birth of Christ, the prevailing cultural influence and language was Greek.

The text leads us to the most significant portion of Daniel's vision. Out of one portion of the fourfold division of Alexander's empire came forth a 'little horn' which waxed exceeding great toward the south and towards the East, and towards the *pleasant land*. The first truth to be realized in understanding the vision is that we are taken historically from the dividing of Alexander's empire after his death to the end of this age. *"for at the time of the end shall the vision be"* (Daniel 8:17). As we would look at the territory captured and controlled by the victories of Alexander we would clearly see that within the geography of the empire the land, which we know as Israel, fits perfectly the description *"towards the South and towards the East and towards the pleasant land"*. We further see in verse ten of the eighth chapter that it waxed great even to the host of heaven, and it cast down of the host and the stars to the ground and stamped upon them. Yes, he magnified himself even to the prince of the host (Jesus Christ) and by him the daily sacrifice was taken away, and the place of his sanctuary was cast down. Under the tenets of the new covenant we understand that the place of his sanctuary is not a temple or building made with hands, but the dwelling place of the Lord is in the spirits of his people. *"Know you not that you are the temple of God and the Spirit of God dwells in you?"* (I Cor. 3:16). So we see that the purpose and acts of the "little horn" in league with the unbelieving world is to *"cast down the host and the stars to the ground and stamp upon them"* We have already seen this language and action operative in the eleventh and twelfth chapters of Revelation. Lets briefly review . . . *"and his tail (the dragon) did draw the third part of the stars of heaven and did cast them to the earth."* (Rev.12:4). We have previously covered the metaphors and symbolic language in the passage in the chapter entitled the woman and the man-child. In Revelation chapter eleven we covered under thee two witnesses that the court, which was without, was not measured and it was given unto the Gentiles to be trodden under foot forty and two months. In returning to Daniel's vision we read that *"yea he magnified himself eve to the Prince of the host* (Jesus Christ) *and by him the daily sacrifice was taken away, and the place of his sanctuary (the Lord's) was cast down"* (Dan.8:11). We have now seen clearly in four separate texts of Scripture: Rev.6 under the fifth seal in the chapter covering great tribulation; Rev 11:2 on the measuring of the temple; Rev12: 4 with the dragon drawing to the ground a third part of the stars down from heaven; and here in Daniel's vision casting down of the host and the stars to the ground and stamping upon them.

Again, we must understand the stars of heaven are a metaphor for the people of God. Thus, each are a representation of the church being overwhelmed during the period of the tribulation and this persecution and martyrdom beginning as we believe even a short time prior to that final three and one-half year period which the Scripture identifies as great tribulation. Is it not clear that the instrument of this execution upon the host, and upon the stars, and upon the saints (Rev 6:9 under the 5th seal) is the little horn? Moving on a little further in verses 13 and 14 of the chapter we read, *"When I heard one saint speaking, and another saint said unto that certain saint, how long shall be the vision concerning the daily sacrifice and the transgression of desolation to give both the sanctuary and the host to be trodden under foot? And he said unto me unto two thousand and three hundred days, and then shall the sanctuary be cleansed.* "As the point has been made before it is clear that one of the principle purposes of the tribulation and God allowing for the people to be trodden on by the forces of darkness and the Gentile world is the process of purifying a people through trial and affliction that they might stand before the Lord with a pure and undivided heart. The period of the purification is here stated to be twenty three hundred days, which equals six years and five months. This exceeds the period defined in chapters eleven, twelve and thirteen of Revelation, all of which are dealing directly with the tribulation by 1040 days. This time does not reach to a period of seven years, which is the length of the tribulation as proclaimed by many evangelicals who hold the dispensational view of theological interpretation. Also nowhere else in Scripture do we find a seven year tribulation period except as pronounced by a faulty interpretation of Daniel's "seventy weeks" which will be fully explained in a subsequent chapter. All of the references in the book of Revelation clearly state the tribulation period to be exactly three and one-half years. (One thousand two hundred and three score days). Chapter six of Revelation in which six of the seven seals are opened does not specify an identified period of time. We dare not assume anything which is not clearly stated in Scripture but we may consider that those seals being opened in chapter six and which are clearly leading to the return of the Lord that possibly the opening of the seals exceeds in time the otherwise defined period of three and one-half years at least in so far as it deals with the persecution of the saints. In support of that concept and reaching to the two thousand three hundred days given here in Daniel's vision it is worthy of taking note that the woman in chapter twelve of Revelation is *in travail* as a precursor to bringing forth the man -child. The concept of travail is the effort and pain, which proceeds childbirth. It is in the travail of the woman (church) that the man-child is delivered. The saint in the text here in Daniels's vision states the how long question posed here is referencing the two issues of the transgression of desolation, and the cleansing of the sanctuary. The work of God in cleansing his sanctuary at the end of this age may be focused in these twenty three hundred days. I am mot asserting this dogmatically but it appears to fit.

We will now pass to the conclusion of the vision for some further important observations. And in the latter time of their kingdom, when the transgressors are come to the full, a king of fierce countenance and understanding dark sentences shall stand up. And his power shall be mighty, but not in his own power (the power and authority is given by Satan, See Rev. 13:2). And he shall destroy wonderfully and practice and prosper, and shall destroy the mighty and holy people. *"Through his policy he shall cause craft (deceit and fraud) to prosper, he shall magnify himself in his heart, and by peace (Hebrew- prosperity) shall destroy many, and he shall stand up against the prince of princes (Christ) but he shall be broken without hand."* (Daniel 8:23-25). The little horn of Daniel's vision is the son of perdition, the Antichrist. It is very noteworthy that *"he waxes exceeding great toward the south, and toward the east and toward the pleasant land"*. **the land of Israel**. There is a very good reason for placing this very strong emphasis on the land of Israel. The prophet Daniel is telling us that the Antichrist, the son of perdition will emerge in relation to the *"little* *horn", i.e the nation state of Israel.* Dispensationalists see Jewish Israel as the "chosen people". Do you understand how crucially deceptive this erroneous doctrine will be as we approach the end of the age and earthly Israel begins to move to recover the *"pleasant land."* The stated and planned New World Order is to be centered around the emergence of a 'Greater Israel"

Chapter Nine

DANIEL'S SEVENTY WEEKS

We move on now to the ninth chapter of the book of Daniel to examine one of, if not the most pivotal passages in the prophetic Sscripture, the proper understanding of which changes dramatically the popularly held "rapture" theory of today's evangelical churches. In a nut shell the doctrine of the pre-tribulational "rapture "theory rests entirely on the premise that the last seven years of the age (Daniel's seventieth week) involve the necessary removal of the church so that God can fulfill promises to the nation of Israel, which they say are separate and distinct from the New Covenant church. It is necessary to state unequivocally that this present writer rejects the "gap" theory of the fulfillment of Daniel's prophecy. There are many profoundly important truths which are affected theologically if we are to accept the theory that the entire church age is a "gap" or parenthesis in God's ultimate plan for Israel, and that the last seven years which they proclaim to be the period of the tribulation are focused exclusively on the Jews i.e. the natural posterity of those we would identify with Israel. Many of these theological issues will be explored within the context of future chapters; Who then Is Israel? and further commentary on Dispensational Theology. The thrust of this chapter will be to provide an orderly understanding of Daniel 9:24-27.

The setting for the revelations of Daniel chapter 9 is at the time of the reign of Darius the Median king in the first year of his reign.

These Prophets

It comes into Daniel's understanding from the books and that which was revealed to Jeremiah the prophet that the time of the captivity was to be seventy years.

Daniel became fully aware that the time of judgment upon Judah had been fulfilled. He then humbled himself greatly before the Lord and entered into diligent and fervent prayer confessing the sins of the people and their departure from the Lord and his precepts. His prayer is a lengthy rehearsal of confession, repentance and supplication on behalf of Judah and all Israel seeking forgiveness. He continues beseeching the Lord that his face might turn again towards Israel and the sanctuary that is desolate, and that he might do so for his own name's sake. Daniel was a righteous man who poured out his whole heart to the Lord. And while Daniel was in prayer about the time of the evening oblation the (man) appearing as Gabriel came unto him and gave him assurances that his prayers and supplications had been heard. He spoke with Daniel saying that he was come to give Daniel wisdom and understanding and to consider the vision. The following four verses of scripture cover the revelation of the wisdom, which was given Daniel concerning the seventy weeks.

First, it is to be understood that the weeks were weeks of years and within the provisions of the law the Hebrew mind was clear in the understanding that each week represented seven years. There was an understanding that God's law had established for them a system of sevens in which matters and times were resolved and completed. Each seventh year was a Sabbath and when the people were in the land they were to allow the farmland to lie fallow on the seventh year. Then when seven Sabbaths had past or forty-nine years on the fiftieth year was declared a Jubilee. The year of Jubilee was a special time in Israel for every debt was forgiven and every form of bondage was released including land that may have become indentured. Each person recovered his possessions and freedom from any debt or servitude. (See Lev. 25:10). Understanding this background with its periodic Sabbaths and Jubilees will help us in understanding the seventy weeks.

The text of the Scripture begins: *"Seventy weeks are determined upon thy people, and upon the holy city, to finish the transgression, and to make an end of sins, and to make reconciliation for iniquity, and to bring in everlasting righteousness, and to seal up the vision and prophecy, and to anoint the most Holy"* (Daniel 9:24). Now with this understanding that the weeks are weeks consisting of seven years we would conclude from the first phrase in the verse that four hundred and ninety years are in view, that is seventy times seven. Then we would be able further to understand from the first phrase that the prophecy and the weeks are determined upon the people of Israel and not on the world empires and kingdoms where the previous prophesies in Daniel have been focused. The second phrase would then be understood to refer to Jerusalem which at the time of the prophecy lay in ruins. Finishing the transgression and making an end of sins and to make reconciliation for iniquity then most certainly points again to the Redeemer. Israel was promised a kinsman Redeemer and those who were truly in faith were waiting for the promise as a means for the finishing of sins and reconciliation for iniquity. The tenets of the law were a detailed system of sacrifices and offerings which were a constant reminder of the sin, which separated them from a holy God. Within the seventy weeks would be brought in everlasting righteousness, a *sealing* of the vision of prophesy and the anointing of the Most Holy. Knowing then that the Jewish Messiah even our Lord Jesus Christ and his work of redemption on the cross, and both the person and the work he accomplished as the perfect sacrifice for sin there on a hill called Calvary outside the city of Jerusalem is in view in the verse.

"Know therefore, and understand that from the going forth of the commandment to restore and build Jerusalem unto the Messiah the Prince shall be seven weeks and three score and two weeks: the street shall be built again, and the wall even in troublous times." (Daniel 9:25).

It is of utmost importance that we are able to glean from the scriptures the times and seasons of these prophesied events. Daniel was given the vision and understanding at the end of the captivity about 536 B.C.E. The fulfillment of the prophetic words were not to be realized immediately, that is to say that the seventy weeks did not begin at the time of Daniel's vision.

It is true that under the regime of the Medes and Persians there was a release of some Jews to return to their homeland. In the closing verses of II Chronicles and the introductory verses of the book of Ezra we see the decree of Cyrus king of Persia concerning a release of a remnant of the people to return to Jerusalem and begin to rebuild the temple. The return to Jerusalem of a remnant, and the beginning to build is not that decree which is in view in this prophecy. We know this because of the preciseness of the time period which is view in the prophecy, and this earlier return would have been given and allowed at a time which exceeds the seventy weeks. There were several more to come after this early migration to Jerusalem for the purpose of restoring the Lord's house and the tenets of the law. After careful study, I have settled on the account given us in Ezra chapter seven as that which answers to *from the going forth of the commandment to restore and build Jerusalem.* I would encourage you to look at this text, the directives and the provisions which were provided to Ezra in Chapter seven and see if it is not clear that the decree of Artaxerxes in the seventh year of his reign having commanded a complete provision for the restoration of the city. Mark the significant date of this decree which is in 457 B.C. and the decree has allowed Ezra's arrival on the first day of the month of Nissan, which is the first day of the Hebrew year and historical scholars have tracked this date.

Significance is added to the time, as it was the beginning of a Jubilee year, which was a time of great celebration for the people as it marks a return to possession and a release from all manner of debt or bondage. As we read in Ezra 7:10, *"Ezra had prepared his heart to seek the law of the Lord and to do it. and to teach in Israel statutes and judgments".*

So now we have the beginning point of Daniel's prophetic seventy weeks, keeping in mind that they apply solely to the Jews. The text of the prophetic verse continues by stating *"that unto Messiah the Prince shall be seven weeks and sixty and two weeks"*. The twofold designation of time is significant in two regards. The original forty-nine weeks was the necessary time involved in restoring Jerusalem, the temple, the street and the wall.

The further involvement of Nehemiah in the building of the wall is significant for we see there were many adversaries and indeed it was carried out and completed *in troublous times.* Also we see significance is the fact that the seven weeks or forty-nine years brings them to another Jubilee.

The remaining portion of the verse designates an additional sixty-two weeks unto *the Messiah the Prince, i.e. the anointing of Christ and the beginning of his ministry.*

Now it was in the fifteenth year of Tiberius Caesar, Pontius Pilate being governor of Judea when John the Baptist came baptizing. The year is 27 A.D. ppecisely it carries us to his anointing when he was baptized by John the Baptist in the river Jordan. Now it is at that event and point in time where the father declares him to be his beloved Son in whom He is well pleased. And the heavens were opened and the Spirit of God descended on him like a dove. This is" *the anointing of the most Holy"*, and sixty-mine of the seventy weeks are fulfilled. Again we repeat that the baptism of Jesus took place precisely at the end of the 69 weeks or 483 years.

"And after three score and two weeks shall Messiah be cut off, but not for himself: and the people of the prince that shall come shall destroy the city and the sanctuary; and the end thereof shall be with a flood, and unto the end of the war desolations is determined." (Daniel 9:26). The text of the vision written down here tells us that Messiah will be cut off i.e., killed, crucified, and that not for himself, but for our sins.

Afterward shall come the prince and his people and they shall destroy the sanctuary and unto the end desolations are determined. This is, of course, a reference of the Roman legions under Titus who came and destroyed the temple and the city in 70 A. D.

"And he shall confirm the covenant with many for one week: and in the midst of the week he shall cause the sacrifice and the oblation to cease, and for the overspreading of abominations he shall make it desolate, even until the consummation and that determined shall be poured out on the desolate." (Daniel 9:27).

He came to confirm the covenant—to make good on all of the promises of God for all of the promises of God are fulfilled and realized in him. The covenant with the Jews that is to say Israel,

These Prophets

Daniel's people as identified in Daniel 9:24. He confirmed the covenant in the midst of the week with his death on the cross as the perfect and complete sacrifice for sin. He was *cut off in the midst of the week* to put an end to sins and the system of sacrifice which had been committed unto the Jews under the old covenant? He *caused sacrifice and oblation to cease* by his own perfect sacrifice for sin. He died on the day of the Jewish Passover as the Lamb of God in the spring of 31 A.D. or the common era for your sins and my sins.

Even at His death when He gave up the ghost, the veil of the temple was rent in twain signifying that access into the holiest of all had been provided by a new and living way through the blood that he had shed on the cross. The Scripture says that *"He will confirm the covenant with many for one week"*. He was crucified in the middle of that last week of the seventy.

The Jews were given every opportunity to believe the gospel, to see and understand who he was, and to embrace him as their promised Messiah.

The twelve apostles entered into prayer and fasting and on the day of Pentecost the Holy Spirit descended on the vast crowd of Jews who had come to the temple from all countries to worship and observe the feast as they had been commanded to do under the precepts of the law. For the next three and one-half years the message of their Messiah and his deliverance from sin was thoroughly ministered to the Jews by Christ himself. They had three and one-half years of the ministry of the Lord as he moved and taught among them performing miracles and wonderful works. They also had the testimony of his crucifixion and the coming of the Holy Spirit in power.

They had the ministry and testimony of the twelve Apostles as representing the twelve tribes of Israel spreading the word among them. They were given an entire week (seven years) on top of all of the law and the prophets to believe on him whom God had sent into their midst. The gospel was spread to the Jew first. At the end of the week (seven years) Stephen appeared before the counsel, the Jewish Sanhedrin and gave powerful testimony to them concerning the Christ, and recounting their history laid it all before them to understand, but they would mot. *"Ye stiff necked and uncircumcised in heart and ears you do always resist the Holy Ghost. As your fathers did so do you also"* (Acts 7:51). They stopped their ears, cried out together with a loud voice and ran upon him with one accord, casting him out of the city and proceeded to stone him to death.

This was the official rejection and denial of Jewry concerning their Messiah. The *seventy weeks determined upon thy people* expired with this violent expression of murder. From that time forward Jewish people can be saved as individuals and many have believed in Christ, but as a nation, and a s a covenant people of God or collectively it was over forever. God has not dealt with the nation as a whole since that day, and as it becomes notable in the book of Acts immediately after there was a recognition that the promises of God were to all peoples and nations and tongues and to as many as truly believed, and we begin to see the movement of the Holy Spirit to spread the gospel of Jesus Christ. Stephen was the first Christian martyr, murdered by the unbelieving Jewish council of elders—the seventy—the Sanhedrin.

This is the fulfillment of Daniel's seventy weeks.

The last portion of verse 27 is not within the time line of the seventy weeks. The subject of this portion of the prophecy is the judgment of God falling upon the Israelites collectively. Of course, in infinite wisdom and foreknowledge he knew that there would only be a small remnant out of the nation who would embrace his Son but the people as a whole would continue in their sin and abominations. It has always been so with the people who God has called. There is a remnant, sometimes a very small remnant that will faithfully endure. And so the proclamation of the prophecy is for the *"overspreading of abominations he shall make it desolate, even unto the consummation, and that determined shall be poured out on the desolate* (vs.27) *"And the people of the prince that shall come shall destroy the city and the sanctuary"* (Daniel 9:26).In 70 A.D., almost a full generation later Jerusalem, the walls, and the temple were destroyed by Roman legions under Tutus *(the people of the prince that shall come)*. This desolation represents the consummation of any covenant relationship, which the Lord previously established with the nation of Israel. Because as we have seen with the over comers God's promises and God's covenants are conditional in nature. It is required of us, as with Israel of old that we are found not only obedient but also faithful.

As a footnote to this chapter, I feel constrained to make a few points for those who have been taught that a 2000 year "gap" comes between the sixty-ninth and seventieth week. I would ask them: Where in the clear setting forth of the prophecy is it possible to interpret a gap of any duration?

Where in the four verse text does the Antichrist, as it is supposed, make a covenant with Israel, and in the middle of the week he breaks that covenant?

Is Messiah the Prince in verse 25 who comes at the end of the sixty-nine weeks the Antichrist? Is Messiah in verse 26 who is cut off in the midst of the week the Antichrist? Can evangelicals and anyone else who holds this view not see how wrong and unsupported it is by the Scripture text and then where it leads? That is to say, to make the clear pronouncements of the coming of Christ and his crucifixion and then to twist into the working and manifestation of the evil one? This gross perversion of the Scriptures has occurred because in the dispensational scheme of theology because promises to Abraham's seed are not understood. They believe the seed of Abraham to be plural i.e. the whole of Israel, and also that the promise s to Abraham's seed our unconditional. They do not understand that those Promises point to their fulfillment in the person of Christ and that the "seed" is spiritual and not natural. We will see the proof of that statement and the fallacy of this interpretation unfolded in the next chapter, **Who Then Is Israel?**

Chapter Ten

Who Then Is Israel?

Before we return to the prophetic subject matter of Daniel, John and the Lord Jesus Christ we must answer this critical question. Who then is Israel? Until we are each one clear on this matter our understanding of the overall plan of God through the Scripture will be greatly hindered. The Holy Scriptures are contained in one book having two covenants, the old and the new. These two covenants are perfectly joined together in the Person of Christ and as the promise of Messiah were central to the hope of the people under the Old Covenant, so the promise of Christ is the foundation and center of the New Covenant. We are not looking at two fundamentally and completely different things when we look at the old and the new covenant.

In order to fully understand the plan of God we will need to go back four thousand years and begin with Abraham. If you have familiarity with the Scripture you will know that Abram (before his name change to Abraham) was called of God to leave his place of habitation and go to a place where God would lead him. And because he believed and obeyed the calling he was given some very precious promises. God made a covenant with Abram saying, *"I will make thee a great nation, and I will bless thee and make thy name great an thou shalt be a blessing; and I will bless them that bless thee, and curse them that curse thee: and* **in thee shall all of the nations of the earth be blessed"** (Genesis 12:2-3). This is commonly known as the covenant with Abraham for it involved God making promises to Abraham on the condition the he would believe, and that he would obey the voice of the Lord. Abram, become Abraham, left Ur and most of his family to hearken unto the calling of God. There came to pass later a separation between Lot his nephew and Abram, and at that juncture the Lord spoke again to Abram saying, *"And the Lord said unto Abram after that Lot was separated from him. Lift up now thine eyes, and look from this place and look from where you are northward, and southward and eastward and westward: for all of the land which thou seest, will I give unto thee and to thy seed forever: and I will make thy seed as the dust of the earth: so that if any man can number the dust of the earth, then thy seed shall also be numbered".* (*Genesis* 13:14-16). Now we know that Abram eventually had a son, Isaac, who in turn had two sons Esau and Jacob. Now because Jacob esteemed the promises and the blessing of the Lord he had a name change to Israel (meaning a prince with, or to rule with God, Strong's Concordance) and he begat twelve sons who became the progenitors of the twelve tribes of Israel. Because of a famine Jacob and his family were constrained to go down into Egypt where his younger son Joseph had been raised to the position of prime minister. These twelve tribes ultimately grew into a great nation, and this great nation after four hundred years of living in Egypt became slaves and fell under oppression by the bondage of Pharaoh. God rose up Moses and it was within his purpose to redeem and deliver them and he did so by the blood of the Passover lamb. The whole nation was miraculously set free and they crossed over the Red Sea and sojourned in the desert. The law was received at Mount Sinai and they were given opportunity to enter into the land of promise, but because they rejected the testimony of the two faithful witnesses, Joshua and Caleb, they were denied the blessing of their inheritance. Their unbelief condemned that whole generation to wandering in the wilderness for forty years where they all perished except for Joshua and Caleb. The generation which followed were led by Joshua and by the hand of the Lord upon them and they went into the land that God had promised Abram. We read in Joshua 21 as follows: *"and the Lord gave unto Israel all of the land which he sware to give unto their fathers; and they possessed it, and dwelt therein. And the Lord gave them rest round about, according to all that he sware unto their fathers, and there stood not a man of all of their enemies before them; the Lord delivered all of their enemies into their hand. There failed not ought of any good thing which the Lord had spoken unto the house of Israel; all came to pass."* (Joshua 21:43-45).

Now we see that the Lord was faithful to his promises, but we need now to continue to look briefly at the history of this great nation after they entered and possessed the land. They passed through a period of about four hundred years under the Judges and there was a continual falling away and then God would periodically raise up a Judge who would serve to deliver them out of the bondage they as a people had fallen into as a result of sin and apostasy. These temporary deliverers raised up by the Lord brought a measure of revival and were called Judges. The people finally insisted of Samuel, the last of the Judges and some say the first of the prophets, that God would give them a king so they could be like the other nations. The Lord consented knowing the corruption of their hearts, and through Samuel the first king was anointed when Samuel anointed Saul to be king. He was subsequently rejected because he blatantly disobeyed the Lord and afterward David was then chosen to be king. David was a man after God's heart, and he was also a great warrior who consolidated the dominion and power of the nation so that by the end of his forty-year reign Israel briefly ruled over all of the nations round about.

Under the reign of Solomon the kingdom reached its apex of power and glory and the magnificent temple was built in Jerusalem. Towards the end of Solomon's reign he fell away from serving the Lord by taking many strange wives and concubines. The nation was soon sliding back into apostasy and a departure from the Lord and he caused the kingdom to be divided into two parts, the northern ten tribes, who retained the name of Israel and the southern two tribes known as Judah consisting, or the tribe of royal lineage Judah, and little Benjamin. Each division continued with its own kings. Judah continued to occupy Jerusalem but the northern tribes set up their false and idolatrous worship in Samaria. Through a shameful deterioration and being ruled over by a succession of evil kings the

Lord finally brought judgment on the northern tribes and they were carried away captive by the Assyrians and ultimately were scattered so as to have totally lost their identity as a nation, and as those that were once known as the people of God.

Judah survived for a short time and actually had a few good kings mixed in with those that were evil. But apostasy and their sins found them out as well and the Lord raised up the Babylonian empire and his judgment fell upon them carrying them captive into their enemy's domain, and bringing about a destruction of the temple. Babylon also destroyed the Assyrian empire and dominion. After the seventy-year captivity was completed the Lord again raised up the empire of the Medes and Persians and they in turn destroyed the kingdom of Babylon. The purpose of the Babylonian empire and its seventy-year reign was to bring judgment upon an unfaithful people, and to completely withdraw from them. Afterward the Lord put it into the hearts of some of the kings of the Medes and Persians to allow the return of a small remnant of the Jews to Jerusalem. It was at this juncture in their history that Daniel had the vision of the seventy weeks giving understanding to the purpose of God with Israel and he recorded dreams and visions prophetically defining the history of the world in advance. According to the prophecy of Daniel the seventy weeks were fulfilled including a rebuilding of the temple at Jerusalem and a restoration of the city and the wall. It would appear that revival under Ezra and a repentant remnant was realized in Jerusalem. We do not know how long-lived it was because the Scriptures are mostly silent, but we clearly see by the coming of their Messiah that the people were again apostate and corrupted.

The law of the Lord had been corrupted and perverted into a religious system and the Jews had fallen under the dominion and control of the Roman Empire. We have already covered the rest of this history leading up to the anointed Messiah, and we have seen the demise of the second temple, and the city at the hands of the Roman legions. The seventy weeks unto the desolation of the Jews has been fully accomplished as they have as a people continued to demonstrate their unbelief, idolatry and their rebellion against the God of heaven. They were the demanders of the crucifixion of the one who was sent to be their Redeemer, and in so doing brought about the purpose of God in Christ to die for the sins of the faithful and repentant ones from all of the nations. We are answering the question of Who then Is Israel, and I believe it worthwhile to review this earthly history of those who were meant to be a vessel of truth and a light and testimony to the nations. Among them were always a few for even in a day of great apostasy Elijah discovered seven thousand who had not bowed their knee to Baal. The point is that in reviewing the history of the nation it is easy to see that except for some very brief periods and the existence of a small remnant in their history Israel was a reproach and a blasphemy to the name of the Lord.

Please do not believe by this review of the history of Israel that I am anti-Semitic. You must understand that God is not a respecter of persons as is brought out so poignantly in the early chapters of the book of Acts. Our purpose here is to bring into clarity in each heart that the Lord has always had in his purpose to bring forth a people of faith and conviction who would love and serve him. Does he love and accept any of his children on the basis of their national or ethnic origin? The New Covenant becomes a clarification of the purpose of God in Christ. Do you remember at the beginning when God called Abram he said unto him "*...**in thee and in thy seed shall all of the nations of the earth be blesse.*" To whom was that promise made and how was it fulfilled? "*Now to Abraham and his seed were the promises made. He saith not as to seeds as many; but as one. And to thy seed which is Christ. And this I say that the covenant, that was confirmed before of God in Christ, the law which was four hundred and thirty years after, cannot annul, that it should make the promise of none effect. For if the inheritance be of the law, it is no more of promise; but God gave it to Abraham by promise. Wherefore then serves the law? It was added because of transgression till the seed should come to whom the promise was made.*" (Galatians 3:16-18). All of the promises of God are in him, Yea and Amen. The seed then is a spiritual seed and is not a natural seed. As we have seen the promise God made to the nation of Israel is that he would bless them in a physical land of inheritance of they would obey His laws and precepts. At a point in time when they first entered the land those promises were all completely fulfilled as we have read in the twenty-first chapter of Joshua. Israel as a nation and as a people, and through their history did not keep their covenant with God and did not retain their inheritance which was laid waste and suffered desolation being overrun by the pagan nations, and at the end of Daniels prophecy of the seventy weeks we see the desolation came by the overspreading of abominations and unto the end of the war desolations were determined. And we also see the end of Israel insofar as they retained any kind of covenant relationship with the God of heaven or existence in covenant with him.

Who then is a *Jew* in the eyes and heart of God, *"He is not a Jew which is one outwardly, neither is that circumcision which is outwardly in the flesh, but he is a Jew which is one inwardly; and circumcision is that of the heart, in the spirit and not in the letter; whose praise is not of men, but of God".*(Romans 2:28-29). *"Not as though the word of God hath taken none effect. For they are not all Israel which are of Israel: neither because they are the seed of Abraham are they all children: but in Isaac shall thy seed by called; (Gen.21:12) that is <u>they which are the children of the flesh, these are not the children of God</u>, but the children of the promise are counted for the seed."* (Romans 9:6-8).*" For as many as have been baptized into Christ, have put on Christ. There us neither Jew nor Greek; there is neither bond not free; there is neither male nor female; for you are all one in Christ Jesus; and <u>if you be Christ's then you are Abraham's seed,</u> and heirs according to the promise."* (Galatians 3:27-29). *"But God forbid that I should glory save in the cross of our Lord Jesus Christ, by whom the world is crucified unto me, and I unto the world, for in Christ Jesus neither circumcision availed anything, nor uncircumcision, but a new creation. And as many as walk according to this rule, peace be on them, and mercy, and upon* **the Israel of God**". (Galatians 6:16).

There is only one people of God (not two) and they include all of those faithful ones under the Old Covenant such as Daniel, Elijah and Moses, and many more who we do not know. They are those whose circumcision was of the heart. We have all been gathered together into one, in Christ, and to as many as walk according to this government, peace and mercy be upon you, for if we abide faithful unto the end, and live according to the leading of the Holy Spirit we will be counted among those who are the **Israel of God**, and we will inherit the kingdom as joint heirs with Christ who is the firstborn among many brethren. Yes, Jew and Gentile becomes one in Christ but the distinction of their natural posterity disappears as a new creation in Christ.

Chapter Eleven

Free Masonary
The Order of the Illuminatti
and The Revelation of
Mystery Babylon

Many deep mysteries are contained in the prophetic words of John in the Revelation. We understand that the Revelation is of, by, and through our Lord Jesus Christ, and as we will see moving through the text of John's revelations in particular, Christ is seen again and again clothed in a shroud of glory and power. But to understand the complete message of the prophets and gain the fullness of his awesome power and glory, we must take a close up look at the adversary and his plans of deception. The text of the book of Revelation is not unfolded in an exact chronological order as most who have offered us commentaries have tried to logically reason. You cannot read from chapter one through chapter twenty-two and assume that it is all laid out with each verse following in a forward progression upon the previous one, and the text does not necessarily give you a warning that this is the case. What we have is a series of visions of what John saw as placed in the order that the Holy Spirit revealed them to him. There exists a chronology from the beginning of chapter four up through the end of chapter nine, and then the Holy Spirit pauses to review and recount things, which have already been introduced.

When we are introduced to Mystery Babylon for the first and only time we are taken forward to later chapters, seventeen and eighteen, and yet to see how Mystery Babylon fits into the overall scheme of end time events we need to understand her formation and role is much earlier in terms of the chronology of events. Many have identified her as America. Others still believe she has a geographic connection to the Babylon of old; and still others believe that she is the apostate religious system existing at the end of the age. When we fully examine the Scripture I believe that you will find that none if these explanations are accurate. You will take notice that the referral to Mystery Babylon is in the feminine as the Scripture deals with her as a woman in a figurative sense. This is because she is personified as a fornicator and a whore in all of her interactions with the kings of the earth. Discovering her true identity is an important piece of the revelation mystery. As we develop the argument for her true identity and role it will be necessary to look carefully at the Scripture, but in preparation we must first lay a rather extensive background of her development and history in the secular world.

America has changed, and the change is continuous, escalating and dramatic. Once the land of freedom, we are now a country of moral decadence, arrogant politicians, and sorcery. America is not now a Christian nation even though there are many in America who professes Christ. The Christian churches are generally in a state of moral and spiritual compromise going through a form of religious observance, but mostly they no longer bear the light of a testimony as we saw with most in chapters two and three of Revelation. We are a nation on the edge of collapse—morally, spiritually, financially and constitutionally. How did this happen? Did these changes happen by chance or has there been in place a plan and design which has brought them about? President George Bush (senior) announced clearly and unequivocally in the fall of 1990 at the time of the first Gulf War where we are headed—to a **New World Order**. I was a careful and intent follower of all of the events surrounding Desert Shield and Desert Storm because my only son was a platoon Sergeant and an Airborne Ranger with a charge of 38 rangers under his command. I carefully observed this operation and the first public proclamation by an American President that there was a plan in the works to bring forth a New World Order. This plan has been in process for many decades, but it has now become very clear that there is a systematic plan for the destruction of America, as we have known it, and that plan is well advanced, as well as reaching out internationally to other nations ("the "world community"), and it is becoming ever more obvious reality through the subsequent administrations, whether Republican or Democrat. Developing world events, wars, including the so called "war on terrorism", civil unrest in many nations, economic turmoil and impending economic crisis in America and other industrialized nations, and many other indicators testify to a changing world scene. How is it possible that America has become the debt slave of the largest communist country in the world, namely China? We are now as a nation enslaved by an impossible debt burden created by the privately owned and controlled Federal Reserve. The Federal Reserve Act legislated into law in 1913 gave the money power and control of the money and financial destiny of America into the hands of a privately owned and international banking cartel. The debt began to build and subsequently led to the international bankruptcy on March 9, 1933 (Stat 48—1)with the passing by the Congress of the Emergency Banking Relief Act. Pursuant to the Fourteenth Amendment to the Constitution, Article 4 (1868), which says in part: "The, validity of the public debt, authorized by law . . . shall not be questioned." And therefore, the validity of the debt of the United States, for which the citizens are fully responsible, cannot be protested or questioned. This allowed the government to pass the sixteenth amendment to the Constitution, i,e, the unconstitutional income tax. Subsequently the admitted debt now has risen to some twenty-one trillion dollars, (more than $50,000.00 for every man, woman and child who are United States citizens pursuant to the amendment) and the citizens are directly responsible for it's payment pursuant to the fourteenth amendment and subsequently the sixteenth amendment, neither of which were ever ratified by three fourths vote of the states. Thus, Americans are the debt slaves of the Federal Reserve (a private banking entity) in league with an international banking cartel, which owns America. Many other facts whether political, social or economic could be raised in this discussion, but the bottom line again is to answer the question, how did this happen? A cartel of international criminals gained control of international finance and their agenda has been controlling the entire world through their control of Banking and finance in all of the nations of the world including America. This is the entity which *sits upon many waters*' (Rev.17:2) and *'that great city (MYSTERY BABYLON) which 'reigneth over the kings of the earth."* (Rev.17:18). The truth is that this satanic entity owns America and most of the world through the system of international banking including the Federal Reserve. Their icon for establishing world government is centered in the nation state of Israel which will emerge through the numerous Middle East wars as a "Greater Israel", i.e. the 'little horn' of Daniel's prophesies.

What lies behind this dramatic change, and what will be the final condition and state of America, as well as the other nations of the world? The answer to these questions are critically important to our understanding of this study in prophecy because the emerging order of things in the world will be fully confirmed as the fulfillment of Daniel's fourth beast described in his vision, and this fourth beast will be seen as that beast which rises up out of the sea in Revelation chapter 13, and dominates the world for three and one-half years.

In each city or town of any significant size in America you are likely to find a Masonic temple. These are the meeting places and organizational centers of Freemasonry. The organization is passed off publicly as a service and philanthropic group holding a high standard of morality and devotion to community service. The membership is made up of those in the professions, businessmen and others holding respected positions in the community. Inside the temple fellowship and practice we would find, if we had access, something of a somewhat different character. The oaths and practices of Freemasonry are secretive, as well as religious and esoteric in nature. The essence of the philosophical and religious content and nature of the organization flows directly from the tree of the knowledge of good and evil, which was the downfall of man in the Garden of Eden. The initiates are taken into a mysterious realm of teaching, secret oaths and indoctrination into pure Gnosticism. Gnosticism is the doctrine of salvation through knowledge, that is, knowledge of the mysteries of the Universe and of magic formulae indicative of that knowledge. The object of the ancient mysteries was to make men like gods. The Gnostics derived their leading doctrines from men like Plato and Philia. The occult Kaballah of the Hebrews is an important source of the so-called ancient wisdom coupled with the ancient mysteries that once illuminated the minds of men including Egyptian and Babylonian mysticism. The direct object of Freemasonry is to bring its own members to the "gnosis" of which the assertion is as being the only possible method of obtaining the divine essence. The supreme human purpose is the perfection of man that he will become a god. The practices, ceremonies, secret oaths, and indoctrinations of the initiates are to this end. The idea of the universal brotherhood of man is a cardinal doctrine of Freemasonry and Masonry is seen as the Universal Religion. The initiates assist, promote and protect the "brotherhood" in business, in finance, in law and in every endeavor of life. These men are engaged in the worship of humanity. Humanism means the moral and spiritual autonomy of man completely separated from any higher authority. But this also becomes a deception for in the higher orders and degrees of Masonry clearly the director and the one being worshipped is Lucifer. The lower degrees of Masonry provide a cover for the truly illumined ones at the higher levels of the 32nd and 33rd degrees. Their observable purposes and practices would seem to men in general to be worthy and honorable. They function under a cloud of secret deception the perception and guise of which is to leave the impression of legitimacy. The higher Order is reserved for the adepts—the truly enlightened ones. Found proximately in the lodges of Freemasonry is the six pointed star, i.e. the symbol and flag of the nation state of Israel. It is not the Star of David as is proclaimed but an ancient occult symbol of Babylonian mysticism.

Who are the Illuminati? "The world is governed by far different personages from what is imagined by those who are behind the scenes". Benjamin Disraeli. There exists in essence a cartel of international bankers, industrialists, and elitists based in Western Europe and North America who hold the money and power strings over the nations, their politicians, and recognized leaders and rulers. The names of certain families stand out including Rothschild, Rockefeller, Warburg, Lazard, Morgan, Schroeder, and Schiff to mention a few. The pivotal family for two hundred and fifty years has been the House of Rothschild. Some have numbered the elitist families at thirteen at the top of the pyramid of power but it is to be realized that there is a hierarchy of evil power supporting and interacting with the upper echelons. There exits in the power structure secret societies separate but yet networking with the apex including Skull and Bone, Knights Templar, the Bilderberg Group, the Committee of three hundred, and other societies and organizations which are involved and two numerous to mention all in a common Luciferian conspiracy to control the entire world. The power structure has been built through money lending and manipulation of national governments, through wars, created depressions, political manipulations and any other covert activity, which would benefit the elitists in the areas of wealth and power. The nations of the world are constantly in debt and they must go to the source for financing, thus creating the concept of "national debt", via fiat money and currencies.(Federal Reserve Notes-evidences of debt to name just one). And it is the age-old truth as is expressed in the Proverbs; the borrower is always the servant of the lender. America is under their control. The Presidents have been selected-not elected- by the Luciferian "enlightened" for decades and probably even generations. Name them; Obama, both of the Bushes, Clinton, Reagan, Carter, Nixon, Johnson, Eisenhower, Truman, Roosevelt, Hoover, Taft, Wilson and maybe even further back into the history of America. There was a break with John Kennedy and he sought to dismantle the Federal Reserve System, and introduced United States Treasury Notes, honest national money bearing no interest to the Federal Reserve. And, he had begun the printing of this debt free United States Treasury Notes. He also intended to end the conflict which became the Viet Nam war. He was assassinated by the occult power structure as you cannot interfere with their banking power and fraudulent fiat money and survive. Robert Kennedy was assassinated later because the power structure comprised of the illuminati and associated secret societies did not want him to gain the presidency and he was very popular.

The name of Lucifer, the fallen angel is also known as the bearer of light, hence the "illuminati" which means the enlightened ones. Lucifer is also known as the father of lies, hence a master deceiver, and a degree of pride that has caused him to declare that he will be as the Most High. The illuminati have always been based on the lodges of Freemasonry, which was taken over at the higher levels in the eighteenth century by the illuminati. So called "good deeds" are carried out by the middle and lower levels of the Society. The higher and enlightened ones are in direct fellowship with Lucifer and the fallen powers of darkness whose final intent and purpose is not only to be worshipped but also to gain dominion and control over the entire earth. In closing this brief resume of the hidden gnosticism of the evil occult powers of darkness that control the world, the reader must understand that the satanic goal will be realized, and their program is already well advanced. Prior to the Lord's return there will be a ten-region **communistic** world government controlling all of mankind. I emphasize the fact of its communistic nature for we see the goals of the occult powers are to destroy monarchies, and the sovereignty of nation states; to abolish the ownership of all private property; to abolish all patriotism; to gain total control of the world's wealth and commerce; to abolish the family; and to abolish all religions except for the purpose of directing all worship to Lucifer. Wake up America! Wake up Christian if you know the Christ! The ten planks of the Communist Manifesto have already been established, and are in place in America. Take notice that the elitists who are responsible for orchestrating world government including the planned destruction of America, as we have known it is Zionist (Khazarian) Jews (certainly not all people who are Jewish for the writer does not endorse anti-Semitism), and their recruited political and financial gentile lackeys. They seek to establish a "Greater Israel".

With this background having been laid, we will move now more specifically to deal with the subject of Mystery Babylon as revealed in the Scriptures in the seventeenth and eighteenth chapters of Revelation. *"Come hither and I will show you the judgment of the great whore that sits upon many waters with whom the kings of the earth have committed fornication, and the inhabitants of the earth have been made drunken by the wine of her fornication*" (Rev.17:1-2.) We begin to see immediately the character of the harlot, and certain things are disclosed. First, she sits upon "many waters", which means by metaphor that she is international in nature. This eliminates a popular perception that she is America, as well as a second idea that her manifestations are from the regions of ancient Babylon. We clearly see that she is involved in an unclean union, (metaphorically fornication) and the inhabitants of the earth have been deceived as made drunken by her union with the kings (world leaders) of the earth. John was then carried away in the Spirit and he saw a woman sitting (note that she is riding upon the top of the beast) upon a scarlet colored beast full of names of blasphemy, having seven heads and ten horns. We will explore this beast in greater detail when we examine the content of Revelation 13. For now we will simply state that this is a metaphorical expression of the final world kingdom of Daniel chapter seven and it is in fact world government, which is the goal and purpose of the Luciferian Illuminati. Thus, the scarlet (sin) colored beast of prophecy, which will gain dominion at the end of this age. The nations and the inhabitants of the earth have been deceived, and they are drunk having lost any possible perception. As we continue we see the woman arrayed in purple (royalty)and scarlet (sin) color decked with gold and precious stones (possessing great wealth), "*and having a cup in her hand full of abominations and filthiness of her fornication; and upon her forehead was written* MYSTERY BABYLON THE GREAT THE MOTHER OF HARLOTS AND ABOMINATIONS OF THE EARTH".(Rev 17:4-5).

And John saw the woman drunken with the blood of the saints, and with the martyrs of Jesus. We saw the souls of them who were martyred for the testimony of Jesus under the altar when we examined the firth seal in chapter 6. We also observed the martyrdom of the saints when we explored the testimony of the "two witnesses" in chapter 11. This martyrdom will be taking place on a large scale during the period of the tribulation, and the persecution and martyring of the saints may in fact actually begin prior to that last three and one-half year period, and then greatly intensify as the tribulation begins. Many will die during that time at the hands of the beast as motivated and deceived by the woman, the whore, sitting on top of the beast, and in control of the beast through the wine of her fornication. A portion of that wine is the blood of the saints as Lucifer's goal and purpose is to destroy anything that speaks out for the Lord, gives testimony, and stands for him against *"the wiles of the devil"*. The wine is also the drunkenness of deception not only of the kings of the earth but also the inhabitants of the earth who will rejoice over the death of these saints. *"They that dwell on the earth shall wonder whose names are not written in the book of life when they behold the beast who was, and is not, and yet is"*. (Rev. 17:8). Continuing with the text of the chapter in verse nine we are told: *"Here is the mind which has wisdom, the seven heads are seven mountains on which the woman sits"* Now we need to pause from the text of chapter seventeen briefly for we are needing to make some identifications.

We have seen that Mystery Babylon sits not only upon the beast, but also upon *many waiters, a*s well as *upon seven mountains.* To solve the mystery as to how this is possible we conclude that the many waters speak of an entity, which is international in scope. We further would conclude that the seven heads are seven mountains where the beast has power and control through the beast's relationship with the whore. The mountains speak metaphorically of a structure of power either spiritually or politically or probably even both of these. We see in Scripture often the mountain of the house of the Lord or Mount Zion. The mountains upon which the woman sits are an expression metaphorically of the same dominion principle. There exists here a structure, which is both spiritual in the sense that it is controlled by spiritual wickedness, and also political in the sense of demonstrating dominion and control world wide (many waters). So we see the whore overriding, controlling and sitting upon the beast which has attained an international power structure being expressed with seven heads (mountains). We laid a foundation with the secret societies and network of occultism headed by the Illuminati (enlightened ones-so called). This is the essence of MYSTERY BABYLON. Even as this treatise is being written this elitist occult, devilish structure controls much of the entire world politically and economically through banking and commerce. The conclusion we are drawing is that the secretive occult power structure seeking total world dominion includes Freemasonry, numerous secret societies, and this network of secrecy and all evil being controlled by the Illuminati is Mystery Babylon. By definition the Greek translation of the word for mystery "is to shut the mouth, as a secret, and when it is used in a spiritual sense it is secretive and to be known only to the initiates". (Strong's Concordance). So this perfectly describes the Illuminati and the network of secret societies it controls along with the political, banking and financial system. It is religious for we have already said they se themselves as the universal religion based upon the "gnosis". They have networked, infiltrated, and gained control over the *ecumenical* churches of Christendom, as well as political control over all of the nations of the West, not to exclude their controlling influence over the other institutions such as international corporations and banking institutions critical to the function of society, namely law, medicine, the media, agriculture, and last but not least education,

Now we have the elements of description identifying **Mystery Babylon**. Ultimately Babylon had its expression first at the tower of Babel when men universally cooperated in the building of a tower ostensibly to reach up into heaven. God judged and destroyed this effort, brought about a confusion of languages to separate the human race and it has taken the scattered peoples in the "confusion" of Babel to reconstruct itself into the emerging form of world government, and as with the first effort it is inspired by Lucifer. It is Babylonish in its cultic mystery religion, and in a sense represents the renewal of ancient Babylon for it is built of the same mysticism and practices. The ancient Jewish Babylonian Talmud and Kabbalah are principle text books on eastern and ancient mysticism having its origins in ancient Babylon and Egypt. We see at the end of chapter seventeen that God will put it into the hearts of the kings of the earth to destroy and overthrow the fabric and essence of Mystery Babylon for they have discovered her whoredom and they turn on her who has been their controller to bring about her destruction, and give all power to the beast which is both for the purpose of the establishment of the system of the antichrist and the person of Antichrist himself. The text says: *"And the ten horns (*the regionalized governments of the world will be tenfold) *which you saw upon the beast, these shall hate the whore, and shall eat her flesh, and burn her with fire, for God has put it in their hearts to fulfill his will, and to agree, and to give their kingdom unto the beast until the words shall be fulfilled. And the woman which you see is that great city which rules over the kings of the earth".* (Rev. 17:16-18). Those who have been controlled because God has purposed it to be so will dethrone the very Illuminati, which have conspired to control the world, of power. This will fully open the door for the Antichrist to come forth and manifest himself as the savior of the world and enable him by his satanic power to direct all worship to himself.

We will now move on into chapter 18 to make further discoveries concerning Mystery Babylon which will become dominant at the end of the age and which will prepare the way for the whole world and the revelation and worship of the Son of Perdition, the Antichrist. There is a declaration of the fall of Babylon at the outset of chapter eighteen by a mighty and glorious messenger (angel) who makes that declaration saying *"Babylon the great is fallen, is fallen, and become the habitation of devils and the hold of every foul spirit, and a cage of every unclean and hateful bird, for all nations have drunk of the wine of the wrath of her fornication, and the kings of the earth have committed fornication with her, and the merchants of the earth have waxed rich through the abundance of her delicacies"* (.Rev.18;2-3.) I believe that the messenger making the declaration is the Lord Jesus, and the statement is made in retrospect of her judgment which we see to have taken place in the previous chapter. The issue to be emphasized and heightened that it is of utter necessity that the Lord's people escape not only from her evil influence but from her control. We se this admonition brought forth clearly in verse four when the voice from haven says with clarity, *"Come out of her my people, that you be not partakers of her sins and that you receive not of her plagues".* The warning is solemn and definite to the saints for Babylon is the epitome of evil and under the judgment of the Lord. She is the ultimate expression of the final order of things in the world system.

If the people of God are ensnared in her web of deception they most certainly will not escape the judgment of the Lord. "*Love mot the world neither the things that are in the world, for if any man love the world the love of the Father is not in him*" (I John 2:15).

When she is overthrown and fallen the kings of the earth who have committed fornication with her shall bewail her with great wailing and lamentation, and the merchants of the earth shall mourn and weep for her. Seeing she had set herself up as a queen ruling over the world's financial system and from that place of power directing the international world of commerce. We see a résumé' of her trafficking and commercial activities in verses 12 through 14 consummating in merchandizing in slaves and the souls of men. Consider the many trade organizations which have been set up internationally to encourage trade and commerce world wide including the World Trade Organization, North American Free Trade Association, The Central American Free Trade Association, and the Asian equivalents of these trade treaties and associations. It is all about promoting world commerce and engaging the nation's participation for there is a monetary reward for them as well as for the merchants of the world. Now it ultimately does all flow back to the international bankers who control most of the world's central banks, and exercise power and control over nations and corporations through their control of fiat currencies, the World Bank and the International Monetary Fund. Also, the bank of International Settlement in Basil, Switzerland, which is the central banker's ultimate bank. Is it not clear that she is already *arrayed in purple and scarlet and decked with gold, and pearls and precious stones* signifying her great wealth? This evil system of commences and world control through fornication with the kings of the earth is already well established covering and monetarily enslaving the vast majority of nations.

Some of the Moslem nations have still not been completely subdued (Syria and Iran) but all of that is in process even as we review this Babylonian whore. Consider the invasion and defeat of Iraq allegedly to free her from the tyrant Saddam Hussein. The real reason for the invasion was that Saddam was resisting the United Nations and their efforts to include oil rich Iraq in the worlds monetary exchange system (International Monetary Fund) and to gain rule over the oil revenues and profits. Awaken if you are asleep concerning these issues for we are rapidly approaching a time of international slavery under the precepts and platform of complete communism. If you believe that a communist nation cannot fully engage in commerce take a long look at where China has come even to having a large control over America through a long history of trade imbalance and accumulated debt. Every time you walk into a Wal-Mart store and buy goods made by slave labor in China a contribution is being made to the system of the emerging communistic world government all of which is being orchestrated by the cultic elitists and their large network of secret societies. America is under their control and the control and power of the Zionist movement is working diligently and progressively to produce a one-world order which will answer completely to Daniel's revelation of the fourth beast and the feet and ten toes of revealed in Nebuchadnezzar's dream. Yes, this is Mystery Babylon in control of the financial systems of the world through debt and fiat money.

Chapter Twelve

BEHOLDING HEAVEN'S THRONE

It is necessary to establish some order so that the forward movement of events as unveiled in the Revelation so that we can begin to understand in context the whole text, as well as in relation to Daniel's valuable supporting contribution. By way of a brief review we previously saw that John had his initial vision of the Lord in chapter one. He described the vision, which he beheld of His glory in the midst of the seven golden candlesticks, which, were identified as representing the seven churches in Asia. When the Lord spoke with John he told him to" *write the things, which he had seen, the things, which are, and the things, which shall be hereafter."*

There is a chronology here to be discerned. In the beginning we have the introduction and John's vision of the Lord Jesus Christ in the midst of the seven golden candlesticks. It is after this initial vision of the Lord that the instruction comes for John to write *the things, which he has seen.* Then, follows those things, which are covered in chapters two and three. Although the spiritual instruction is to the seven churches and was directed to them individually there is a general admonition and exhortation to the church as a whole. These letters to the churches again speak to *the things, which <u>are.</u>* Beginning with chapter four the *things, which shall be <u>hereafter</u> begin* to be addressed. It is very important to understand that the next six chapters of the book (chapters 4, 5, 6, 7, 8 and 9) of Revelation are unfolded for us in a chronological order in the successive chapters.

THESE PROPHETS

But then there is a pause at chapter ten, which we will examine in detail, and John is told that *he must prophesy again* concerning other perspectives upon which the Word of God has established further detail, and which is added concerning portions of that will add to this explanation at appropriate points as we move through the book. But now the plan is to follow the text in order at least until we accomplish a complete commentary on chapters four through nine. One of the major failures of the popular expositors on the text as a whole is to make the erroneous assumption that everything from chapter one through chapter twenty-two happens in a chronological sequence. This approach results in connecting things and events, which cannot be connected. These distinctions will be explained at the appropriate time when we reach those points in the Scripture. For now we will return to chapter four and behold the heavenly throne.

Before the various issues of tribulation, spiritual conflict, and ultimately the righteous judgment, which most certainly must follow it is incumbent upon us to understand, and for it be established with us that there is a sovereign God and that He does reign eternally in heavenly places. Further the authoritative basis for judgment and justice must be clearly discerned by each one who is the subject of his sovereign throne. There exists the need and requirement of our examination and assent of truth so that when the actual judgment is meted out we recognize and understand its purposes, justice, righteousness and necessity of execution, as well as that a spiritual dividing of all things is established in our hearts. And that we may say, Amen, and so be it, to all that is faithful and true. Chapter four begins with the vision of an opening door in heaven, and a voice as the sound of a trumpet as it were speaking to John saying. *"Come up here and I will show thee things, which must be hereafter."* (Rev.4:1),. We have been introduced to see heaven through an open door. Many who have interpreted this passage have applied it to the alleged pre-tribulational "rapture" of the church. Clearly there is no vision of the church in view in the text and the one being addressed is the apostle John as the one to *come up here*. This false interpretation, if accepted, opens the door, not to heaven, but lays a foundation for the erroneous interpretation of much of what is to follow. We will clearly see that the gathering of all of the saints in the resurrection which follows immediately after the period which we have termed according to Scriptural authority the "great tribulation". (Comp. Math. 24:29-31).

John being immediately in the Spirit beheld a throne, which was set in heaven, and he describes the glory and beauty of what he beheld. Around about the throne he beheld four and twenty seats and upon the seats he beheld four and twenty elders clothed in white raiment and having upon their heads crowns of gold. We are assisted in our interpretation here with the white raiment and crowns of gold which we see from other Scripture in the larger text of the book would identify the elders as being a representation of the people of God. Three of those references are already established in the letters to the churches. At Revelation 3:18 the saints are admonished of him to buy gold tried in the fire as well as white raiment that they might be clothed. There are other references at Rev. 2:10 and 3:11 to the possessing of a crown by virtue of faithfully overcoming, There are also other confirming references later in the text so that we mat conclude that the identity of the elders are those who are out from among the whole company of God's people. We are not saying that they are specifically from the churches referenced in these texts, but their being in possession of the white raiment and crowns of gold clearly designates them as belonging to a faithful company of believers who have overcome. The number twenty- four also bears an impotent symbolic meaning not necessarily to be interpreted literally. The kingdom of Israel of old established by David provides a spiritual reflection having elements, which foreshadow the kingdom of our Lord. We see that what was set up were courses of the priesthood to function in the ministry even before the temple was built by Solomon. These priestly courses were twenty-four in number functioning in the orderly fulfillment of the priestly duties. You may read of these courses of the priesthood and their divisions in I Chron. 24:1-18. What we are saying is that these twenty -four elders represent a priestly company ministering before the very throne of God, and the number twenty- four connects us to that ministry established by king David of old who in many ways prefigures as

These Prophets

a type the ultimate King and Lord of the heavenly kingdom. We would conclude that they are not disembodied spirits but appear as whole having heads and bodies with the symbolic covering of white raiment and crowns of gold. The resurrection of the saints has not yet occurred at this point in time even though we are dealing with things, which are hereafter. We purposely examined the early portion of chapter twelve prior to this portion because of the importance of establishing the 'man child' who was caught to the throne and the woman who was left behind having found a place prepared for her in the wilderness. If you will return to that portion you will find that our clear declaration was that the man child represented a faithful remnant out from among the general company of the whole church. That company was caught to the throne and warfare issued, which resulted in that dragon the Devil being cast out of haven.

There are two precedents (witnesses) in the Old Testament which bear witness to faithful ones being translated and caught up to God without first experiencing physical death. They are Enoch and Elijah. It is abundantly clear from the text of chapters four and five that we are beholding in this vision at a time immediately prior to the beginning of the great tribulation as is evidenced by the opening of the seals of the book, that the twenty-four elders and the man child are synonymous and of the same company. Those who have held the doctrine of a pretribulational "rapture" will no doubt need to struggle through this concept, but it becomes clear with study that no scripture can be found which supports the concept of the entire church being so "ruptured" prior to the period of the tribulation. Those who hold that doctrine also erroneously hold to a seven-year tribulation based on their misinterpretation of Daniel's seventy weeks.

We will now move on with John's vision of the heavenly throne. Out from the throne proceeded lightening and thundering and voices, and there were seven lamps burning before the throne which were the seven Spirits of God, i.e. the Holy Spirit (Cp. Rev. 1:4, 3:1, and 5:6). Also round about the throne were four beasts (living creatures) with eyes before and behind. The first was like unto a lion, the second like unto a calf, the third like unto a man, and the fourth like unto a flying eagle. The living creatures full of eyes also had six wings and they ceased not to worship before the throne saying holy, holy, holy is the Lord God which is and which was and which is to come. Their worship was to give glory and honor and thanks to Him that sat upon the throne.

We need to identify the living creatures and to do so we will need to look at the prophetic visions of Ezekiel beginning in the first chapter. You will find here a more elaborate description of the living creatures, but we clearly see from verse ten that Ezekiel was beholding in his vision the same ones who are identified here in chapter four of Revelation. Moving to chapter ten of Ezekiel you can read about more of their function and activity around the throne of God and in verse ten of the chapter reference is made to the original vision which Ezekiel had by the river Chebar in the beginning of the vision in chapter one. Here we see the living creatures are identified as the Cherubim. The Cherubim are angelic beings who have a very special place and function near the throne of God. We see representations of them watching over the mercy seat on the Ark of the Covenant watching intently over the matter of the covenant contained therein that God had made with his people. Their ministry before the Almighty is seen to be forever and ever. We also see the twenty-four elders (in reality an indefinite number symbolized by the number twenty-four) before the throne with their hearts filled with worship and giving worthy praise and honor to him who is the Creator and who occupies the throne, and all that it encompasses.

The text of chapter five begins with a focus on the Book sealed with seven seals. The Book which we will see contains all of the judgments which are to be released not only during the period of tribulation, but also after the resurrection when the Day of the Lord is manifest on the ungodly and the entire unregenerate world system and its peoples. The question is posed by a strong angel: *"Who is worthy to open the Book and to lose the seals thereof?"* (Rev 5:2). No man was found to open the Book, neither to look therein, and John wept much until he perceived the truth that there was one who was worthy to open it. Behold the Lion of the tribe of Judah and the Root of David has prevailed to open the Book. The Scriptures teach us that all judgment has been committed to Jesus Christ. He who has experienced all of the trials and temptations if the enemy, and he who has walked the earth as a man and maintained his sinless purity and righteousness, and he who has shed his own blood and died on the cross for the sins of men is worthy to loose the seals of judgment. And we behold him in the midst of the throne as a Lamb having been slain having seven eyes, which are the seven Spirits of God taking the Book out of the right hand of him who sits upon the throne. We are allowed to observe the four and twenty elders falling down to worship having everyone of them harps and vials full of odors, which are the prayers of the saints. And they sang a new song. You are worthy Lord to open the Book and loose the seals thereof because you have redeemed us by your blood out of every kindred and tongue and nation, and have made us to be kings and priests and we shall reign.

All heaven is worshipping and a myriad of angels are praising Him saying with a loud voice *"Worthy is the Lamb who was slain to receive power, ruches, and wisdom, and strength and honor, glory and blessing"* (Rev. 5:12).And this occasion around the throne elicited worship form all including the angels, the four beasts (Cherubim), and the twenty -four elders who fell before him that lives forever and ever.

Chapter Thirteen

Daniel's Final Vision-Tribulation

Daniel's Vision

John's vision of the heavenly throne with the Book having been taken by the Lion of the Tribe of Judah as the one worthy to open the seals thereof immediately precedes the great tribulation. The sixth chapter of this discourse deals specifically with the loosing of he first six seals binding the Book. In the tying together of the visions of these two prophets it seemed expedient to attach the sixth chapter of Revelation to Daniel's vision in the seventh chapter of Daniel. Now we will return to Daniel's later vision set forth in chapter eleven of Daniel to correlate the account of John's vision in chapter six of Revelation (this narrative is covered in chapter four) dealing with the opening of the first six seals to see what was revealed to Daniel concerning the experience and testimony of the saints during this time of trouble. We have previously also sought to open up to our understanding the truth concerning the testimony of the two witnesses in the first twelve verses of chapter eleven of Revelation. We would reference your attention back to the chapter entitled Measuring the Temple to incorporate these truths into the proper framework. The objective here is to compare Scripture with

Scripture so that an overall understanding of the portions that are related to each other may be achieved.

We are now going to focus on the later portion of Daniel chapter eleven for it is this portion that specifically details much of what is symbolized in the first five seals of Revelation chapter six. The symbolism being employed in Revelation chapter six is that of horses of color as in the first four seals each one representing elements of the trials and difficulties experienced on the earth by it's inhabitants. The fifth seal specifically discloses the martyrdom of the saints, which will occur throughout the tribulation period. As we examine the text in Daniel you will see the relatedness of the vision to both chapter six and the first portion of chapter eleven (vss.1-12) of John's visions in the Revelation.

We will begin our examination of the text beginning with verse thirty; of Daniel, 11. The reason for this being that this portion correlates with the loosing of the seals; *"For the ships of Chittim will come against him; therefore, shall he be grieved, and return, and have indignation against the holy covenant; so shall he do; he shall even return and have intelligence with them that forsake the holy covenant. And arms shall stand upon his part and they shall pollute the sanctuary of strength, and shall take away the daily sacrifice, and they shall place the abomination that makes desolate."* (Daniel 11:30-31). Several elements of the conflict are revealed to us in these two verses. First, we see the movement to take power and controls for the ships of Chittim are coming against him. The word Chittim translates to mean "an islander", and more specifically the shores opposite of Palestine. We place the action and activity geographically in the Middle East at least in the close proximity of the land of promise given to Israel under the old covenant. Secondly, there are many who have set forth commentary on these prophetic Scriptures who believe that there will be a rebuilding of the temple in Jerusalem. Some of the thought concerning that position is questionable as the only support for that thinking and doctrinal conclusion turns around what Daniel has spoken of as the "abomination of desolation." If we take it as a given that this final conflict and movement will ultimately focus on Jerusalem and the establishment of a throne of power in that location, then we must present to those that hold the position that the seventieth week of Daniel deals more or less exclusively with Jewish people for an answer to some searching questions concerning the abomination of desolation. As a precedent to the causing of the daily sacrifice to cease they would hold as a necessity a rebuilt temple in Jerusalem, and a covenant allowing the Jews to resume ritual sacrifice under the tenets of the law. They would further hold according to their view of Daniels' seventieth week that the Antichrist breaks the covenant in the midst of the week and from that point forward he issues an enforceable decree forbidding the continued offering of animal sacrifices in the temple.

Is this the meaning of the abomination of desolation? What effect would such a decree have upon the multitude to whom such animal sacrifices hold absolutely no spiritual significance? How then could the Antichrist engage and have intelligence with them who are (supposedly Jews) who forsake the holy covenant assuming that the covenant made was for the Jews only? Most certainly their doctrine declares that the tribulation period is to reach lost Israel, and they affirm very dogmatically that "all Israel shall be saved" specifically referring to natural Jews and secular Israel.

It is necessary at this juncture to address the true meaning of the "abomination of desolation" for it plays a role which must be understood by the saints of God lest we be carried away with flatteries and deceptions.

Fundamentally the term has to do with the issue of worship and what or who is the object of worship. For it is foundational for us to understand that the most basic element of our relationship with the Lord is that of worship. When the Scripture speaks of that which is an abomination we understand that by the meaning of the Hebrew word we are dealing with something which is *filthy, defiling* and *idolatrous*. When we consider the aspect of desolation we find that it carries the meaning of *devastation* and *destruction*. So we find in the phrase combined an act of filthy and idolatrous destruction. We will find the timing of the abomination of desolation spoken of here in Daniel 12:11 where we are told that: *"And from the time that the daily sacrifice shall be taken away and the abomination that market desolate set up shall be a thousand two hundred and ninety days."* This places the occurrence just thirty days before the beginning if the tribulation, which lasts for a thousand two hundred and three score days. Let us look at another reference to this pivotal event at Mathew 24:15-21, *"When you therefore shall see the abomination of desolation spoken of by Daniel the prophet, stand in the holy place, whoso readeth, let him understand . . .*

For then shall be great tribulation, such as was not since the beginning of the world unto that time, no, nor ever shall be". We see then the abomination of desolation as a sign for our understanding occurring very shortly before the onset of the great tribulation. Drawing upon another important Scripture dealing with identifying the act of abomination we look at II Thes.2: 2-4, *"Let no man deceive you by any means: for that day will not come, except there be a falling away first, and that man of sin be revealed, the son of perdition; who opposes and exalts himself above all that is called God, or that is worshipped; so that he as God sits in the temple of God, showing himself that he is God".* How then do we define the manifestation of that which the Scripture refers to as the abomination of desolation? The temple of God is the place where worship takes place. Under the old covenant it was in the holy place inside the temple. Under the new covenant God does not dwell in a temple made with hands but enters into the "true tabernacle" (See Hebrews 9:11-12), which is in the spirits who embrace him. I personally do believe that there will be a rebuilding of a third temple in Jerusalem and my basis for that conviction is found at Daniel 11:45 where we read *"And he shall plant the tabernacle of his palace between the seas in the glorious holy mountain (Zion) yet he*(Antichrist) *shall he come to his end, and none shall help him."* So that would be strong evidence to further deceive the masses and certainly those Zionist Christians who have bought into the Israel deception.

What I do know is that the true worshippers of God must worship him in spirit and in truth.(See John 4:23-24). I also believe that by a masterful deception that the Antichrist will bring the whole world to worship him and the spiritual power behind him, which is Satan, the Devil, the Dragon, and Lucifer. To take away the daily sacrifice is to decree that we cannot offer ourselves daily to worship the true and living God, but will need to take a position that we will worship him whom Satan has set forth. This may be found to be closely related to the actual acceptance and taking to ourselves the "mark of the beast". Understand the abomination of desolation in the light of this eternal truth, and refuse it with all of your being.

Continuing with the account following in Daniel we are instructed and understand as above that *"such as do wickedly against the covenant shall he corrupt by flatteries, but the people who do know their God will be strong and do exploits, and they that are wise among the people shall instruct many: yet they shall fall by the sword, by flame, by captivity and by spoil many days. Now when they shall fall they shall be helped with a little help; but many shall cleave to them with flatteries. And some of them of understanding shall fall, to try them, and to purge, and to make them white even unto the time of the end; be4cause it is yet for a time appointed"* (Daniel 11:32-34). This text provides us with a classic confirmation of the trials and settings of the saints during the time of trouble come upon the whole world, This provides a clear comparison of the account given under the fifth seal at Rev. 6:9-11 as well as the testimony of the "two witnesses" at Rev. 11:3-12. It would be helpful for you to read these portions again for your own clarification of the truth.

The king (Antichrist) shall do according to his own will exalting himself, and magnifying himself over every god, and he shall speak with a great mouth against the God of heaven, and he shall prosper until the indignation shall be completed. He shall not regard the **God of his fathers,** or the desire of women, and he shall magnify himself above all. It becomes clear from this passage that the Antichrist will be Jewish for the word used for God is a reference to the true and only God of Israel, i.e. the God of his feathers. It is referred to here using the same word as is used numerous times and translated God in the Old Testament. This would be fitting and proper for he us emulating the Jewish model and expectation of a savior, but in his estate shall h honor the god of forces (a fortified place, a defense-Strong's Concordance) and a god who his fathers knew not. From the passage we see that he will be taken up with riches, material values and pleasant things, as well as total glory and power. This is quite the opposite of our Lord and Savior who was meek and lowly of heart and possessed no material wealth at all.

Even up to the time of the end there remains battles and conflict with the king of the south pushing at him, and the king of the north (Antichrist) shall come against him like a whirlwind with chariots and horsemen, and many ships and he shall come into the countries and pass over. The text here does not identify for us who the king of the south might be so we can only surmise that it is an ancient enemy in the conflict which has ragad in the area historically for literally thousands of years. He shall stretch forth his arm upon the counties and the land of Egypt shall not escape. He shall enter into the glorious land and many shall be overthrown. The glorious land is that beautiful land of splendor possessed by Israel under the original promises of God to them as their inheritance. He is in control of great riches and over all of the precious things of Egypt, Ethiopia and the land of the Libyans shall be at his steps. Messages of trouble coming from the north (conceivably Iran or Russia) will trouble him, and he shall go forth with great fury and overcome many. *"He shall plant his tabernacles of his palace between the seas (Mediterranean and Dead Sea) in the glorious holy mountain. Yet shall he come to his end and none shall help him."* Read again (Daniel 11: 36-45).

We have in the text further elements of the seals as represented by the horseman. In the first seal we saw a white horse; and him that sat upon had in his hands a bow, and a crown was given unto, and he went forth conquering and to conquer. Clearly this scenario under the first seal recaps what we have just followed in the campaign of conquering revealed to us in Daniel's vision, The horse revealed under the second seal is a red horse and it speaks metaphorically if much blood shed and death through warfare. We have observed at least a portion of that warfare and blood shed in the progression of Daniel's vision. Warfare and conflict are significant elements of the great trouble coming upon the earth in those coming last days of tribulation. Within the context of the third and fourth seal we do see famine and pestilence (diseases) covering the earth and we have spoken of these in the earlier chapter on the great tribulation. We see our Lord's commentary on this period in Mathew 24 where at verse 22 He says; *"and except those days should be shortened, there should no flesh be saved; but for the elects sake those days shall be shortened"*. We have reviewed Daniel's perspective on that period from the point of the abomination of desolation even to the end, and we have sought to cross-reference this period with the first five seals of the sixth chapter of Revelation. These two prophets graphically depict the reality pf the great tribulation for us here. Let us not be deceived by the awesome difficulties to be faced in this relatively brief and final chapter of human history. Let us also not be deceived by the ascent of Antichrist to a throne in Jerusalem because we are holding to a falsified version of Daniel's seventy weeks and fail to see who Israel really is in truth.

Chapter Fourteen

SHAKING OF THE HEAVENS AND THE EARTH

The end of this age is coming with very cataclysmic events including a complete disruption of the natural order of the creation. We have previously reviewed the unfolding of the tribulation period in two chapters. The first chapter was viewing the great tribulation in the context of the first five seals which are revealed in chapter six of Revelation. In the chapter previous to this one we examined the same period of time as revealed to Daniel in he last several verses of chapter eleven. We will continue now by returning to Revelation chapter six and looking at the last several verses of the chapter attempt to understand the issues and meaning of the sixth seal.

"And I beheld when He had opened the sixth seal, and lo, there was a great earthquake and the sun became black as sackcloth of hair, and the moon became as blood, and the stars of heaven fell unto the earth, even as a fig tree casts its untimely figs, when she is shaken with a mighty wind. And the heavens departed as a scroll when it is rolled together; and every mountain and every island were moved out of there places. And the kings of the earth, and the great men, and the rich men, and the chief captains, and the mighty men, and every bondman, and every free man hid themselves in the dens and in the rocks of the mountains;, and said to the rocks and hide us, and hide us from the face of him that sits upon the

throne; and from the wrath of the Lamb; fir <u>the great day of his wrath is come</u> and who shall be able to stand?" (Rev. 6:12-16).

    Several important spiritual truths are contained within the passage and we will need to examine each one. The shaking of the heavens and the earth are an announcement to all that the great day if His wrath is come. Notice that this was not the pronouncement given at the outset of the tribulation before the first seal was opened, but rather at the time of the sixth seals opening. The book of Revelation is dealing in considerable measure of detail with two separate realities which are divided and can only be understood in there appropriate contexts. As we have already stated in previous considerations the great tribulation has duration of three and one-half years, and this period is measured in real time as we have come to understand it i.e. a definite number of days, months and years in which it will run its course precisely as we are told several places in Scripture. The signal signs of the *end of that period* are announced with the opening of the sixth seal and its attendant description of the great cataclysmic events described in the text. We then see clearly after those events with their vast consequences upon the heavens and the earth that those evil men that are not numbered with the saints are brought to an acute awareness that the great day of his wrath is come. So in discerning the overall content of the chapters of the book beginning with chapter six we will not be confused if we understand there exists these two distinct designations, the first of which happens in time, and the second of which is not defined by time. The great day of his wrath is referred to in Scripture numerous times and is understood as a period consisting of the Lord's final and absolute judgment on this present world as well as wicked men. It is variously referred to as The Day of the Lord, the day of Christ, the day of God, the day of the Lamb's wrath, and the Day of Judgment all of which are referring to that time when the Lord Jesus Christ undertakes the final and complete judgment upon all of this present creation. These signal events and signs also announce the Lord's return to gather all of his people in resurrection. This is not a "rapture". It is a full and complete resurrection of the faithful dead in Christ and a translation of those of his own that remain alive on the earth. There is no pretribulational rapture as such, although there is a partial catching up to the throne of a remnant of faithful servants as we have seen in our treatment of the "man -child" being caught to the throne in chapter twelve of Revelation. In that context we saw the woman (the church) was driven into the wilderness for a thousand two hundred and three score days. This brings us back to the end of the age and the general resurrection of the saints. By looking at several Scriptures we can correlate the signs and wonders, which happen with the opening of the sixth seal with the gathering of the saints to the Lord.

Let us look at several of them: *__Immediately after the tribulation__ of those days, shall the sun be darkened, and the moon shall not give her light, and the stars shall fall from heaven and the powers if the heavens shall be shaken. And then shall appear he sign of the Son of man in heaven; and then shall the tribes of the earth mourn, and they shall see the Son of man coming in the clouds of heaven with power and great glory. And He shall send His angels with a great sound of a trumpet, and they shall gather together His elect from the four winds and from one end of heaven to the other.* (Mathew 24:29-31).

"For if we believe that Jesus died and rose again, even so them also which sleep in Jesus will God bring with Him. For this we say unto you by the word of the Lord that we witch re alive and remain unto the coming of the Lord shall not prevent them which are asleep. For the Lord Himself shall descend from heaven with a shout, with the voice if the archangel, and with the trump of God; and the dead in Christ shall rise first; Then we which are alive and remain shall be caught up together with them in the clouds, to meet the Lord in the air; and so shall we ever be with the Lord." (I Thes. 4:14-17). *These* are the verses that the dispensationalist pretribulational "rapture "people use to prove their theory of the "rapture". Do you think that these verses speak of rapture or do they speak of the resurrection? Is there anything in the context that indicates that a period of a seven year tribulation (they hold to a seven year period of tribulation) is to follow?

"But the Day of the Lord will come as a thief in the night; in which the heavens will pass away with a great noise, and the elements will melt with a fervent heat, the earth also and the works therein shall be burned up. Seeing that these tings shall be dissolved, what manner of persons ought you to be in all holy conversation and godliness, looking for and hasting unto the day of God . . ." I(I Peter 3: 10-12). This is Peter's general

description of the cataclysmic destruction of the havens and the earth which will occur during that designated period of judgment known as the Day of the Lord, and having as its dramatic announcement the content of the sixth seal.

It would b additionally supportive to look at Old Testament prophet texts of the same announcement. *"Behold the day of the Lord comes; cruel both with wrath and fierce anger, to lay the land desolate: and he shall destroy the sinners thereof out of it. For the stars of heaven and the constellations thereof hall not give their light: the sun shall be darkened in his going down, and the moon shall not cause her light to shine. And I will punish the world for their evil and the wicked for their arrogancy; and I will cause the arrogancy of the proud to cease, and will lay low the haughtiness of the terrible. And I will make a man more precious than fine gold; even a man than the golden wedge of Ophir. Therefore, I will shake the heavens and the earth shall remove out of her place, in the wrath of the Lord of hosts, and in the day of his fierce anger."* (Isaiah 13; 9-13). The prophet Joel adds to the commentary: *"Multitudes, multitudes in the valley of decision: for the day of the Lard is near in the valley of decision. The sun shall be darkened, and the stats shall withdraw their shining. The Lord also shall roar out of Zion, and utter his voice from Jerusalem; and the heavens and the earth shall shake; but the Lord will be the hope of his people, and the strength of the children of Israel."* (Joel 3:14-16). "*And again the word of the Lord came unto Haggai in the four and twentieth day of the month, saying Speak to Zerubbabel governor of Judah, saying I will shake the heavens and the earth; and I will overthrow the throne of kingdoms, and I will destroy the strength of the kingdoms of the heathen . . .* (Haggai 2:20-22).

It should become clear from these scriptures that there is coming upon the creation a great shaking announcing the Day of the Lamb's wrath.

These judgments are brought by the Lord and come at the consummation of or immediately after the great tribulation. As we go forward with our study there will be a continual emphasis to delineate between the events and occurrence of the tribulation and those that are associated with the Day of the Lamb's wrath.

Chapter Fifteen

THE GATHERING

The seventh chapter of Revelation contains the vision which John saw concerning the resurrection and translation of the saints to the throne of God. All aspects of their judgment have not been fully made manifest at this event, but the fact of their glorification and putting on that new body of resurrection and the righteousness of Christ is set forth here. Anticipation of this event is the goal in view all through the pages of Holy Writ. It will be edifying for us to trace that glorious expectation through several of the scriptures helping to place this vision in its perspective.

While on the one hand the blessings to be enjoyed will fall to a great multitude, which a man cannot number in the overall scheme of God's dealings with mankind they are but a relatively small remnant of mankind, and have become worthy of this distinction by faith and by their endurance translating into faithfulness. We see this clearly typified by Joseph in the forty-ninth chapter of Genesis where the blessings conveyed by his father Israel came to rest upon him. *"Joseph is a fruitful bough even a fruitful bough by a well whose branches run over the wall. The archers have sorely grieved him, and shot at him and hated him: but his bow abode in strength, and the arms of his hands were made strong by the mighty God of Jacob; from thence is the shepherd the stone of Israel; even by the God of thy father who shall help thee; and the Almighty who shall bless thee with blessings of heaven above; blessings of the deep that lieth under, blessings of the breasts, and of the womb; the blessing of thy father have prevailed above the blessings of my progenitors unto the utmost bound of the everlasting hills: they shall be on the head of Joseph, and on the head of him who was separate from his brethren.* (Genesis 49:22-26).

The conduct and character if Joseph is set forth as a type and illustration of those who will be gathered into the eternal kingdom of God. This gathering unto *the utmost bounds of the everlasting hills* was anticipated in the heart of Jacob become Israel and he spoke in the place of God when he uttered these blessing upon Joseph. *And it shall come to pass when all of these things are come upon thee, the blessing and the curse, which I have set before thee and thou shalt call them to mind among all of the nations where the Lord thy God has driven thee. And shall return unto the Lord thy God, and shall obey his voice, according to all I command the this day, thou and thy children with all thy soul; that then the Lord thy God will turn thy captivity, and have compassion upon thee, and will return and gather from all of the nations, whither the lord thy God has scattered thee . . . And the Lord God will circumcise thine heart, and the heart of thy seed, to love the Lord thy God, with all of thy heart and with all of thy soul".*(Duet. 30:1-3f.). We take note again that the covenant of God is always conditional and always resting upon faithful obedience to him. Clearly the text is referring to a future gathering of this manner of people from the nations who have embraced the covenant and had their hearts circumcised by the Holy Spirit.

This is not the so-called Palestinian covenant to an earthly Israel as held by dispensational teaching, but has its fulfillment in the new and everlasting covenant.

The Psalmist has said: "*Out of Zion the perfection of beauty. God hath shined. Our God shall come and shall not keep silence; a fire shall devour before him and it shall be very tempestuous round about him. He shall call to the heavens from above, and to the earth that he may judge his people.*

Gather my saints together unto me; those that have made a covenant with me by sacrifice." (Psalms 50:2-5).

"*Immediately after the tribulation of those days . . . And then shall appear the sign of the Son of Man in heaven: and then shall the tribes of the earth mourn, and they shall see he Son of Man coming in the clouds of heaven with power and great glory, And he shall send his angels with the sound of a trumpet, and they shall gather together his elect from the four winds and from one end of heaven to the other."* (Matthew 24:29-31).

"Behold, I show you a mystery; we shall not all sleep, but we shall all be changed, In a moment, in the twinkling of an eye, at the last trump: for the trumpet shall sound and the dead shall be raised incorruptible and we shall be changed." (I Cor. 15:51-52).

Now let us correlate the seventh chapter of Revelation with the scriptures that have been cited above. Immediately after the signs of the sixth seal John sees four angels standing the four corners of the earth holding the four winds that he wind should not blow on the earth or upon the sea. And he saw also another Angel ascending from the East having the Seal of the living God; and this Angel cried with a loud voice to the four angels to whom it had been given to hurt the earth and He said to them hurt not the earth or the sea until we have sealed the servants of God in their foreheads. Several points are to be made here concerning the Angel (messenger) ascending from the East. *"For as the lightening shines out of the East unto the West even so shall the coming of the Son of Man be."* (Mathew 24:27). The Lord's return is described as occurring from the East unto the West. It is the Angel ascending from the East who has the seal of the Living God. The seal is a signet of protection as well as a testimony of genuineness." *Him that overcomes will I make a pillar in he temple of God and he shall go no more out; and I will write upon him the name of my God, and the name of the city of my God which is New Jerusalem . . ."* (Rev 3:12). So we see that the Lord himself has made this promise of sealing his saints and the promise is confirmed twice in later verses, here in chapter seven and again in chapter fourteen. *"And I looked, and lo, a Lamb stood on the Mount Zion and with Him an hundred and forty four thousand having his Father's name written in their foreheads,"* (Rev. 14:1). We can only conclude in this *text* as we have seen before and as we will see again in other places that the *Angel* is the Lord Jesus Christ ascending from the East and with the full and *only* authority from God to seal and gather his servants into the kingdom. His cry is to hurt not the earth until we have sealed the servants of our God in their foreheads. The numbers which are sealed are metaphorically stated as being one hundred and forty four thousand of all the tribes of Israel. I say that the number stated is metaphorical and not literal because the tribes of Israel are twelve as established to be the whole house of Israel under the order set forth in the old covenant. So twelve is a number representing fullness or completeness and the metaphorical significance is carried on by the sealing of twelve thousand from each of the twelve tribes. Please *understand* that these are not Israelites according to the flesh or any natural distinction. This is a representation of the whole house of the *Israel of God*. The sealing proceeds through the next few verses and then a conclusion is reached: *"After this I beheld, and lo a great multitude, which no man could number, of all nations and kind reds and people and tongues, stood before the throne, and before the Lamb, clothed in white robes, and palms in their hands; and cried with aloud voice salvation to our God which sits upon the throne and unto the Lamb."* And then issues forth from them blessings and thanksgiving, and honor for these are those who have come out of great tribulation who have washed their robes in the blood of the Lamb and made them white and they are thus before the throne of God and will serve him day and night as a kingdom of priests. This is the glorious hope of the saints and the consummation of resurrection and translation into the eternal kingdom. A complete deliverance makes provision for their every need for the lamb *"shall feed them, and shall lead them into living fountains of waters: and God shall wipe away all tears from their eyes."* (Rev. 7:17).

Chapter Sixteen

THE SEVENTH SEAL
(FIRST FOUR TRUMPETS)

The Day of the Lamb's Wrath

The opening of the seventh seal announces the beginning of judgments upon the earth and upon evil men commencing after the gathering of the saints and will be consummated with the sounding of seven trumpets and later the opening of seven vials. Be very clear now that all that relates to the Day of the Lord or the Day of the Lamb's wrath comes **after** the three and one-half years of tribulation, and **after** the return of the Lord to gather all of His saints to the throne in resurrection. If you do not get these distinctions clear in your mind you will not be able understand the Revelation. Remember that the Revelation is the Revelation of Jesus Christ. It is all about him so we see him again and again identified by the word **angel** (a messenger or one that brings tidings).

As we look into chapter eight we first see that the Lord has opened the seventh seal. In this vision John first sees seven angels, which stood before God and to them were given seven trumpets. At this point we need a little review of truth we have already covered but are now critical to our continued understanding of the execution of judgments which will be executed during the Lamb's wrath. The identity of the angels are established in the content of the first chapter as John makes his initial pronouncement to the churches of Asia saying *"Grace be unto you, and peace from Him which is, and which was, and which is to come; and to the **seven spirits which are before his throne**; and from Jesus Christ who is the faithful witness..."* (Rev1:4-5a). We see here at the outset that the blessings of grace are extended from the triune Godhead, Father, Holy Ghost and the Son. The notable thing is that the Holy Spirit is sevened. That, of course, does not mean that there are seven Holy Spirits but rather it is the Spirits means of expressing the absolute and fullness of the Holy Spirits involvement with all that is to follow. Again at the end of chapter one we read. "The *seven stars* (which John observed in the right hand of Christ) *are the angels* (messengers) *of the seven churches*". As we follow the text of the messages to the seven churches we see that each message begins by saying that it is *unto the angel of* the church at Ephesus, and so on through all of the seven. And at the end of each admonition the church addressed is exhorted *"he that has an ear to hear what the Spirit says unto the churches"*.

Our previous observation which is established by the teaching of Christ concerning the ministry of the Holy Spirit is that he is the Comforter, the instructor and that Person of the Godhead who leads us. For further confirmation of the true identity of the seven angels we can go to Rev 3:1 *"These things sayeth he* (Christ) *who has the seven Spirits of God and the seven stars..."*-these being one and the same. The stars represent in metaphor light from heaven. Let us go a step further to Rev. 4:5 where we read: *"And out of the throne preceded lightening and thundering, and voices: and there were seven lamps of fire before the throne, which are the seven spirits of God."* And again at Rev.5:6: *"And I beheld and lo in the midst of the throne and of the four beasts, and in the midst of the elders, stood a Lamb as it had been slain, having seven horns and seven eyes, which are the seven Spirits of God sent forth into all of the earth.".* This foundation has been laid again so that it might be clearly understood that the seven angels which stood before God and to whom were givens even trumpets are not angelic beings but rather are the seven Spirits of God i.e. the Holy Spirit manifest sevenfold and sent forth into all of the earth as executing judgment under the directives of the Lamb of God now become the

Lion of the tribe of Judah. Angelic beings, as marvelous and full of wisdom and beauty as they may be, have not been ordained to bring judgment upon the earth and mankind. They have never experienced a falling into sin and therefore were not subject to the redemption of Christ. They are without a subjective comprehension of the working of salvation, and therefore have no basis for rendering judgment on the issues of mankind. All judgment has been committed unto the Son and He therefore has directive authority to send forth the Holy Spirit in authoritative directed manifestations of judgment. These are the seven angels sounding with the seven trumpets of judgment beginning the execution of the Day of the Lord. In the next verse we see another Angel come and stand at the alter. This is the great High Priest of the new and everlasting covenant the Lord Jesus Christ. He has in His hand a golden censor to minister by placing the much intense on the golden alter as with the prayers of the saints. The golden altar of incense stood before the veil leading into the Holy of Holies where the Ark of the Covenant rested. It was used for offering up incense to the God of heaven by the high priest of the Old Covenant foreshadowing the work of Christ." *By so much was Jesus made a surety of a better covenant . . . hath an unchangeable priesthood, wherefore he is able to save to the uttermost that come unto God by him seeing he ever lives to make intercession for them."* (Hebrews 9:22f.).

In the context here he is responding to all of the prayers of all of the saints through the ages to avenge and vindicate them as their Advocate and great High Priest. These prayers are typified by the cries of those who were slain for he Word of God and the testimony which they held under the fifth seal: *"How long o Lord, holy and true, do you not judge and avenge our blood on them that dwell on the earth?"* (Rev. 6:9-10). *"And the smoke of he incense, which came with the prayers of the saints, ascended up before God out of the Angel's hand. And the Angel took the censor, and filled it with fire of the altar, and cast it into the earth: and there were voices and thundering, and lightening, and a great earthquake and the seven angels which had the seven trumpets prepared themselves to sound."* (Rev.8:4-6).

The sounding of a trumpet is the announcing or proclamation that something of significance is about to happen, Notably the first four trumpets sounded by the first four angels are addressing judgments which are executed in bringing destruction upon earth. *"Hail and fire mingled with blood, and they were cast upon the earth: and a third part of all green trees were burnt up, and all green grass was burnt up."* (Rev.8:7) *"And when the second angel sounded, as it were a great mountain burning with fire was cast into the sea: and the third part of the sea became blood. And a third part of the creatures which were in the sea, and had life, died: and a third part of the ships were destroyed."* (Rev. 8:8-9). And with the sounding of the third angel: *"There fell a great star from heaven, burning as it were a lamp, and it fell on the third part of the rivers. And the name of the star is called Wormwood: and the third part of the waters became wormwood, and many men died of the waters because they were bitter."* (*Rev* 8:10-11). And when the fourth angel had sounded,*" the third part of the sun was smitten, and the third part of the moon, and the third part of the stars; so as the third part of them were darkened, and the day shone not for a third part of it, and the night likewise"*. (Rev.8:12). And John beheld: He heard an angel fling through heaven saying with a loud voice, *"Woe, Woe, and Woe to the inhibiters of the earth by reason of the other voices of the trumpets of the tree angels which are yet to sound."* (Rev.8:13).

Chapter Seventeen

WOE, WOE . . . AND WOE

There has been a cry from heaven announcing *"woe, woe, woe unto the the inhibiters of the earth by reason of the voices of the three angels, which are yet to sound"* (Rev. 8:13). Woe is an expression of extreme calamity having great consequence. We have stretched out the third woe because it will be separated somewhat in manifestation and consequences from the first two woes. The ninth chapter of Revelation deals only with the first two of the three woes. The ninth chapter of Revelation is deeply shrouded in metaphor, and it cannot be interpreted unless you are able to follow the metaphorical meaning of the symbolism used. I have spent many hours of study over the years in this portion of Scripture to be able to fully understand it, and some of the keys to this understanding must necessarily be found in other scriptures not only within the text of Revelation but within the Old Testament prophesies, and then under the direction of the Holy Spirit seeing the significance and application of the metaphorical language. I will be seeking by the grace of the Lord to lead us through it, and bring its message into focus. We understand that it falls in order behind chapter eight and the sounding of the first four trumpets of the seven angels. Two more things are necessary to repeat: the first is that it takes place in the context of the Day of the Lamb's wrath and not in the tribulation period; secondly that the soundings are Holy Spirit announcements declaring an order and content of judgment under the direction of the Son of God.

Let us begin by emphasizing that there are two phases or aspects to be understood in the Lord's return. We have already stated much to establish the fact that his return is after the tribulation. The first phase or aspect of His return is to gather together and translate his people from all the ages in the power of resurrection. Chapter seven of Revelation and many other relevant scriptures establish this glorious reality. The saints are caught up in resurrection and carried away in glory into the very presence of God. The second phase or aspect of his coming is understood from the perspective that all of the saints are with him in heaven before the second phase or aspect of his coming is manifest. That reality needs to be stated first before elaborating on the details. It is a clearly established fact revealed in Scripture that Jesus Christ intended that there would be a participation of all of the saints in a return to the earth with him to engage them in a battle and warfare of a spiritual nature to be waged against the "inhibiters of the earth".

To introduce that doctrinal truth let us look first at Psalms 149 beginning with the firth verse and moving on through to the end of the Psalms 149 "*. . . let the saints be joyful in glory: let them sing aloud on their beds. Let the high praises of God be in their mouth, and a two edged sword in their hand; to execute vengeance upon the heathen, and punishments upon the people; to bind their kings with chains, and their nobles with fetters of iron; to execute on them the judgment written: this honor have all of His saints. Praise ye the Lord.*" There are many other scriptures, which confirm this fact, and they will be brought into consideration as we move along with the exposition of subsequent texts.

For now let us go forward with the first the two woes in chapter nine. "*And the fifth angel sounded and I saw a Star fall from heaven and to him was given the key to the bottomless pit* " (abyss). (Rev.9:1). In the beginning we must see that the Star is a person, and in the possession of him is the key to the bottomless pit. We will quickly identify the Person to be Jesus Christ for in the first instance we know and have already established that God has committed all judgment to him, and he is here seen to have the key to the bottomless pit. We can reference Rev. 20:1; "And *I saw an Angel come from heaven having the key to the bottomless pit and a great chain in His hand.*" We recognize that this Angel and this Star come down from heaven is our Lord Jesus Christ consistent with his role and his actions for He is the one to whom all judgment is committed. We must be able to see the metaphor being expressed in the passage including the key (the power and authority to open and close). This authority is verified at Rev. 1:18. Clearly in the two passages he is come from heaven (not the heavens of the universe, but the heaven which is the dwelling place of God). The use of the metaphor of the star is reasonable and necessary for our understanding in that we know that the stars in the physical creation are heavenly bodies of light. We are helped in our interpretation of identify the Star as our Lord by the prophesy of Balaam at Numbers 24:17 and following where he proclaims: *"I shall see him but not now: I shall behold Him but not nigh: there shall come a Star out of Jacob, and a Scepter shall rise out of Israel . . . Out of Jacob shall come he that shall have dominion, and shall destroy him that remains of the city."* Clearly this prophetic passage is spoken n reference to the Lord and his coming in judgment. We see that the Star is spoken of as falling from heaven. The word for fall can be understood in its definition to mean to fall either physically and carrying with it the idea of *alighting*. Our conclusion is then from verse one that this is Christ come from heaven and he is holding in his power and authority the key to the bottomless pit. Moving forward with the text we see in verse two that he opens the abyss as he also did at Rev. 20:1. The difference here is that the great chain of binding spiritually has not yet become fully manifest. In this text we see that smoke arises out of the pit as a great furnace. Smoke then become the evidence of fire (or judgment as we understand it in its metaphorical meaning). Would it not be seen even by the "inhibiters of the earth" that the great day of his wrath is come? *"And the air was darkened by reason of the smoke".* Joel adds commentary when he says at Joel 2: 2. *"A day of darkness and gloominess, a day of clouds and thick darkness, as the morning spread on the mountains".*

'And there came out of the smoke locusts upon the earth and with them was given power as the scorpions of the earth have power. And it was commanded them that they should not hurt the grass of the earth, neither any green thing, neither any tree; but only those men who have

not the seal of God in their foreheads. And to them it was given that they should not kill them, but that they should be tormented five months, and their torment was as the torment of a scorpion, when he strikes a man." (Rev.9:3-5). Here again we must be able to see the meaning of the metaphorical language being used by the prophet and it is drawn from the writings of the prophets of old, and tenets given in the law. First we would learn from more than one reference in the law and the prophets that a plague of locusts was a mode and instrument of judgment exercised in the judgment by God. References include Exodus 10:4, 12-14, 19. Duet. 28:38, Joel 1:4, and Joel 2:5. The locusts also symbolize as an event of being overwhelmed by a great and powerful army. Cp. Judges 6:5, 7:12. There are other Old Testament references but the essence of our argument for interpretation can be gleaned from the ones listed. What is in view in the text is a great and powerful army, which has come upon the inhibiters of the earth i.e. those who have not the seal of God in their foreheads. They have been typified as a plague of locusts for the sake of illustration. Joel adds supporting commentary at Joel 2:5 "*. . . the land is as the garden of Eden before them and behind then a desolate wilderness, and nothing shall escape them*" as he advances and confirms the metaphor before us. As a means of dispelling the idea that they are actually locusts John sees in the vision that they are commanded not to hurt any green thing on the earth but "*only those men which have not the seal of God in their foreheads."*

The further metaphor is added with the description of their power being as the power of scorpions. The scorpions, which live in the Middle East, possess a sting of deadly poison but death does not come immediately with the sting. There is a lingering and agonizing torment for the fact of death is a given but it is consummated over time if there is not an antidote provided. So we see that the locusts whose sting is as that of a scorpion brings the inhibiters of the earth to seek death and yet they will not be able to find it. The picture is very clear. The Lord returning with all of his saints will place every man outside of that covenant in the agonizing recognition that all they may have thought about a possible judgment has now become manifest before their eyes and understanding.

These Prophets

Our further confirmation of the identity of the army is made more clear in the following verses numbers seven, eight, nine and ten. *"And the shapes of the locusts were like unto horses prepared for battle."* The prophet Joel assists us again in our understanding at Joel 2:4 when he reveals:" *The appearance of them is as the appearance of horseman, and so shall they run."* John adds significantly to the vision at Revelation 19:11-14 and following context when he proclaims : *"And I saw heaven opened and beheld a white horse; and he that sat upon him was called Faithful and True, and in righteousness He does judge and make war. his eyes were as a flame of fire, and on his head were many crowns; and he had a name written that no man knew except he himself. And he was clothed in a vesture dipped in blood: and his name is called the Word of God. And the armies, which were in heaven, followed Him on white horses, clothe in white linen, white and clean . . ."* The metaphor of the army led by the King of Kings is completed here but we will also draw again from the prophet Joel where he gain additional commentary beginning in the text of Joel 2:5-11: *"Like the noise of chariots upon the tops of mountains shall they leap, like the noise of flames of fire that devours the stubble, as a strong people set in battle array . . . And the Lord shall utter his voice before his army: for His camp is very great: he is strong that executes his word: for the day of the Lord is great and very terrible; and who can abide it?"* The metaphorical language identifies the Lord leading His army in judgment becomes increasingly clear.

The commentary in the text goes on: *"and on their heads as it were. crowns like gold, and their faces were as the faces of men".* Where else do we encounter the crowns of gold (again remember these are metaphors). At Revelation 4:4 we found the twenty-four elders before the throne were clothed in white raiment and had on their heads crowns of gold. The symbolism is that of the saints having received a precious crown from the Lord. They had faces as the faces of men. Sarong's concordance tells us that the face is the countenance, the appearance, the presence or the person. It is the preeminent characteristic for identification. Hopefully by now you have already concluded that this vast band of locusts are the people of God come out of heaven with him, and are presented here to us with a metaphorical description, to collectively make war on the unbelieving inhabitants of the earth.

In the next phrase we have two more metaphors presented to further confirm the army which ahs been set in battle array. *"And they had hair as the hair of women. And their teeth ere as the teeth of lions."* What significance does the long hair of women have to add to this metaphorical picture? Again we must go to the Old Testament to find our answer. In Numbers chapter six we have set forth for us the vow of a Nasserite, which comes from the Hebrew "nazir", which means a separation, or to consecrate oneself to the service of God. The details of the vow are special, and it always had to do with one who would solely consecrate his life unto the Lord. One of the most wonderful studies that I have ever done came out of this passage and then having pursued the beautiful concept of separation and consecration through the other Scriptures. The notable example in Scripture of one who became a judge in Israel was Samson who slew one thousand Philistines with the jaw bone of an ass and in his final act of consecration brought down the temple of Dagon on the worshippers of Baal. The secret of his strength was in the length of his hair because that was bound up with his vow. When his hair had been cut off by the subtle deception of Delilah he was as any other man, but when the hair had grown long again he was imbued with supernatural strength from God. Again we are given a metaphor by example from the days of Israel by the Holy Spirit choosing to identify these faithful ones in the army of their Lord as having, as it were, taken the vow of consecration to serve the Lord, and then being likened in the vision to the Nazarites of old.

Moving on we see them as endowed with teeth as the teeth of lions (Cp. Joel 1:6) having the ferocity of the king of beasts. They were dressed with breastplates of iron, and are we not admonished in the Ephesian epistle to put on the breastplate of righteousness protecting our hearts from the fiery darts of the wicked, which has been provided to us in Christ. And the sound of their wings (using the locust metaphor) was as the sound of many chariots running to battle. Again the metaphor is as many chariots running to battle as the prophet Joel saw it in Joel 2:5. I would urge you to read the whole book of Joel as a commentary on the Day of the Lord but certain passages in chapters one. And much more in chapter two to show us clearly that John's vision here was drawn from those same descriptive phrases, and there can be no doubt as to who the Scripture is referring to in this passage. The metaphor of the army is completed by referring back to the stings in their tails and they had power to hurt men for five months. I confess that I have never become completely or absolutely settled concerning the significance of the period of five months. I strongly suspicion that it is throw back to the flood and a preacher of righteousness who we know as Noah. If you track the flood in Genesis chapter seven you will find that in the first destruction of his earth by water that *"the waters prevailed on the earth an hundred and fifty days"*. (five months- Cp. Genesis 7:24). I would not say that you would then take the five months here to necessarily be literal for if this is the Scriptural connection then the message is that a second destruction of the earth is underway and the first one which was by water prevailed over the earth one hundred and fifty days. Time as we understand it in this context may not be if the essence for we are in a framework of God's judgment being executed by his Son, but the Scripture will always provide us with information that we may understand what is being conveyed by the Holy Spirit.

    The absolute clincher to our contention as to the assembly and identity of this army is found in verse eleven. *"And they had a king over them, which is the angel of the bottomless pit* (Cp. Rev. 20:1) *whose name in the Hebrew tongue is Abaddon, but in the Greek tongue has his name Apollyon"*.(Rev.9 11). The word in both the Hebrew and the Greek coincide and in each case mean a Destroyer. Many, if not most, of the commentaries on this portion would identify the destroyer as Satan. This conclusion comes from a failure to understand the context, as well as in many cases holding doctrine, which is unscriptural. Clearly the Destroyer in the Day of the Lamb's Wrath or in other terminology, the Day of the Lord is the Lord Himself, Jesus Christ. He is the King of Kings and certainly is the King over his army. He came the first time as the Lamb of God, which takes away the sin of the world. His return is as the Lion of the tube of Judah.

"One woe is past; and behold there comes two woes more hereafter." (Rev.9:12).With the sounding of the sixth angel a voice is heard from the four horns of the golden alter which is before God. This golden alter which is before God is a representation of the alter of incense which stood before the veil in the temple adjacent to the holy of holies, and we know that in that context the veil had not yet been rent in twain. But it represents symbolically the place where the high priest worshipped and offered up incense before God. At this juncture based on the prayers (incense) which has gone before the restraint which had been bound before is released allowing those beyond the river Euphrates to be enjoined in the battle. *"And the number of the horseman were two hundred thousand thousand . . . i.e.* The word is a myriad which simple means an uncountable number. The common interpretation if this with most Christian expositors is that this is the military might of China two million strong coming to attack the Lord. While I would agree that if they are saying that Armageddon is in view here, I believe that this identification of the event would be consistent with other Scripture which we will consider soon. However, to identify these as the armies if China is without merit or without any support. We see the horses in the vision *"having breastplates of fire, and of jacinth, and of brimstone and the horses heads were as of lions; and out of their mouths went fire and smoke and brimstone"*. It is clear that this is not an earthly army or they do not have weapons, which are launched from their mouths which are constituted in terms such as fire and brimstone. Clearly this battle is being waged by the Lord's army who can speak the word of God, and is understood in terms of judgment (i.e. fire and brimstone). The classic Old Testament example is given in the destruction of Sodom and Gomorah. *"For their power is in their mouths an in their tails; for their tails were like unto serpents, and had heads, and with them they do hurt."* (Vs.19). So I would see the second woe as an extension of what we covered under the first woe carried out in open spiritual warfare. There is absolutely nothing here, which would identify these warriors as Chinese. There is a preparation by way of the drying up of the river Euphrates to prepare the way for the kings under the pouring out of the sixth vial at Revelation 16:12. I believe that this passage parallels

the one in chapter 16, and both are focused on the last great battle, which we know to be Armageddon. We will deal with that subject by adding some detail from that further text later on. What we do reasonably discern is that the second woe involves the same army which we have attempted to thoroughly describe under the first woe. It is not different nor is it made up of the "inhibitors of the earth", and the second woe is an extension in kind of the first woe bringing forth the intensity of the battle. Also the final conflict, which is in view, is that of Armageddon, which is later, named at Rev. 16:16. The closing verse of the ninth chapter reveals that there is no place of repentance remaining within the hearts of these wicked men.

Chapter Eighteen

THE LITTLE BOOK OPEN

After the progression of the opening of the seals(chapter six) followed by the sounding of six of the seven trumpets(chapters 8 & 9) we come upon a vision which will prove to be an interruption in the progress of events. Briefly then reviewing we have covered the opening of the seven seals. Six of those seven seals, as has been discovered deal primarily with that period which is identified as great tribulation. Then we have covered the gathering of the saints in resurrection as is captured by the vision of the prophet in chapter seven. After the saints have been gathered to the throne we are introduced to the Day of the Lord or The Day of the Lamb's Wrath whichever way you are comfortable in referring to that time when Jesus Christ is revealed in judgment upon the physical creation and ultimately upon the evil "inhibiters of the earth". The visions concerning the Day of the Lord are introduced at the beginning of Revelation chapter eight and we find within the covering of that seventh seal when it is opened there are revealed to us seven trumpets which will be sounded as the day of his wrath proceeds. The content of chapter eight takes us through the first four of those trumpets sounding which are under the direction of our Lord and are in execution by the seven Spirits of God, i.e. the Holy Spirit. The first four of the trumpets are dealing primarily with the judgment and destruction of the physical creation. Then as we moved into chapter nine we have been confronted with three woes and two of those three woes are revealed within the content of the chapter. All of the trumpets proceed from the seventh seal, which introduces us to his judgment. Those two woes are bound up with the truth of the Lord's return to the earth after the resurrection and gathering. He comes leading his army, which are those who have been found faithful and who thus have participated in the first resurrection. Man's day is concluded at the end of the tribulation. We are now well into the day of his wrath, but with the introduction of chapter ten we will find a pause in the forward movement of the narrative, and will be taken back to the tribulation to reveal that period from three separate perspectives. As we have said early on the Revelation is not entirely set forth in a progressive chronology and certain keys if interpretation is necessary to avoid our getting completely lost, and thus failing to rightly relate the order of the visions. Having provided this brief review so that we can remain properly focused we are ready now to examine the contents of chapter ten.

If you look at the first portion of each of the three proceeding chapters (7, 8, & 9) you will find that a certain Angel distinctly headlines them all.

That Angel will be found to be identified as Jesus Christ in each of those contexts. We laid a foundation in chapter one identifying our Lord as that Angel. He is God's Messenger in the context of the Revelation, and he is the object of the book revealing a lengthy series of messages in the progressive contexts which are unfolded for us by the visions of the prophet John. Chapter ten also opens with the vision of "another angel". It is not another in the sense of being a totally different entity, but another in a difference of manifestation and with a different message. This is a critically important distinction for us and as the Holy Spirit reveals this truth you will se that the whole of the book is really all about him.

Proceeding with the text of chapter ten we see another mighty Angel coming down form heaven clothed with a cloud, and having on his head a rainbow. We know from the ascension of Christ in chapter one of Acts that he was taken up in a cloud and several references show that he is to return in like manner. I believe that what we have here in chapter ten is the symbolism of that return, and not the literal return itself. That thought will require further explanation as we proceed through the chapter. A rainbow in Scripture stands as a sign of covenant. We have all witnessed beautiful rainbows after a refreshing rain caused by the refraction of the sunlight through droplets of the rainwater. The precedent is established in Genesis 9: 8-17 where we see that God made a covenant that he would not destroy the earth again by water and he sealed that covenant with the appearance of the rainbow. The rainbow appears again as a symbolic expression of covenant expressing the glory of the Lord round about the throne of God at Ezekiel 1:26-28. The Lord God is a God of covenant and the vision we see here is an expression of covenant for he has not only promised his return but also executes righteous judgment, and so we see here early in chapter ten *a rainbow was on his head.*

"*His face was as it were the sun, and His feet as pillars of fire*". We have two other references of visions in Scripture, which provide physical attributes of his appearance. Daniel describes his vision of the Lord is chapter ten at verses 5-6. "*His body was like the beryl and his face as the appearance of lightening, and his eyes as lamps of fire, and his arms and feet like in color to polished brass*". John provides a further description of his appearance in chapter one of the Revelation . . ." *His eyes were as a flame of fire; and his feet like unto fine brass, as if they burned in a furnace . . . his countenance was as the sun shines in its strength*".(Rev. 1:14-16). The Angel at Revelation 10:1 entirely fits the description. In the second verse we see that he had "*in his hand a little book open: and he set his right foot upon the sea and his left foot upon the earth*".

In explaining the little book open we go back to the narrative in chapter five concerning the book containing all of the judgments and being in the hand of God. We further see from the narrative that there was a great concern as to who was worthy to open the book. The Lion of the tribe of Judah prevailed to take the book and as we have seen subsequently began to open the seven seals thereof. Now, the little book here in the text is a diminutive of the book in chapter five held and opened by the Lord. It is in reality the same book but so much of the content has been unsealed and released that there remains a much smaller portion yet to come; and so the metaphor is consistent with describing it as a little book open. The same one is in control of all of the content of both the complete book in chapter five and the lesser portion of it appearing in the vision in chapter ten. It is, of course, he that is worthy. The placing of his feet, the one on the sea and the other on the earth is symbolic expression of his dominion over all of the creation. After this he cried with a loud voice likened metaphorically to the roar of a lion, and of course as the one to whom all judgment is committed he has taken the identity of the Lion of the tribe of Judah. When He cried there were seven thunders, which uttered their voices. As John was about to write what they had uttered he was restrained for they will come along at a later time in describing further developments of judgment in the day of his wrath. For this current vision other details are at hand to be revealed which have their relationship to the great tribulation and not to the Day of the Lord. Thus, the seven thunders are abated for a time. As we go forward with the text of the chapter this will hopefully be seen by the reader. The Angel speaks with great authority lifting up his hand to heaven (Comp. Daniel 12:7) and swearing by him that lives forever and ever, maker of heaven and earth and all that are therein. We are enlightened that it will be in the days of the voice of he seventh angel when he shall begin to sound the mystery of God will be finished as was declared by his servants the prophets. John then hears a voice from haven telling him that he must take the little book opened from the hand of the Angel. He speaks to the Angel and asks for the little book. The Angel responds by telling him to take the little book and" *eat it up, and it shall make your belly bitter, but shall be in your mouth sweet as honey*" (vs. 9). This is the Word of God to be taken in as food in metaphorical sense. In so doing as the Psalmist has said the word is more to be desired than gold and it were is sweeter also than the honey of he honey comb. Cp. Psalms 19:10. Because of the nature of the content of these words of judgment it became bitter in the stomach for it is in this instance hard to digest as food eaten and creating an acidic condition in being digested. When John had taken it and eaten it was in his mouth sweet as honey, but in his belly it became bitter. A similar situation is paralleled in the experience of

Ezekiel in chapter three as he was also instructed to *eat this roll* (scroll) *and go speak to the house of Israel*. It was in Ezekiel's *mouth as honey for sweetness.* Cp. Ezekiel 3:1-3. Understanding that Ezekiel's words to Israel were words of judgment for their rejection of the word of the Lord; so likewise that which will follow from John continues in that vein and has application to the church at the end of the age. The last verse of the chapter is key to placing into right context that which will follow. *"And He said unto me you must prophesy **again** before many peoples, and nations, and tongues and kings".*(Rev.10:11).

We are placing a special emphasis on the word again because in the meaning of the word in the original Greek it conveys a specific meaning needed to be understood for the following text. The word is rhetorical in nature indicating moreover, also indicating a statement to be added in the course of an argument. (See Strong's concordance). The significance here is that the following three chapters returns us rhetorically to a point of beginning which is the great tribulation before concluding with the narratives of the further visions of John to take us to the final consummation of things as pertains to this earthly scene and the establishment of the new heavens and the new earth. John will prophesy again taking us back to the three and one-half years of tribulation in the following texts: Revelation 11:1-12; all of chapter 12 of Revelation; and all of chapter 13 of Revelation. Although we have previously covered the portion of chapter eleven under the topic of the two witnesses and officered some of the content of chapter twelve under the heading of the man- child; I believe it will be profitable for us to return to these texts and cover the details again with some supplementation of the issues involved. We also need to consider in much detail the important content of chapter 13 by focusing on the beast.

Chapter Nineteen

THE ABOMINATION OF DESOLATION

What we have seen with this interruption of the Angel come down from heaven (Christ) with the little book open in His hand and it is that rhetorically the Lord has much more to show us concerning things to come. We desire to know the whole story and he wants us to have a full understanding. The text in Revelation follows a continuum beginning with chapter four and following through to the end of chapter nine. The subject matter opens from a heavenly perspective seeing the four living creatures (cherubim) and he twenty- four elders round about the throne offering praise and worship to the Father and the Son. We have seen the Lion of the tribe of Judah take the book with the seven seals from the Father and having been found worthy He will loose them one at a time. The first six of those seals take us through the period of the tribulation as captured in the visions of John in chapter six. The resurrection and sealing of the saints is found in the seventh chapter and the faithful having been secured in heaven; the Day of the Lord is introduced under the seventh seal in the following two chapters. Six of the seven trumpets have been sounded before the Angel interrupts in chapter ten to share the little book with John with the explanation that he must prophesy again to many peoples, and nations, and tongues and kings. The text returns to the tribulation period in the first twelve verses of chapter eleven, all of chapter twelve and all of chapter thirteen. We will depart from this point to lay some additional important foundations before we rejoin the progression of the text.

An understanding of the spiritual phenomenon known as the abomination of desolation needs to be brought into focus for it is of significant consequence as an introduction to the coming "great tribulation".

We would insert this portion revealing the abomination of desolation here as being timely for we will see that it will proceed the time of the tribulation period. We return to Daniel to find what he saw in a vision from the Lord to place its occurrence in proper perspective of time and then the need will be to look at other Scriptures which will be necessary to help us in our understanding. The text of Darnel chapter twelve beginning at verse nine: *"And He said, go thy way Daniel: for the words are closed up and sealed till the time of the end. Many shall be purified, and made white and tried; but the wicked shall do wickedly: and none of the wicked shall understand; but the wise shall understand. And from the time the daily sacrifice shall be taken away, and the abomination that makes desolate set up, there shall be a thousand two hundred and ninety days. Blessed is he that waits and comes to the thousand three hundred and five and thirty days"* (Daniel 12:9-12). These verses give us the timing for this every significant milestone event. There being one thousand two hundred and ninety days measured, we have already determined that the great tribulation lasts one thousand two hundred and sixty days so we can place the timing at thirty days <u>prior to</u> the onset of tribulation. Other Scriptures will add understanding in the defining of the content of the occurrence but one thing that is brought out in this portion is the taking away of the daily sacrifice. (the continual worship in translation—not the old testament practice of animal sacrifice) What would that mean in terms of a new covenant application seeing that there is no sacrifice and oblation under the tenets of the covenant for Christ has provided the one sacrifice which is sufficient forever? We are here engaging the old covenant counterpart to his death on the cross for the new covenant was not yet revealed or understood in the days of Daniel's prophesy. Daniel has prophesied concerning an event in future time that he does not possess an ability to fully explain theologically. But we can gain from this passage the timing of the event and the facts that only the wise will understand its significance and the wicked will be blinded as to its meaning. Satan weaves a masterpiece of deception for he deceives those who are undiscerning.

Moving to Daniel 11:31-32 we read: *"And arms shall stand on his part and they shall pollute the sanctuary of strength, and shall take away the doily sacrifice* (no Greek word in the original for the word sacrifice*) and place the abomination that makes desolate. And such as do wickedly shall he corrupt with flatteries but the people that do know their God shall be strong and do exploits."* More of this text will be considered at a later time but our purpose now is stay focused on the abomination that makes desolate. We see from the text that he is mightily exercising force and power. Who is this? It is the son of perdition, the Antichrist. He is enabled by this power and deception o pollute the sanctuary of strength and to take away the daily sacrifice and place the abomination that makes desolate. What then is the sanctuary of strength? Is it is a building? A temple as dispensational teaching would lead us to believe? As Stephen aptly declared prior to his being stoned to death: *"Howbeit the Most High dwells not in temples made with hands; as says the prophet, heaven is more throne and the earth is my footstool: what house will you build me? Says the Lord or what is the place of my rest? Hath not my hand made all of these things. You stiff-necked and uncircumcised in heart and ears, you do always resist the Holy Ghost."* (Acts 7:48-52). Are you able to see that the *"sanctuary of strength"* cannot be a rebuilt Jewish temple for the veil of the same has already been rent in twain and sacrifice and offering have been put away forever and *"Christ is not entered into the holy places made with hands, which are the figures of the true; but into heaven itself now to appear in the presence of God for us"*. (Heb. 9:24).

Satan seeks universal worship. His incarnate representative on the earth is the Antichrist, the son of perdition. How is that goal to be accomplished in these last days and leading us into a time of great trouble and persecution as he seeks to eliminate the worship of the true God from the face of the earth? We will need to gain some assistance from the writings of the apostle Paul to the Thessalonians to gain this insight into the meaning of these truths which Daniel prophesied concerning for they have their application under the new and everlasting covenant. This cannot be construed to be some supposed return to an Old Testament economy dependent upon having its fulfillment in a rebuilt Jewish temple at Jerusalem. **<u>I will not say</u>** that there will not be a temple rebuilt in Jerusalem and the resumption of animal sacrifice at the end of the age to fabricate a deception upon the peoples of the earth, but <u>I will say dogmatically</u> that the abomination that makes desolate cannot have its application in an earthly temple which God has clearly not ordained to have any place or function under the new and everlasting covenant. *"Now we beseech you brethren, by the coming of our Lord Jesus Christ, and by our gathering together unto Him, that you be not shaken in mind, or be troubled, neither by spirit, nor by word, not by letter as from us, as that the day of Christ is at hand. Let no man deceive you any means: for that day shall not come, except there by a falling away first and that ma of sin be revealed, the son of perdition; who opposes and exalts himself above all that is called God, or that is worshipped; so that he as God sits in the temple of God, showing himself that he is God"* (I Thes. 2:1-4). This is Paul's description of the abomination of desolation. How are we then to interpret it in application? *"The mystery of iniquity does already work; only he that letteth, will let until he be taken out of the way. And then shall that wicked be revealed, whom the Lord will consume with the spirit of his mouth and the brightness of his coming even whose coming is after the working of Satan with all power and signs and lying wonders, and with all deceivableness of unrighteousness in them that perish because they received not the love of the truth that they might be saved".* (II Thes. 2:7-10). We have seen <u>the when</u> part of the abomination of desolation from the revelation of days in Daniel chapter 12. Now from the new testament explanation by Paul we need to have a revelation of <u>the how and the why.</u> The why is relatively simple to understand if we are clear on the concept that Satan since prior to his fall has continually sought to be worshipped and exalted above the Most High for he has said in his heart." *I will ascend into heaven, I will exalt my throne above the stars of God; I will sit also in the mount of the congregation, in the sides of the north; I will* *ascend above the heights of the clouds; I will be like the Most High".* (Is.14:13-14).

How then will this be manifest and come to pass? In the Thessalonians passage it is clear that the mystery of iniquity has always been at work but even though Satan has usurped a dominion over this world's system and has a certain access to work his evil devices within the hearts of men, we do see from the passage that he is and always has been under restraint by the Holy Spirit and he cannot fully manifest his desire for complete control over mankind. At a point in time, which is totally under the control of God: *"He that letteth will let until he be taken out of the way; and then shall that wicked be revealed."* (II Thes. 2:7). The Holy Spirit has unlimited and marvelous power both to bring about positive actions within the will of God, but also acts as a restraint upon the evil workings of the powers of darkness as they act to subvert, deceive and control mankind. What the passage is conveying to us is that there is a restraint being exercised over the mystery of iniquity but when the restraint is removed the lesser, but still great power of the enemy will be allowed to be manifest. God will continue to protect those who are committed to him to a walk according to the Spirit and so they will possess the wisdom to understand. But, at the same time, when the Spirit ceases to restrain the powers of evil literally "all hell will break loose". God dwells in us by His Spirit, but should we be deceived, the powers of darkness can take control by being allowed access to the mind, and ultimately to gain access to the spirit of a man.

I have in my own experience seen a man once given to Christ, and then through the use of drugs, and the enemy's powers of deception I observed him to be given over to demon possession, and complete control by the powers of darkness. Satan gains access to us first by deceiving us by lies placed in our minds. If we succumb to those deceptions it is possible to allow a complete desolation of the man in his spirit. I have observed it and I know it to be true. Are we not admonished to put upon ourselves the whole armor of God that we may be able to stand against the wiles of the evil one? I believe that with the removal of the restraint of the Holy Spirit any man can and will be captured by the enemy. When he has gained an entrance to the inner man he will destroy the man spiritually and completely from the inside. A man was intended to be possessed and be guided by the Spirit inwardly, but in forsaking the covenant or rejecting the conviction of the Holy Spirit he bares his own spirit to be dominated by the powers of evil. This will have a wholesale and worldwide expression when the wicked one is revealed who intends to sit in and possess the spirit of a man, which is the sanctuary or the true temple of God under the tenets, and provision of the new covenant. This I believe to be the abomination of desolation spoken of by Daniel the prophet and the sanctuary of God (a man's most inward being- his spirit) will be totally defiled, made desolate and profaned if he turns back from or away from a covenant relationship with the Savior and the Holy Spirit from whom we derive our protection.

Jesus himself adds commentary on the subject of the abomination of desolation as he instructs His disciples in Mathew 24." *And because iniquity shall abound the love of many shall wax cold. But he that endures to the end shall be saved. And this gospel of the kingdom shall be preached in all of the world for a witness to all nations; and then shall the end come. When you therefore shall see the abomination of desolation spoken of by Daniel the prophet stand in the holy place, whoever reads let him understand. Then let them in Judea flee unto the mountains . . . For then shall be great tribulation, such as was not since the beginning of the world to this time, no nor shall be"*. Mathew 24: 12-21. We discover in this passage the condition of hearts and the closeness in proximity of the abomination of desolation to the onset of the great tribulation. Those that be in Judea would have its application as those who in a spiritual sense are in relationship with the Lord. A counter part verse is found at Revelation 12:6 where it says: *"And the woman* (the church) *fled into the wilderness, where she has a place prepared of God, that he should feed her there a thousand two hundred and three score days"*. It is with soberness of heart that these truths are presented for it is of a certainty that the fabricated pre-tribulation "rapture" is a fantasy and serious heresy of the first order, which has led many of God's people astray from an understanding of the truth. There will be a company of those who have been utterly committed to Christ and are walking with him in a Spirit led life that will escape the tribulation. This is the man- child of Revelation 12:5 who shall be caught up to God and to His throne and will provide the spiritual ground to cast Satan out of heaven.

Chapter Twenty

THE CHURCH IN THE WILDERNESS

Briefly reviewing the ground we have covered in our spiritual journey through a significant portion of Daniel' revelations, and likewise about half of the Revelation given to John; Daniel's prophesies as we have seen give us background in understanding the development of world empires as well as specifics as relates to the nation of Israel under the old covenant. Daniel has provided us with the specifics of the history of an earthly people as God's plan has included Israel and has pronounced an end to them as a people under and/or in a covenant relationship for the simple fact that they not only failed as a people to receive their Messiah, but also bear accountability for his rejection and ultimately his death by crucifixion. Daniel has added complimentary details of events on the earth as they develop to the end of the age including that time of great tribulation.

We have followed the development of John's prophesy through the messages to the seven churches in Asia and into the prophetic portion beginning with the heavenly scene immediately prior to the opening of the seals of the book by the Lion of the tribe of Judah. We have tracked the seals opening through the tribulation, and considered the gathering of the saints at the end of that period of trouble focused on the earth prior to his return to bring about the general resurrection carrying the saints to the glory of heaven. Then under the opening of the seventh seal we have seen revealed that great and awesome Day of the Lord. With the sounding of six of the seven trumpets revealed with the opening of that seal. As we reached to chapter ten we saw that other Angel who had in his hand a little book opened and we were able to realize that it represented an as yet unrevealed portion of the original book having the seven seals. The Angel directed John to eat up the book for it was given unto him to prophesy again rhetorically speaking and to add additional details to all that has already been seen and examined. Consideration and detail has also been examined to discover the meaning, the activities and the judgment of Mystery Babylon. Chapters eleven, including the first twelve verses, and all of chapter twelve have been disclosed for an understanding of the measuring of the temple including the two witnesses and the significance of the man-child who was caught to the throne precipitating war in heaven and the casting of Satan from the heavenly realm. It would seem to me to be valuable to add emphasis to the experience of the Church during this period of three and one half years of tribulation as it is captured for us in this portion in chapter eleven dealing with the two witnesses and the whole of chapter twelve. Reading again these portions of Scripture at this time would be helpful as we approach this subject. (see chapters five and six in the book).

The vast majority of those who would confess Christ hold very tenaciously to the concept of a "pre-tribulational rapture" and therefore hold a passive apprehension of the great tribulation as their doctrine holds that if he should return and they are yet alive on the earth they will be in heaven and will have no part or participation n those difficult times to befall the earth. An interpretation of Scripture that allows for an escape from trouble, affliction, and trial receives reception and great popularity in the writings of Hal Lindsey's title, *The Late Great Planet Earth* and Tim LaHay's treatment of the subject of the "rapture" in *Left Behind* so much so that a popular movie was made. This does not reflect the reality of the matter of an unprecedented time of trouble on the earth and further treatment of the subject matter is probably needed because those who have held this erroneous interpretation will not be easily persuaded to the contrary. What is abundantly clear in the accounts of John's vision in the first portion of chapter eleven of Revelation and the whole of chapter twelve is that while the Church is to have a great and powerful outreach during that period of one thousand two hundred and three score days it will be at a great cost of persecution and martyrdom, and so it is appropriate that we borrow the words of Scripture *"As the woman fled into the wilderness where she has a place prepared of God that they should feed her there a thousand two hundred and three score days."* (Rev. 12:6). The wilderness spoken of here is to be understood in its metaphorical sense which is borrowed from the literal account of Israel under the old covenant after they passed out of Egypt under the provision of the blood of the Passover lamb. These saints in view in the passage have also availed themselves of the blood o the Passover Lamb, i.e. the Son of God. However, to be born again into the kingdom of God does not mean that we are abiding there by faith. The wilderness is a place of testing where God allows us to be for a time for the purpose of proving our faith to be genuine and through the testing a process of purification takes place if we abide faithful.

As Israel of old did not enter the lad of promise because they believed not, so the Lord must prove us each one in the fire of testing. Many Old Testament as well as New Testament verses bear witness to this truth, and if you know the scriptures at all you also know that this is the testimony of the Word of God. Traversing though the last five verses of the text let us read: *"And when the dragon was cast out unto the earth, he persecuted the woman that brought forth the man-child. And to the woman was given two wings of a great eagle that she might fly into the wilderness into her place where she is nourished for a time, and times and a half of time from the face of the serpent. And the serpent cast out of his mouth water as a flood after the woman that he might cause her to be carried way by the flood. And the earth helped the woman, and the earth opened her mouth, and swallowed the flood that the dragon cast out of his mouth. And the dragon was wroth with the woman and went forth to make war with the remnant of her seed who keep the commandments of God and the testimony of Jesus Christ."* (Rev. 12:13-17). The text is, of course, written in metaphor and not to be interpreted by each literal meaning of the words. This is the pattern of the Revelation. What is being portrayed is that the woman is under severe and extreme trial and testing but that the Lord is faithfully nourishing and protecting her. Testing is a necessary prerequisite to the purification of the heart. The prophet Isaiah confirms the metaphor and it's meaning at Isaiah 43:2: *"When thou passest through the waters, I will be with thee; and through the rivers they shall not overflow thee; when thou shalt walk through the fire, thou shall not be burned neither shall the flame kindle upon thee."* That which is at stake and that which is being tested is the faith of those who keep the commandments of God and the testimony of Jesus Christ.

When we move back one chapter to eleven and the first twelve verses of the chapter we see some of these same principals involved because the testimony of the witnesses comes out from the woman or the church from which there are those who are keeping the testimony of Jesus Christ. The cost to may will be martyrdom when they have finished their contribution to the testimony. This does not mean that God has forsaken them but there are those things which he allows to befall his faithful saints but in it all we are nourished spiritually and we are preserved for *"to be absent from the body is to be present with the Lord"* if we were to be found faithful.

Under the fifth seal at its opening which is within the context of great hribulation we see *under the altar the souls of them that were slain for the word of God, and for the testimony which they held, and they cried wth a loud voice, saying how long oh Lord, holy and true, shall thou not judge and avenge our blood on them that dwell on the earth And white robes were given to every one of them; and it was said unto them, that they should rest yet a little season until their fellow servants also and their brethren that should be killed as they were should be fulfilled.* (Rev.6:9-11).

Daniel takes us to this same time in the later part of their kingdom speaking of the fourth beast in chapter eight we begin to read at verses 23 through 25. *"And in the latter time of their kingdom, when the transgressors are come to the full, a king of fierce countenance and understanding dark sentences shall stand up. And his power shall be mighty, but not by his own power* (but by the power of his master Satan); *and he shall destroy wonderfully, and shall prosper and practice, and shall destroy the mighty and the holy people. And through his policy also he shall cause craft* (deceit) *to prosper in his hand; and he shall magnify himself in his heart, and shall destroy many: he shall also stand up against the Prince of princes; but he shall be broken without hand.* Daniel takes the whole matter to the end of days that is to say through the tribulation period and references the destruction of the Antichrist by the Prince of Princes and that to be done not with physical power but by the authority and power of the Almighty. We will later see the confirmation of his destruction in the Revelation as we move towards the end of the book. Remember that Daniel does not deal with prophecy issues that extend outside the time frame of the tribulation (the end of days) while John takes us on into the Day of the Lord (the Day of the Lamb's wrath) and judgments and events occurring outside of time. With the opening of the sixth seal of Revelation chapter six the sun and the moon is darkened and time as we know it ceases to be measured by days and nights. This is the signal event that initiates the Day of his Wrath. The tribulation is obviously still measured in time i.e. three and one-half years. Let us move on to Daniel chapter eleven to review more the experience of the "church in the wilderness Daniel11:32-36 reads as follows:

> "*And such as do wickedly against the covenant shall he* (Antichrist) *corrupt by flatteries: but the people who do know their God shall be strong and do exploits. And they that understand among the people shall instruct many: yet they shall fall by the sword, and by flame*(the head of a spear-Daniel must speak in the language of warfare conversant with his days), *captivity and by spoil many days. Now when they shall fall, hey shall be helped with a little help; but many shall cleave to them with flatteries. And some shall fall to try them and to purge, and to make them white even to the end; because it is for a time appointed. And the king shall do according to his will; and he shall exalt himself and magnify himself above every god, and shall*

speak marvelous things above the God of gods, and shall prosper till the indignation be accomplished; For that determined shall be done."

In conclusion of this portion concerning the Church in the wilderness it will add clarify to the words of the pervious prophets by haring the Lord speak from the Mount of Olives in what is called the Olivet discourse by theologians as is found in Mathew chapter 24. "*Then shall they deliver you up to be afflicted, and hey shall kill you, and you shall be hated of all nations for my name's sake; and then shall many be offended, and betray one another and shall hate one another; and many false prophets shall arise and shall deceive many. And because iniquity shall abound the love of many shall wax cold. But to he that endures to the end, the same shall be saved. And this gospel of the kingdom shall be preached in all o the world for a witness to all nations; and then shall the end come. When you shall therefore see the abomination of desolation spoken of by Daniel the prophet, stand in the holy place (whoso reads let him understand).* "1 "*Then if any man say unto you. Lo, here is Christ or there; believe it not; for there shall arrive false Christs, and false prophets and shall show great signs and wonders; in so much that it were possible they shall deceive the very elect.*

Behold I have told you before. Wherefore if they shall say unto you, Behold he is in the desert; go not forth: behold he is in the secret chambers; believe it not. For as the lightering comes out of he east, and shines even unto the west; so shall the coming of the Son of man be. For wherever the carcass be there shall he eagles be gathered together. Immediately after the tribulation of those days, shall the sun be darkened, and the moon shall not give her light, and he stars shall fall from heaven, and the powers of the heavens shall be shaken.(sixth seal of Revelation six)

THEN *shall you see the sign of the Son of Man in heaven: and then shall the tribes of the earth morn; and then shall you see the Son of man coming in the clouds of heaven with power and great glory. And He shall send His angels with a great sound of a trumpet, and hey shall gather together His elect from the four winds, from one end of heaven ttheother.* (9--31)(.Compare with I Thes. 4: 14-18).

Beloved this is **not** the pre-trbulational *rapture* of the entire church for <u>that is a non-event</u>. This is the resurrection of all of the saints at the end of the tribulation excepting only those who were partakers with the man-child three and one-half years earlier.

Chapter Twenty-One

THE ZIONISM DECEPTION

Now it becomes necessary that we change our focus from the study of Biblical prophecy to ongoing developments in the secular world. These significant developments are definitely related to an understanding of prophetic fulfillment but are obscure to most who observe unfolding world history. The world is in a state of dramatic change. This is true in the world at large, and certainly profoundly evident in America. This change is affecting all Americans, but at the same time are not being discerned by the masses even though it will have a profound effect on everyone. In the days and years to come these changes both political and economic will continue to do so in an even more dramatic fashion. We will be exploring the nature and effects of these changes again in a future chapter under the Epilogue. But before elaborating on those details it is necessary to explore the root cause behind these changes and hen develop that subject matter in a way that it will bring an understanding to the reader. The critical issues to be understood lie in a phenomenon which is being orchestrated internationally and which can be summarized in one word. That word is Zionism.

In order to comprehend the more recent historical and current developments in the international secular world it is basic to arrive at an informed understanding of the modern day phenomenon of Zionism including its recent history. As we know the Jewish people had a legitimate and long history ordained and controlled by the God of Abraham, Isaac and Jacob. The record of His calling and dealings with the nation of Israel is written down for our admonition in the Old Testament, The spiritual principles and resulting consequences have been set forth by way of example and instruction using the history of the nation of ancient Israel as our teacher. We see clearly in His purpose the promise of a land of permanent sojourn and the providing of an inheritance for a people centered around a city of habitation where He desired to place His name for His own glory, and the potential blessings for a people to whom He had revealed His law and precepts establishing the clear parameters necessary to hold His favor and experience those promised blessings.

The land of Israel has come to be known as the "holy land" by virtue of these promises and dealings initiated by the mighty God of Jacob. He chose a city, which is named Jerusalem where He purposed the building of a temple, the functional spiritual operation of priesthood, and a place of gathering for worship for a people to bring praise, honor and glory to His name. Under the tenants of the old covenant this became known as Zion. The Jews as a collective people (not necessarily individually) have had a sordid history of failure in general to maintain the testimony of their God. The temple which was built, destroyed, rebuilt and ultimately destroyed a second time in seventy AD by the legions of the Roman armies under Titus to bear witness to the failure of the people to maintain their covenant with their God. The people have been scattered and dispersed among the nations, and the testimony is that ultimately they collectively rejected God's promise and the incarnation of their intended Messiah, Jesus Christ, the Son o God. The twice-experienced destructions of the temple and their ultimate dispersion into the nations of the world give honor and credibility to the words of God and were clearly prophesied in the Torah, not to mention the many warnings from the prophets. These events have been realized historically to the vindication of the righteousness of God and the execution of justice directly drawn from the Torah, and the prophets. The consequences of destruction and desolation are attributed directly to the failure of the people to honor, obey and perform the tenants of this covenant, and the collective rejection by the people of their Redeemer. They truly were historically and ultimately a people who were" *stiff-necked and uncircumcised in heart you do always resist the Holy Ghost"* (See Acts 7:51)), as Stephen so aptly pronounced in his sermon before the Sanhedrin.

They have been a tenacious people in that they have labored diligently to retain their national identify and after almost nineteen hundred years to reestablish a homeland in the place of its ancient origins. Their return to the land of Israel has nothing to do with a reaffirmation of any covenant with God beyond their insistence that the historical promises of a land of habitation still holds credence and viability, and holding aggressively to the concept that <u>they have the right of habitation</u> because God gave the land to them millennia ago. There is no recognition by them or even by the majority of the Christian community that the loss of the land and the promises were directly related to their breach of the covenant God made with them. He very clearly expressed the covenant to them as being conditional upon the faithful performance of the people to all of the tenets of that covenant. The nation was again reestablished politically on May 14, 1948 and has grown out of a long struggle for national identity and a progressive occupation of the historic homeland. This movement of Zionism or the reestablishment of the historic homeland has a significant history in its own right and has continued aggressively through violent resistance by the Arab nations and millions of Palestinian peoples occupying the immediate region. There truly exists a modern day conflict over Zion, but the question to be posed is does this have something to do with the immediate or direct relationship to the workings or directives of the God of heaven? We need to examine what really lies behind the effort and advancements of modern day Zionism.

Although the reestablishment of a national identity has been now placed in the context of the historical geographical location of the ancient people of Israel only in relatively recent times; the movement of what we now identify as Zionism has a much longer history. There has existed behind the scenes for centuries a plan and a purpose to obtain world dominion by a collective movement of Jews with the ultimate intention to gain control again of the historic lands centered in Israel. This is not well understood by most for the plan and intentions remain in the secret realm of the secret societies. (See Chapter eleven). As you read this and believe that what is being stated here is preposterous I would encourage you to do a little of your own research on this movement and subject matter which we are addressing known as Zionism. A most important foundational document, which will be of great assistance to you and can be found on the Internet. It is entitled **The Protocols of the Learned Elders of Zion.** This treatise is very educational and somewhat shocking when you realize the wisdom and planning which has gone into its composition. Basically laid out therein is the plan and methodology behind the movement to establish a world government, which ultimately will be governed from Jerusalem. Key passages in the book of Daniel give us insights into this reality when you have been able to put the prophetic puzzle together to sufficiently understand the meaning of an important passage in Daniel chapter eleven. The entire chapter is significant in recounting the historical developments in the regions, which emerged from the dividing of the empire of Alexander the Great. We will focus on the verses that conclude the chapter beginning with verse thirty- six and continuing to the end of the chapter. Some significant points are to be gained in our understanding of events, which will occur at the very end of the age. *"And the king shall do according to his own will; and he shall exalt himself and magnify himself above every god; and shall speak marvelous things against the God of gods and shall prosper until the indignation be accomplished; for that that is determined shall be done."* (Daniel 11:36). What we are seeing in this passage is the movement of the Antichrist to gain ultimate dominion. In verse thirty-seven we read: *"Neither shall he regard the God of his fathers, nor the desire of women, nor regard any god: for he shall magnify himself above all."* Now the word used for God here is a reference to the God of heaven and the God of his fathers. We discern from this reference that the Antichrist will be a Jew. This is clearly supported within the context of Scripture. Tracing down through the passage we see his power and wealth being manifest. I would encourage you to read through this portion concluding at verse forty-five where we read: *"And he shall* *plant the tabernacles of his palace between the seas **in the glorious holy mountain**"* (Zion); *yet shall he come to his end and none shall help him."* This clearly is a reference to Jerusalem or Zion between the seas (the Dead Sea and the Mediterranean Sea) in the *glorious holy mountain, which* is exactly what it represented in Daniel's day. So we conclude two major points from the passage along with several less significant ones. First, the Antichrist will be Jewish. Is that not totally reasonable? The Jewish people and even the world at large would not be able to accept a coming messiah, as he will present himself to be, unless he had the credentials of a Jew. Second, his dominion will be established in Jerusalem for he shall set *'the tabernacle of his palace between the seas in the glorious holy mountain'*

Some foundations for our understanding of these events have been laid, and that being that the "little horn" spoken of by Daniel in Chapter 8 and verse 9 is a reference to the small nation of Israel as it has been reestablished and has a current political identity in its ancient homeland. Citing the scripture beginning at that location we read: *"And out of one of them came forth a little horn, which waxed exceeding great, toward the south and toward the east, and toward the pleasant land,"* Horn in Scripture carries the meaning of a kingdom or politically defined entity whether large or small. It is not difficult to see that Israel at this current time in history is a small political power resting exactly where it was in ancient history with its principal city identified as Jerusalem positioned as it were toward the south and toward the east, and toward the pleasant land and that geographically it sets it within the historical division of the empire of Alexander the Great. This is the object, the purpose and the intent of Zionism, i.e. to reestablish Israel and Jerusalem and a "Greater Israel" at the center of a world government. Only this time it will be governed by the Son of Perdition, the Antichrist who will be accepted as the Jewish messiah and a return of the messiah of virtually the whole world who will have succumbed to the powers of deception perpetrated by Satan and *the powers of darkness.* Now we know from our study of theology and specifically eschatology that the belief of many, if not most, of those people who claim to adhere to the Christian faith is that Christ will rein from earthly Jerusalem for a millennium after His return.

This is not true and results from erroneous interpretations of the prophetic Scriptures. The point to be made here at this time is that it will be Antichrist who *will set his tabernacle between the seas in the glorious holy mountain* according to Daniel's prophesies. The archenemy of God and Christ is now and will progressively work a masterpiece of deception upon the hearts of those made vulnerable by faulty assumptions and erroneous interpretation of the Holy Scriptures. So we conclude that the important concept of Zionism is well established and has a growing acceptance in today's secular world.

There exists also today a progressive and growing deception as we move rapidly to the end of the age and it is known as Christian Zionism. It is based on the conviction that Israel and the Jews are the "chosen people" of God and that the reestablishment of the nation of Israel in 1948 was a miraculous fulfillment of God's plan for them to be restored into favor and blessing at the end of the age. As we have made note of before; this theological error arises from a misunderstanding in the interpretation of Daniel's seventy weeks around which much of the eschatology is centered. The purpose here is not to spend a lot of time explaining again these theological concepts, but rather to share the truth as I believe God has revealed it in the Scriptures. I would suggest to you that this Christian Zionism movement is more than a century old. It was first presented by a theologian named John Darby in the nineteenth century and was later popularized by C, I, Scofield and the very popular Scofield Reference Bible. Its adherents include some of the more acclaimed Bible schools and seminaries and alleged biblical scholars in America, including Dallas Theological Seminary and Moody Bible Institute, and many more, Many popular Christian writers and teachers are adherents of Christian Zionism, i.e. the theological concept that God will return to a predetermined plan to bring blessings and salvation on the nation of Israel and the Jewish people collectively Consider the popular prophetic writer, Hal Lindsey and his book, *The Late Great Planet Earth,* the popular book and movie *Left Behind.* The Calvary Chapel movement headed up by Chuck Smith (now deceased) is another significant source of this confused doctrine. The Southern Baptist Convention, some sixteen million strong endorse this doctrine. Too numerous to mention are the many other prophetic speculators who are propagating this heresy and misinformation to the so-called Christian establishment. Is it true? If you are still wrestling with some of these issues after having read this far I would encourage you to return to, and reread the following portions again: Who Then is Israel?, and Daniel's Seventy Weeks. We have there proven with Scripture these truths, and they fly in the face of the Christian Zionism movement, which is leading many Christian people into a quagmire of theological bondage and deception.

It is important, I believe, to briefly review the secular Zionist movement and to attempt to explain for our understanding and insight the larger picture of eschatology because at its roots lie in the single most fundamental issue of these last days, i.e. *Novus Ordo Seclorum*— (look at the reverse side of your one dollar bill). It means announcing the New Order of The Ages. This is prophetically the fourth beast of Daniel's dream in chapter seven of Daniel, and the Scriptures clearly reveal that in its ultimate and final expression there is a return to the land of Israel and Jerusalem as a world capitol, i.e. Zion. Again, this is established in the last ten or so verses of Daniel chapter eleven. Read it again if you need a confirmation. It takes review to get it.

There has existed for centuries of Jewish separation form that which they would consider their homeland. This was consummated by an act of God's judgment upon them nationally in 70 A.D. when legions of Roman soldiers under Titus destroyed the ancient city of Jerusalem as well as the second temple as was prophesied by Daniel in chapter nine at verses twenty- six and twenty- seven. This reality is termed by the Jews as the Diaspora, i.e., the dispersion. Since that time there has been a longing among many to restore their identity as a nation for we have collectively a people without a political identity and without a homeland as was exactly prophesied by Moses in the book of Deuteronomy (See Duet. 28: 63-68 and surrounding context) as an act of God's judgment upon a disobedient people. This is not an expression of "anti-Semitism", but rather an expression of Biblical fact. It must be noted that besides the loss of their political identity they have also lost their spiritual identity, and any connection whatsoever with the concept of priesthood. But the modern movement of Zionism is not really identified as a spiritual phenomenon but it has definite spiritual roots in Orthodox Judaism, the Babylonian Talmud, the mystical Kabbalah and other teachings of the Jewish sages and rabbis. These teachings and intrusions into society as a whole will likely undergo dramatic changes and escalations in the not distant future reaching more dramatically into the media, education and law. There is ground for these areas to be advanced as the Jewish world view is that their messiah has never appeared, and as things deteriorate in the world at large people are made vulnerable to the concept of a world savior. It must be noted with emphasis that ate vast majority of 'Jews' in the world toddy as well as those gathered to Israel are not the defendants of Abraham, Isaac, and Jacob; but rather are Ashkenazi Jews who are only recognized as such because they adopted the pagan teaching of the Pharisees which ultimately became the Babylonian Talmud which is an occult masterpiece in total contrast to the Torah. These 'Jews' are counterfeit as is the nation state that they have established, i.e. Israel.

There have been movements of small groups and gatherings of Jews back to the ancient geographical location of the "promised land" over the centuries, and there was the two hundred year (1096-1272 A.D.) medieval history of the Crusades allegedly undertaken for the liberation of the geographical area from Arab and Muslim control. These nine separate crusades were undertaken by elements from England, France and others of European decent as a perceived worthy but misguided religious endeavor. More recently the movement has taken upon a more definitive and focused political effort. What is today called Zionism had its real birth with Theodore Herzel, a Jewish zealot, in the late nineteenth century (1897 and ongoing) and from that point began to gain notable momentum. Herzel was responsible for the organization of the first Zionist Federation, and we find in the Herzel diary a quotation of significance and we quote: "I bring to the Rothschilds and the big Jews their historical mission. I shall welcome all men of good will—we must be united and crush all of these of bad". Zionism took hold and it was backed by the money power of the House of Rothschilds and other extremely wealthy Jewish financiers. The early evidence of this source of political and financial support has continued and become successful because great financial infusions have come from the international banking cartel that now virtually controls the financial world. These same people are the authors, members, propagators and supporters of the Illuminati and a network of secret societies and organizations focused on the purpose of promoting a one-world government. Volumes of books could be written on this theme with the details of its influence and out workings. but the issue here is to demonstrate that Zionism is a world wide endeavor to revive, promote and restore to a place of world domination the precepts and teachings of Orthodox Judaism and establishment of a Jewish "Greater Israel", and its support comes from a cultic conspiracy that will end in the revelation of the Antichrist. One of the most bizarre expressions of world diplomacy was manifest in the Beafour declaration of November, 1917. Arthur James Balfour was a Jewish (and Zionist) member of the English parliament and England at that time had gained political control of Palestine in the Middle East. As a political spokesman for the crown he wrote the following letter to lord Rothschild as the real rulers of the world have been for some considerable period of time, the international bankers and the occultist secret societies and world powers behind the scenes, and we quote:

"Dear Lord Rothschild: I have much pleasure in conveying to you on behalf of His Majesty's government (King George the fifth) the following declaration of sympathy with Jewish Zionists aspersions, which has been submitted to and approved by the Cabinet. His Majesty's government view with favor the establishment in Palestine of a national home for Jewish people, and will use their best endeavors to facilitate the achievement of this object, it being clearly undertook that nothing being done which may prejudice the civil and religious rights and potential status of existing non-Jewish communities in Palestine and the rights or status of Jews in any other country. I will be grateful if you will bring this declaration to the knowledge of the Zionist Federation. Yours Sincerely, Arthur James Balfour"

The movement continues with the establishment of Israel as a nation state in May of 1948. Notably President Truman, a high level Mason (we will make further direct connections between Freemasonry and Orthodox Judaism in a future chapter) was the recipient of a bribe of some two million dollars from the Jewish religious establishment for his part in the official declaration of the United States government giving full credibility and recognition of Israel as a nation state. This information and other contributions on the object can be found in the *Conspiracy of the Six Ponied Star* by Texe Marrs, a long time prophesy researcher. There is of necessity an evolution of the Zionist agenda concerning Israel for the area is inhabited by millions of Arabs and Muslims who hate and oppose the Jews and Israel so that the final establishment of "Greater Israel" has not yet been fully accomplished. The United States and its powerful military are the lackey servants of the Jewish money powers via their control of America through the Federal Reserve. Most of the world is is controlled through the creation of fiat currencies and the various nation's central banks including the Federal Reserve (a private banking cartel which is not controlled by the U. S. Government), the Bank of England, the central banks of Europe, Japan, Canada, and other major industrial nations as well as the International Monetary Fund, the World Bank, the Bank of International Settlements, et al, ad infinitum. The end of this endeavor is an emerging world government regionalized into ten world regions, and ultimately controlled by a false Jewish messiah who will deceive not only Jewry but also the vast majority of the populations of the entire world. Much more detail could be added to validate the argument and define its developments but presented here is the essence of Zionism. It is Satan's plan for a final attempt to be worshipped *"like the most High and to exalt himself above the stars of God"* (Isaiah 14:14), and it will come to pass because the Lord will allow it, for it is to settle the final conflict between the Lord and Satan as it relates to the creation of man, and he has given his people instruction and wisdom available from his Word if they are able to embrace the truth and escape the delusion perpetrated by the evil one but allowed by Him because men general have not embraced truth.

These Prophets

"And with all deceivableness of unrighteousness in them that perish because they received not a love of the truth that they might be saved." (II Thes. 2:10). This portion of this treatise has been withheld for a time and presented here in the hope that enough background has been laid so that the contents can be placed into and incorporated into the whole and be properly understood in context. The writer is fully aware that much of what is written here runs contrary to the traditional conventional Christian worldview of eschatology, and the general conventional wisdom of the day, which has been adopted, by the Christian world at large. While it is admittedly a controversial subject, I believe that it has been adequately documented and it is presented in the spirit of love that the eyes of your understanding might be enlightened and the reader might be renewed in their understanding. We will attempt to build on the concepts set forth here in future chapters. For additional insights into the Zionist phenomenon I would suggest you obtain a copy of my book: **The Israel Deception.**

Chapter Twenty-Two

Understanding The Beast

The prophet Daniel has laid down for us in his interpretation of Nebuchadnezzer's dream and his own dream and visions a prophetic framework for understanding the beast. These were covered early in our study of Daniel, and it became apparent that Daniel was dealing with the kingdoms and empires of this world unfolded in a chronology of time beginning with ancient Babylon. His early prophecies are an overview of world history as revealed to him by the Lord. He provides us with some important details concerning the fourth beast in particular that will help us to understand better the beast we are dealing with in these last days, and we receive latter revelations from the prophet John, which add even further necessary details. Our Lord wants to provide this understanding to his people in these last days so that by referencing the Word of God and receiving grace from the Holy Spirit we may be able to stand in the evil day. We see from Daniel's interpretation of Nebuchadnezzer's dream that the image of world domination comes down to the end of the age in the form of the feet and the ten toes of the image. We know that this brings us to the consummation of the age because the Lord's judgment falls upon the final image of the man.

"*And as the toes of the feet are part of iron and part of miry clay, they shall mingle themselves with the seed of men: but they shall not cleave to one another as iron is not mixed with clay. And in the days of these kings shall the God of heaven set up a kingdom, which shall not be* *destroyed; and the kingdom shall not be left to other people but <u>it shall break in pieces and consume these kingdoms and it shall stand forever"</u>.* (Daniel 2:42-44). Gathering as much insight as the Lord will allow it is clear that this last kingdom is diverse from the ones which have gone before. It is characterized by ten toes, which represent ten kings or kingdoms, if you will. While these entities have a close relationship with one another as do the toes on your feet and yet they are separate and retain a certain function as individual units even though there remains interdependence among them. The world's Zionist and elitist planners of a one-world government have determined to set up a political and commercial system over the entire world governed regionally. As we would view recent international developments we are aware of free trade regions being established which are the forerunners of regional government centered on commerce and trade. Several years ago during the Clinton administration the North American Free Trade Agreement went into effect putting into place and bringing together in commerce the United States, Mexico and Canada. The political union, which will follow behind, will ultimately bring about the loss of the sovereignty of these nations and bind them together under the North American Union. The American Constitution at that point will become null and void and so will what remains of our freedoms.

The internationalist's efforts at the dismantling of the Constitution have been ongoing for decades. Other free trade zones have been established in other parts of the world to bring about a unity and consolidation of regional government. It is always based upon commerce and the geographic proximity of nations. The other regions are now planned and are still in the formative process with the ruling power of the world ever more clearly being the United Nations in concert with the World Bank and the International Monetary Fund. Gathering up the "world community" and the "family of nations" into a composite whole is the objective. The principal engine driving this beast has been America as our military power has been utilized around the world, and yet the people of America continue to live under two illusions, those of freedom and prosperity, neither of which will be long lived. The leaders of nations are beholden to and most often selected by the money power, which holds sway over the political authorities as well as the monetary systems and central banks of all of the major industrial nations including the Federal Reserve in America. The control of the nations in the first instance has been and continues to be in the control of the financial and banking world all of which is perpetrated upon the populations through the blatant fraud of fiat money. With the fiat money system they have gained political control of the nations through enslaving the people with debt, buying and controlling the political systems, and controlling government officials to support their initiatives so as to transform the world into a one world communistic system of tyranny. This world system is well along the way to its final form.

The European Union has led the way with a regional unity and its community currency known as the Euro. The plans for the North American Union also initially included a new currency named the Amero or some other currency contrived by the international banking cartel. The currency reset is in the making and will provide the necessary groundwork for political union. Likewise other regions, which are planned and are being formed around the world until there will come into clear focus the identity ten worldwide regions. These are the ten toes of Nebuchadnezzar's image interpreted by Daniel, and they are likewise identified by John as we will also see as the ten horns of Revelation chapter 13 and other references we have examined in Daniel's later visions.

We can move now to chapter thirteen of Revelation and be further Instructed through John's vision where we read: *"And I stood upon the sand of the sea; and I saw a beast rise up out of the sea having seven heads and ten horns and upon his horns ten crowns and upon he heads the name of blasphemy. And the beast, which I saw, was like unto a leopard, and his feet were as the feet if a bear and his mouth as the mouth of a lion; and the dragon gave him his power, and his seat and great authority."* (Rev.13:1-2).

In Daniel chapter seven we learn that he had a dream and he saw the first three beasts having individual elements of the fourth beast being symbolized by the lion, the bear, and the leopard. Following the analogy we see the lion as representing Babylon, the bear as representing Medio-Persia and the leopard representing the Grecian empire of Alexander. In metaphor the lion represents great majestic ruling power, the bear as having brute power and strength, and the leopard as moving with great stealth and quickness. As these were used to typify the first three kingdoms historically they are again associated with the description of, and all are present in the fourth kingdom of the beast. Further it is clear that the dragon controls this monolithic union, one world government, orchestrating the consolidation of his power and dominion. The ten horns clearly are the final counterpart of the ten toes of the image Daniel interpreted from the king of Babylon's dream. In other words all of these elements are present in this beast, which John perceived as rising up out of the sea. Seven heads are identified as a composite whole of the beast. These seven represent Satan's power as the god of this world and thus having control over the kingdoms of this world. The seven heads represent the historical kingdoms of this world beginning with Egypt and consummating in a "Greater Israel" dominating the world scene. They represent heads of kingdoms and political empires traced down through world history and finalized in the one world government, i.e. the announced New World Order. George H. W. Bush proclaimed this new world order loudly and clearly at the time of the first Gulf War. Interestingly that was at the beginning of numerous wars and insurgencies in the Middle East which are ongoing to this present time. The developing world system is clearly in process in proximity to the nation of Israel but also worldwide in terms of commercial and banking activities. All of these developments are emerging into a unified system with America in decline. We are witnessing the beginnings of this new international system.

And I saw one of its heads as it were wounded to death; and his deadly wound was healed: and all of the world wondered after the beast. And they worshipped the dragon, which gave power unto the beast: and they worshipped the beast, saying. Who is able to make war with him? And there was given unto him a mouth speaking great things and blasphemies; and power was given unto him to continue forty and two months. (Rev. 13:3-5).

Let us examine the elements of this seeming riddle to see if we can solve some of the puzzle. Daniel adds to our enlightenment at Daniel 7:8 where he reveals from his dream:" *I considered the horns and behold, there came up among them a little horn, before which there were three of the first horns plucked up by the roots: and behold, in this horn were eyes like the eyes of a man, and* **a mouth speaking great things.** And again at Daniel 11:38…. *and he shall exalt himself and magnify himself above every god,* **and shall speak marvelous things against the God of gods***, and shall prosper until the indignation be accomplished: and that that is determined shall be done."* This of course is the son of perdition, the Antichrist.

Moving forward with other elements of the riddle we will look at yet another passage from Revelation 17 beginning at verse 9 and continuing through verse 14 reading: *"And here is the mind which has wisdom. The seven heads are seven mountains on which the woman sits. And there are seven kings; five are fallen, and one is, and the other is not yet come, and when he comes he must continue a short space. And the beast that was and is not, even he is the eighth, and is out of the seven, and goes into perdition. And the ten horns, which thou saw, are ten kings, which have received no kingdom as yet; but receive power as kings one hour with the beast. These shall make war with the Lamb, and the Lamb shall overcome them; for he is Lord of lords and King of kings; and they that are with him are called and chosen and faithful."* Let us do an overview and apply it to those Scriptures cited above of the things we do know from the study so far. From the first verses of Revelation chapter thirteen we understand that the ten horns are separate entitieies representing kingdoms or regional governments and the seven heads while being an integral part of the beast are identified separately. One of those heads receives a wound by the sword unto death, and yet by miraculous power he is revived and does live.

We need at this point to elaborate on the seven headed beast which represents world dominions as they are presented and described in the Old Test ament scriptures. The first is Egypt which held the Jews in captivity for four hundred years. The Lord delivered them out of their bondage and after some tine of trial and testing in the wildness they ultimately prevailed and became a great nation as the Lord had promised them. Israel prevailed over the civilized world for a short period of time under King David and into the dominion of his son Solomon before the kingdom declined and became divided due to transgression and apostasy. The Northern ten tribes of Israel were subsequently subdued by the Assyrians and virtually obliterated and scattered as the direct result of their wickedness. This was God's judgment upon them. Shortly thereafter the Kingdom of Babylon arose and took Judah into captivity bringing the world empires under their dominion of the Babylonian Empire. After seventy years this was followed by the Medes and Persians who conquered the world and brought about the demise of Babylon. Subsequently Alexander the Great came from the West and conquered his way eastward to India in a span of about eleven years. He died soon after his conquests from an illness, but his vast kingdom survived until the time of the Romans (about 64 BCE). The Roman Empire prevailed for many centuries before it finally declined into the nations of Western Europe. Out from which emerged America as a product of migration from the residue of the Roman Empire because its migrants were primarily from that region.

The beast which will prevail at the end of the age was already active throughout Europe in the form of a banking dynasty created by what we understand to be the Rothschild dynasty initiated originally by Mayer Anshcel Bauer who through great craft and cleverness and over time gained control of the banking institutions namely the central banks of all of the significant European countries. His network of control was made effective by setting up his five sons in the various nations of Europe eventually bringing it all under a central control. He changed his name to Rothschild (Red Shield) and through their monetary craft of fiat currencies they were able to capture America through the Federal Reserve Act of 1913 and subsequently the passage of the sixteenth amendment (income tax) and the seventeenth amendment which changed the representation of the states in the U.S. Senate taking a giant step forward to destroy the concept of a republican form of government. From there the tyranny has grown exponentially for the Zionist bankers who own and control America through a fraudulent monetary system. Thus the influence of America has gone worldwide and our military is the lackey servants of the Zionist agenda to propagate war and destruction worldwide but specifically in the Middle East. So America is not free as most believe, but rather it has become an instrument economically, politically and militarily for the Zionist plan for world dominion which will be ultimately expressed in the emergence of a "Greater Israel". All of the wars in the Middle East over the last three decades are all about advancing the nation of Israel into a place of dominance in the region.

By Daniel's account as cited above behold there came up a little horn afterward or sometime later, likely prior to the tribulation period, and plucked up three of the first horns. So now there are only eight i.e. that is ten minus three plus one (the little horn). We are asserting again that the little horn as referencing a political identity which is Israel and as it references also the individual coming into universal power which will be Antichrist. This man is a Jew and he ultimately establishes his throne in Jerusalem *between the seas in the glorious holy mountain* as is testified to by the prophet Daniel in chapter eleven. We have previously covered this identification and provided an explanation for our conclusion i.e. it is stated in the Scripture at Daniel 11:36 and following.

We have yet to unravel the rest of the riddle as set forth in chapter seventeen of Revelation verses nine through eleven. *"And here is the mind which hath wisdom. The seven heads are seven mountains, on which the woman* (the woman is Mystery Babylon which has continued to control the pagan empires of this world), *and there are seven kings* (i.e. kingdoms); *Five are fallen, one is, and the other is not yet; and when he cometh he must continue a short space. And the beast that was and is not, even he is the eighth, and is of the seven, and goeth into perdition."* A mountain represents an apex or something rising above the plain and metaphorically symbolizes a kingdom and/or its king as is seen with Mount Zion as a representation of the kingdom of Israel when established under the old covenant. *"The beast which was and is not and yet is, he is the eighth, and out of the seven, and goes into perdition."* It would then seem that the son of perdition is a prominent leader within the scope of the seven heads riding upon the whore prior to his miraculous manifestation from a deadly wound. Israel was destroyed and ultimately scattered as a result of the Roman invasion under Titus in 70 A.D. In recovery from the deadly wound the Antichrist and the reemergence of Israel then becomes wonderment to the world and takes upon himself deity-having cone out of the seven and then is made manifest as the eighth and magnifies himself as supreme over all. In solving this metaphorical riddle form the seventeenth chapter of Revelation we would set forth the following interpretation of the three verses. The kingdoms of this world prominently existing during the Old Testament were five in number, First, there was Egypt (Then Israel came into world domination under the leadership of David and subsequently Solomon. Israel is not counted among the five which are fallen because it was the temporary dominion which God established according to his promise). The s second was the Assyrian Empire which controlled the world and destroyed and assimilated the Northern ten tribes due to their great apostasy. The third was Babylon which was God's instrument to bring judgment upon Judah for a seventy year period. The forth was the Medio-Persian Empire which ruled the world foe significant period, This was followed by their conquest by Alexander the Great, i.e. the Grecian Empire then was the fifth identified collectively as the *"five which are fallen"*: The one which is then existing at the time which John was writing was the Roman Empire controlling the world i.e. *"the one which is"*. The eighth which is of the seven and is to come will be the reemergence of Israel becoming accordance the plan for world dominion can only be a "Greater Israel" to be ultimately ruled by Antichrist.

By him three of the ten horns are "plucked up" or entirely supplanted. We can only speculate that these could be regions of the world in the area round about the Middle East. We would state that only on the basis that the Zionists have in view a "Greater Israel". If you are one who is accepting that premise i.e. that God's original promise to Israel under the old covenant was never fulfilled then you are looking at a vast geographic area from the Euphrates to the Nile and possibly even beyond. We are given information in this expansion of territory at Daniel 11:41-42 reading: *"He shall enter into the glorious land and many countries shall be overthrown: but these shall escape out of his hand, even Edom and Moab and the chief of the children of Ammon. He shall stretch forth his hand also upon the countries and the land of Egypt shall not escape. For he shall have power over the treasures of gold and silver: and over the precious things of Egypt: and the Libyans and Ethiopians shall be at his steps."* The end of all these things being set forth at Daniel 11:45. *"And he shall plant the tabernacles of his palace between the seas in the glorious holy mountain; yet shall he come to his end, and none shall help him."*

Chapter Twenty-Three

Mark Of The Beast

The plan of the Zionists is not really such a complicated thing when it is understood. But there are complications and an extended period of time necessary to move the world into their total control. What it all really comes down to is controlling people both politically and economically. Through the control of fiat currencies internationally and the multiplication of debt which inevitably lies within the power of the bankers, and then first by inflation and then by deflation, and the manipulation of debt they have gained control of the nations. The people are in bondage not only to their own personal debt, but they are likewise in bondage to the debt which their governments have created by borrowing fiat money from the money manipulators (changers). Politicians and political decisions are also controlled by those who hold power over that which we consider to be money. The fiat money scheme never prints the money to pay the interest on any loan but only the principle which is debt on it's face and when borrowed is repayable with interest with no resource with which to repay. Eventually the debt becomes so massive that it is unplayable by the debtor nations. At that point debt becomes total bondage from which there is no relief or release. Once the system comes to total melt down the whore who rides on the beast has accomplished several things. First, all real wealth of substance and value has been transferred into their ownership. All nations have been drained of any valuable resource, and all people have been enslaved by the debt of the nation for which they have been made responsible. *The borrower is servant to the lender* (See proverbs 21:7). So you have been enslaved by this craft and deceit and you have no way of escape.

Now the false prophet has duplicated the image of a man as was seen in our first study in the dream of Nebuchadnezzar. And so you are faced with the reality of either worshipping the image of the beast or being put to death. Signs and wonders will be performed to deceive all that the image is worthy of worship because the false prophet exercises all of the power of the first beast.

The world has been and is still being led into this system of Antichrist which has been arrived at through s a long period of deception. In America it beganwith the Federal Reserve Act of 1913 and then was followed twenty years later by the declaration of national bankruptcy on March 9, 1933 (48 Stat-1)), known as the Emergency Banking Relief Act. All of the gold (HJR 192) was confiscated by he government and the people were given fiat paper money issued by the Federal Reserve which is neither Federal nor were there any disposable reserves for the benefit of the people for it was all debt from the date of issue. And the scourge of this debt was all repayable to the government by virtue of the financial bondage created by the fourteenth amendment to the Constitution and your status as a United States citizen. The fourteenth amendment was never lawfully ratified.

Shortly after the bankruptcy in 1935 the fraud and deception was further advanced through a system of social welfare known as Social Security so that you need not worry in your old age or your disability for the government has promised to take care of you. You were tagged with a 716 digit number that was to mark you throughout your life and be required to identify you for anything governmental and much which was not governmental. In more recent times the numbering system has become more sophisticated through technology and will ultimately require that an RFID (radio frequency identification card) shall be issued to the population and required for providing health care, any government benefit, banking, etc. The people have been led through this vast system of lies and fraud into total bondage. It is Satan's masterpiece of deception. The ultimate identification will be a numbered microchip implanted in your body to identify you to the commercial system so that you will be able to buy and sell to obtain the necessities of life. When this ultimately all comes about you will no longer need Federal Reserve Notes or currency of any description for all transactions will be totally computerized and carried out electronically." *"And he causes all, both small and great, rich and poor, free and bond to receive a mark in their right hand or their forehead: "And that no man may buy and sell, save he that had the mark or the name of the beast or the number of his name. Here is wisdom. Let him that hath understanding count the number of the beast; for it is the number of a man; and his number is six hundred* and *threescore and six . . ."*

(Rev 13:16-18*). "He that leads into captivity shall go into captivity: he that kills with the sword must be killed by the sword. Here is the* patience *and faith of the saints."* (Rev. 13:10).

Chapter Twenty-Four

THE LAMB ON MOUNT ZION

Because of the nature and complexity of the subject matter it is fitting that we gather things together, review, summarize and restate the ground, which has been covered in a manner that will provide a proper focus for moving forward.

Daniel's prophesies have been invaluable to help us understand the revelations of John the apostle of the Lord who was blessed us with the glorious revelation of the Christ. When we reach the subject matter, which takes us through to the end of the great tribulation we no longer can draw on Daniel's visions and dreams for he does not bring us beyond that juncture in the unfolding of God's plans in the final consummation the age. For that reason as we continue on we will necessarily need to draw on others among the prophets because we must carry the truths of these revelations to the very end; but before moving on let us briefly summarize.

Daniel has unfolded for us the kingdoms of this world as they played a role or had bearing upon God's people whether they were Israel of the old covenant or the kingdom of the beast found to be persecuting the church at the end of the age.

We have seen that the God of Israel ceased to deal with the nation of Israel collectively after the complete fulfillment of the seventy weeks (Daniel 9),but He has much to add concerning the emergence of the beast and the trials of the saints during the tribulation. Tracing the chapters of the Revelation we see again the centrality of Jesus

Christ and the operation of the Holy Spirit in revealing him to his people. From chapter one where he is first revealed to John and moving forward we see him being manifest over and over again as yet *"another angel"* i.e., a messenger bringing different yet related messages, all in His role as the anointed Judge of the earth. Chapters two and three were to provide us with a survey of the various spiritual conditions, which existed in the churches of Asia at that time but also they become instructive and encompass issues within the church through the age to the very end of the age.

When we arrive at chapter four we are first taken into "the *things which shall be hereafter.*" The scene in chapters four and five take us into the heavenlies and before the very throne of our God. The text brings us to the Lion of the tribe of Judah who is found worthy to execute the judgments and he takes the seven sealed book form the hand of the Father and prepares to begin opening he seals.

Chapter six takes us through the opening of the first six seals and those are related to the trials and troublous times of the tribulation period. With the sixth seal at the end of the chapter we see the sun darkening and the moon not giving it's light and the men of the earth realize that the great day of His wrath has come. Chapter seven is he gathering of the saints in resurrection to the Lord and following on through chapters eight and nine with the sounding of six of the seven trumpets. These are announcements of judgments occurring within the Day of the Lamb's wrath—not in the tribulation which many expositors are inclined to include as a logical continuation of the same chronology. Making a correct dividing of these two separate realities is critical to our overall broad view of the text of the Scripture, never mind the details because contextually you are lost from any ability to make associations of events. Chapter ten gives us a pause in the forward chronological motion of events which occur from the beginning of chapter four to the end of chapter nine." Another angel' intervenes and tells John that he must eat the little book: and prophesy again to the peoples and tribes and tongues and nations. The prophetic narrative then takes us back from a point near to the consummation of the Day of the Lamb's wrath and gathers together additional needful perspectives on the tabulation period. Three different perspectives are revealed and provided in the texts of the first twelve verses of chapter eleven, all of chapter twelve and all of chapter thirteen. We have discussed the details of these perspectives in earlier chapters, but the purpose here is to put the ordering of the chapters again in a context that will help avoid confusion. Always remember that after chapters two and three concerning the churches and the Church that we are dealing prophetically with things "hereafter" which includes the great tribulation, the gathering of the saints, the Day of the Lamb's Wrath, and the final judgment and the eternal state in the New Jerusalem, then the new heavens and the new earth when the former things a re passed away.

This brings us to chapter fourteen and the Lamb on Mount Zion. The tribulation period has been exposed to the full extent that it will be, and now we see the saints have been gathered into heaven. This portion parallels chapter seven where the one hundred and forty four thousand consisting of twelve thousand each from the twelve tribes of Israel have been sealed and have been translated to appear before the throne in heaven being in actuality "a *multitude which no man can number*". It would be helpful if you read again chapter seven of the Biblical text as well as reading the previous chapter in this treatise entitled "The Gathering". These being parallel passages we discern she similar language and participants. We are told that the singing of the "new song" was reserved to those who had been redeemed form he earth. We see them as not being defiled with women, but as virgins joined to their head, even Christ. These things are set forth in metaphor to illustrate the purity of a bride prepared for her husband being clean and untainted. The numbers again are symbolic representing the whole house of Israel (not Israel after the flesh, but the *Israel of God* being defined as the faithful through the ages) who partake of the first resurrection i.e. *"the first fruits unto God and to the Lamb."* We will later see that there is more than one resurrection, which totally confounds the evangelical eschatology of these last days, but is nonetheless true as will be clearly shown later on in the study. Let us be clear that the Lamb on Mount Zion having with him the one hundred and forty four thousand representing the gathering of his own into the kingdom and are set before the throne of God in heaven. We see their character and spiritual condition described in the symbolism and metaphor of a virgin without guile and without fault as *"having been redeemed from the earth."*

Another angel (messenger)* is seen to fly in the midst of heaven *"having the everlasting gospel to preach to them that dwell on the earth."* The messenger is the Holy Spirit making clear to the living remaining on the earth after the resurrection that there had been a message of salvation from the Creator of the universe, and they having rejected the message they now know that the hour of his judgment has come. And there followed then another angel (messenger)* being of the seven Spirits or the Holy Spirit of God proclaiming the fall of (Mystery) Babylon, and yet a third angel (messenger)* proclaiming that those who have worshipped the beast, and received his mark upon them, *"the same shall drink of the wine of the wrath of God poured out without mixture into the cup of His indignation"."* These three are Holy Spirit messages to the inhibitors of the earth. But the clear contrast is there to be seen, i.e. *"Here is the patience and faith of the saints: here are those who keep the commandments of God and the faith of Jesus."* And John heard yet another voice from heaven telling him to write: *"Blessed are the dead which die in the Lord from henceforth: Yea, says the Spirit that they may rest from their labors, and their works do follow them."* These are each and everyone utterances from the Holy Spirit of the Almighty God.

John then looks and behold another vision of a white cloud and *"One that sat upon it like unto the Son of Man, having on his head a golden crown, and in his hand a sharp sickle."* The one who is the director and Lord of the judgment likened unto the Son of Man has made His glorious appearance and there is yet another angel* coming forth from the temple crying out with a loud voice to Him that is sitting on the cloud and proclaiming to him who has the sickle to thrust it in for the time has come to reap for the harvest of the earth is ripe. *"And he that sat upon the cloud thrust in his sickle on the earth: and the earth was reaped."* And then we see through John's vision yet another angel* come out of the temple also having a sharp sickle; and then also another angel* having power over fire; and crying out to him that had the sharp sickle saying, *"thrust in the sickle and gather the* *clusters of the earth; for her grapes are fully ripe."* The angel then thrusts in his sickle into the earth; and gathered the vine of the earth and cast into the great winepress of the wrath of God.

What we have here in a summary text is the fullness of the wrath of the Almighty having been committed unto the Son in concert with the Holy Spirit and executing the judgments which are elsewhere individually explained as being the portions of judgment which in composite are making up the whole. There has been an asterisk placed by the introduction of each individual angel having a message to bring and in summary we find that there are seven in number. Tracing the Scriptures as follows: *"and the seven Spirits, which are before His throne"* Rev. 1: 4, *"These things says He that has the seven Spirits of God and the seven stars. The mystery of the seven stars, which thou saw in my (Christ's) right hand, and the seven golden candlesticks. The seven stars are the angels of the seven churches."* (Rev. 1:20). *"These things say He that has the seven spirits of God and the seven stars. (Rev.3:1). and there were seven lamps of fire before the throne, which are the seven Spirits pf God".* (Rev. 4:5)." . . . *a Lamb as it ad been slain, having seven horns and seven eyes, which are <u>the seven Spirits of God sent forth into the earth"</u>.* (Rev. 5:6). *"And I saw the seven angels, which stood before God; and to them were given seven trumpets.* (Rev. 8:2)." *And I saw another sign in heaven, great and marvelous, seven angels having the seven last plagues; for in them is filled up the wrath of God."* (Rev. 15:2).So what is the point which is being made in these various Scriptures? Beginning with Rev.1:4 the precedent is established i.e. the Holy Spirit is consistently spoken of as being sevened or sevenfold in manifestation. Note that cited above are seven Scriptures which show us that the seven spirits of God become <u>the seven angels sent forth</u> into all of the earth. Their designation as angels is simply to show that the Holy Spirit manifested sevenfold become the messengers in the text because that is what the word angel means ...*a messenger.* If you grasp this truth it will spare you from misinterpreting the word angel to mean a literal angel because we see in these contexts that the seven spirits perform things which do not lie within the preview, authority or power of the angelic beings. We have previously made the point early in our study that the word angel is also in numerous passages speaking of the Lord Jesus Christ for he is the ultimate messenger of God, and He utilizes the Holy Spirit likewise as an active messenger as He carries out his work of executing judgment as we see here in chapter fourteen. If you are able to grasp these two truths you will have taken a large step forward in unraveling the mysteries of the Revelation.

Having set forth these important keys there is a need to add a summary statement to the fourteenth chapter of Revelation. We see at the outset that the Lamb is on Mount Zion. This speaks of the heavenly kingdom, and he is there with his saints. This demonstrates the truth that the resurrection of the saints occurs *"immediately after the tribulation of those days"* (Matt. 24:29), but also that there is period in between the resurrection of the saints and the return of the Lord with them to bring judgment upon the evil inhabitants of the earth. At the end of the age I believe that we can no longer mark the passage of events with time for another dimension of reality has been introduced. This is clearly seen in the eighth chapter where the first four trumpets sounding are directed Holy Spirit activities prior to the Lord coming with His army to engage in the spiritual battle. This truth will be observed again in chapter nineteen with added explanation. The progression of this chapter does not involve activity of the saints other than to establish their presence in the heavenly realm and the character and purity, which they possessed to attain unto the glory. The rest of the chapter is a summary of preparatory declarations including the announcement of the final judgment of the world (i.e. the Day of the Lamb's wrath) as being expressed as in the gathering of a vine from he earth for her grapes are fully ripe and then they are *"cast into the great winepress of the wrath of God."* The *winepress* is then *trodden without the city.* The saints comprise the city and are safe within the city, that is, the New Jerusalem and they are delivered from these final judgments, which are to come upon the earth. In fact, after a pause they will be participants with the Lord in their execution.

Chapter Twenty-Five

THE SEVEN LAST PLAGUES
(SIX LEADING TO THE SEVENTH)

The text of the subject matter in chapter fourteen, fifteen and sixteen of Revelation are continuous. Our context is within the Day of the Lord remembering that the time of this wrath being poured out on the earth and its inhabitants is <u>after</u> the tribulation and <u>after</u> the first resurrection. As we have seen previously in The Lamb on Mount Zion the saints have been gathered before the throne of God with announcements and proclamations being made and it is becoming clear that a preparation for a reaping of the harvest of the earth is being described and as it is about to be cast into the winepress of the wrath of Almighty God. The foregoing events, activities, and proclamations of chapter fourteen lead us directly into the seven last plagues. In this vision John has seen *"seven angels having the seven last plagues, for in them is filed up the wrath of God."* (Rev.15: 1). First we see those that had gotten the victory over the beast, his image, his mark and the number of his name. Again the Holy Spirit is illustrating that those who have been true and faithful are set in a place of security and separated from the issues of ongoing judgment being poured out on the earth. There comes forth from them a song of praise being described as the song of Moses the servant of God and the song of the Lamb. As we read it is a song or worship, honor and thanksgiving. We are reminded of the song of Moses, which was sung by the children of Israel when the Lord delivered them out of Egypt. Be refreshed by looking at Exodus 15:1-13 for the song of Moses. At that point in their history they to were praising God for at that time they had just experienced his mighty power and great deliverance. *"Great and marvelous are your works Lord God Almighty, just and true are your ways thou King of saints."* (Rev. 15:3).

And after this John looked and beholds the temple of the tabernacle of the testimony was opened. Out from the throne of God in the holiest of all where he dwells the testimony is apprehended by John in the vision for he is granted to foresee the very glory of God in the vision to be fully realized by the saints in that future reality when all judgment has been fully realized. We see that the temple was filled with smoke symbolizing the glory of God and that no man was able to enter the temple until the seven plagues of the seven angels are fulfilled. (Compare Exodus 40: 33-35). We see them symbolically *dressed* in white linen a symbol of righteousness and having their breasts girded with golden girdles. Symbolically the golden girdles speak of that which is of great value because of its purity and that being contained inwardly within the breast (heart). These symbols are to be understood as metaphors of the temple and Holy Spirit acting in righteousness and truth. Again, the need is here to emphasize that the seven angels are the seven Spirits of God, which are before his throne, which we have before set forth and established a chain of references for beginning with Rev. 1:4. Repeating the Greek word for angel which simply means as a noun a messenger, and as a verb to bear tidings or to bring a message. If you have interpreted the word to mean literally an angelic being the doctrine of the book will completely collapse in contradiction for the angelic beings are servants of God that have not been ordained to execute judgment for the elect angels have no experience of sin or any intrinsic understanding of the scope and depth of the Father and the Son's dealings with mankind concerning the issues if sin, righteousness and the judgment to come for they have not experienced the realities of sin and it's consequences and have no authority to bring judgment upon man.(See Heb. 2:5-9 and I Pet. 1:12). So we see through the text first the Angel, God's ultimate messenger Jesus the Christ, and then we see over and over again the action of the Angel and His interactions with the seven Angels signifying the Holy Spirit.

"And I heard a great voice from heaven saying to the seven angels, Go you ways and pour out your vials of the wrath of God upon the earth." (Rev.16:1). When the first angel went and poured out his vial upon he earth, there fell upon those men that had the mark of the beast and those who had worshipped his image a noisome (injurious) and grievous sore (as an ulcer).

And the second angel poured out his vial upon the sea and the sea became as the blood of a dead man and every living soul died in the sea. (Cp. Rev.8:8-9). When the third angel will have purred out his vile upon the waters of the earth the rivers and fountains of water will likewise become as blood.(Cp. Rev. 8:10-11). *"For they have shed the blood of prophets and saints for thou has given them blood to drink for they are worthy,"* (Rev. 16:6). Following this the fourth angel poured out his vial upon the sun; and power was given to him to scorch men with fire. (Cp. Rev. 8:12). Men blasphemed the name of God and they did not repent of their sins nor give God glory. When the firth angel poured out his vial upon he seat of the beast and his kingdom, and the kingdom was filled with darkness, and they again blasphemed the name of God and did not repent of their deeds. And with the action of the sixth angel pouring out his vial, the great river Euphrates was dried up making a way for the passage of the kings of the East.

John observed in the vision then three unclean spirits out of the mouth of the dragon, and out of the mouth of the beast and out of the false prophet.

These are the spirits of devils, working miracles and their mission is the gathering of the kings of the earth together for battle in that great day of God Almighty. *And he gathered them together into a place in the Hebrew tongue Armageddon.* (Rev. 16:16). Before we continue to the pouring out of the seventh vial it may be profitable to consider the development of judgments up to this point. If you will return to chapter eight in the text of Scripture you will note that the sounding of the trumpets of the first six angels have some close parallels to these six plagues described in the putting forth of the first six vials. While they are not identical it can be surmised that the vials are related to the trumpets in their order and dealing with the same progression in the Day of His wrath. First the physical creation experiences destructive judgments by the Spirit of the Lord. And as the judgments progress the effects upon men are more clearly set forth. I believe that the plagues of the vials are an extension of those judgments introduced under the sounding of the first six trumpets.

Before considering those issues related to the seventh vial, and the seventh trumpet as well; it is appropriate that we search and gather some more specific information on the final open battle of warfare for it is a major theme of the Revelation. While it is not detailed in chapter sixteen but is simply brought forth as an event and a gathering to a location where the gathering of some supposed northern army of aggression will be coming against them. There are other texts to give more detail. And there are other Scriptures, which provide us with a background for a fuller understanding.

Chapter Twenty-Six

Armageddon

This significant final encounter occurs in the period before the final judgment just before that of the great white throne which will be the final account and consummation of the Day of the Lamb's wrath. It relates directly to the kings and kingdoms of the earth. The word Armageddon is a compound word from the Hebrew and not the Greek. It has ancient significance and its meaning is the Mount or hill of Megeddo. It is the place where many historic battles were fought and is strategically located about fifty miles north of Jerusalem. It sits on a rise of land that is a gateway to pass through leading into the valley of Jezreel where battles took place in the days of the judges. It is of significance also because it was at Megiddo that two kings of Judah died in battle. First king Ahaziah and later the very good king of Judah named Josiah who engaged the Egyptians there and it cost him his life. Megiddo can be found at first mention in Joshua 17:11 where we see that it was a portion of the inheritance of the tribe of Manasseh but discover at Judges 1:27 that the tribe failed o drive out the inhabitants of Megiddo. A significant battle of the judges under Deborah was fought there against the Canaanites as is recorded in Judges Chapter 5 verses 13 through 20. The only point we are making here is that the location of Megiddo is strategic and played a role in the history of ancient Israel. Later in the history of the kings as we have mentioned was the place of the death of two of the more righteous kings of Judah.

These Prophets

Having looked just briefly at the history of Megiddo and its location a further examination is needed from the Revelation. In review of the clear plan and declaration of the Lord it is seen the saints are participants in this final encounter on the earth when the Lord returns with His saints at the end of the Day of the Lamb's Wrath. Under the sounding of the fifth trumpet which was an announcement of the first of the three woes in chapter nine; we were introduced to the great army of the Lord under their king Abaddon in the Hebrew tongue and Apollyon in the Greek language both of which mean a Destroyer. This is the army of the Lord being described and they are coming ready and prepared to participate in this great consummating spiritual battle with him which we see takes place at Armageddon.

The second woe of Revelation chapter nine adds detail to the encounter. Under the second woe I would encourage you to return to the potion titled Woe, Woe, and…… Woe to clarify in your mind the issues and explanations given there. These two *woes* are directly involving the Lord at the head and as the king of the army of his saints. These passages are very difficult but not obscure containing full descriptions which can be discerned with careful considerations of the metaphorical language contained there, and the Holy Spirit to say amen providing the confirmation that the interpretation given is true.

There is yet another important portion in John's revelations which although written also in metaphor is somewhat easier to unravel. I am speaking now of Revelation chapter 19: 11-20. The account given by John in this vision follows the marriage supper of the Lamb, which subject we will consider later. Now we behold as heaven is opened. Remember from the potion and title of the Lamb on Mount Zion and the references we have previously covered that the saints are in haven with the Lord after the resurrection and prior to the beginning of the Day of His Wrath. We then can take note that the havens are opened and there appeared to behold "*a white horse and He that sat upon it was called Faithful and True. His eyes were a flame of fire and on His head were many crowns; and he had a name written, that no man knew but he himself. And he was clothed in a vesture dipped in blood: and his name is called the Word of God."* (*Rev. 19:11-13*). It is with complete clarity that this is the Lord of glory returning out of haven to engage in the final battle,

You may have some difficulty with the Destroyer in chapter nine identified as Abaddon and Apollyon as King over his people. This is the exact one and the same Lord Jesus Christ revealed in battle array and makes no mistake that he comes as a Destroyer. The horse is used more than once in Revelation as symbolic of warfare and preparation for battle.

Now also as appears in chapter nine he is leading a great army and they are following after him also on white horses and being clothe in fine linen white and clean for this is the righteousness of the saints having no spot or blemish on their raiment. Speaking again of the Lord we see that *"Out of His mouth goes a sharp sword that he should smite the nations; and he shall rule them with a rod o iron: and he treads the winepress of the wrath of Almighty God. And he has on his vesture and on his thigh a name written, KING OF KINGS AND LORD OF LORDS".* He is coming now with his saints to that great rendezvous at Armageddon and there is a gathering of the fouls of prey in the air to come to that great supper of the great God to eat of the flesh of the mighty men, and the flesh of all men on he earth both free and bond, both great and small. And John saw also the beast and the kings of the earth, and their armies gathered to make war against him and the army of His saints. *"And the beast was taken and with him the false prophet that wrought miracles before him, with which he deceived them that had received the mark of the beast, and them that had worshipped his image. These both were cast into a lake of fire burning with brimstone. And the remnant were slain with the sword of him that sat upon he horse, which sword proceeded out of His mouth: and all of the fouls were filled with their flesh."* This is that which the Scripture identifies as Armageddon. It is portrayed for us in the language of metaphor but the essence of the meaning is clearly that of destruction for all that have embraced evil upon the earth. It is a spiritual battle engaged with the spiritual weapons of warfare and righteousness has prevailed.

Chapter Twenty-Seven

THE SEVENTH TRUMPET AND POURING OUT OF THE SEVENTH VIAL...

We took note at the end of chapter nine and after the sounding of the sixth trumpet that there was a pause in he forward movement of judgment in the Day of His Wrath because the Lord appearing to John in chapter ten had somewhat more to reveal in the details of the great tribulation so He instructed him that he must prophesy again to many nations, and tribes and peoples and tongues. And so we came to understand that in the first twelve verses of Revelation eleven, in all of chapter twelve and in all of chapter thirteen we were taken back to before the resurrection to review and see the tribulation period viewed from three different aspects.

If we were to return to chapter eleven and verse fourteen, and then moving on to the end of that chapter we would see the vision from the end of chapter nine is resumed revealing the third *woe* which is equal to and the same as the seventh trumpet. It also parallels the pouring out of the seventh vial at chapter sixteen and verse seventeen. Looking then at the text a Revelation 11:15 and following we read: "*The second woe is past and behold the third woe comes quickly. And the seventh angel sounded; and here were great voices in heaven saying <u>the kingdoms of this world are become the kingdom</u>*

of our Lord and of His Christ; and He shall reign forever and ever, and the four and twenty elders which sat before God on their seats, fell on their faces and worshipped God, Saying we give the thanks O Lord God Almighty, which are and was and are to come; because thou has taken to thee thy great power and reigned." (Rev 11:15-17). Now we understand that the nations were filled with anger for they realized that his great wrath had come, and the time of the dead that they should be judged, and also the time that his servants the prophets, and the saints should receive a great reward. And that the time of final judgment has come when those who have destroyed the earth should be destroyed. *"And the temple of God was opened in heaven, and there was seen in His temple and the Ark of; his testament; and there were lightenings, and voices, and thunderings, and an earthquake and great hail."* (Rev 11:19). Besides those physical things as the lightening, the thundering, a great earthquake and a great hail the key to focus upon here in the text is that *"the time of the dead that they should be judged, and that thou should reward thy servants the prophets, and the saints and them that fear thy name."* (Rev. 11:18). Up to this point we have been occupied with the revelation of mostly physical events, which under the power of the Holy Spirit were executing judgments on the earth, transforming it, changing it, and progressively destroying it. When the conflict of Armageddon was reached we also viewed events that had consequences in the physical realm although their outworking ultimately lies within the spiritual realm.

But now when we reach the seventh trumpet and the pouring out of the seventh vial, while it is true that several physical signs are made manifest when we make the comparison between the last several verses of chapter eleven and he last several verses of chapter sixteen we are now entering another realm of judgment in kind. That realm of judgment is that which falls not upon the body, but upon the souls and spirits of men who have already experienced physical death or as we shall see it is "the first death". In comparing the last portion of chapter sixteen with the last portion of chapter eleven we take note of the parallels between the two.

Looking then when the seventh angel has poured out his vial we would take note that it is not poured out upon the earth, but as it were "in *the air*".

Those former judgments in the Day of his wrath were poured out upon the earth, but now, as with the sounding of the seventh trumpet there is a consummation of greater judgment that transcends the earth that comes into focus for the time has come, the *time of the dead that they should be judged.* (Cp Rev. 11:18). So also with this text in chapter 16 we observe the following. We now hear a great voice from heaven coming out of the temple and from the throne "*it is done*" and there were voices and thundering and lightening; and there was a great earthquake such as was not ever seen on the earth and these things were accompanied with a great hail falling out of heaven. Each of these accompanying signs is paralleled in the closing verses of chapter eleven under the sounding of the seventh trumpet. Additionally we see here that every island fled away and the mountains were not found indicating a destruction of the earth had occurred. It is important to take note of this for these things portend the complete destruction of the physical creation, as we know it, in preparation for a new heavens and a new earth. It is important to recognize this truth for most who have done exegesis on the closing issues of biblical eschatology would have us to believe that Christ is going to reign from the earthly city o Jerusalem for a millennium for one thousand years. This, of course, is impossible when the entirety of this present creation is to be burned up and destroyed. Peter enlightens us concerning this reality when he declares "*the Day of the Lord shall come as a thief in he night; in the which he heavens shall pass away with a great noise, and the elements shall melt with fervent heat, the earth also and the works that are therein shall be burned up. Seeing then that all <u>these things shall be dissolved,</u> what manner of persons ought you to be in all holy conversation and godliness?*" (II Peter 2:10-11). "*For the first heaven and the first earth are passed away and there was no more sea.*" (Rev. 20:1). Let us be perfectly clear that all of the former things are to be destroyed and to pass away as relates to this present order and the physical creation.

It is inevitable that we must move on to issues even more difficult to understand, but nonetheless true and necessary to be proclaimed for we seek to know the whole counsel of the Word of the Lord in order to be rightly prepared for that great day of his wrath. We are told at verse nineteen *"that the great city was divided into three parts, and the cities of the nations fell, and great Babylon came in remembrance before God o give unto her the cup of the wine of the fierceness of His wrath"*. It is not particularly difficult to understand the falling of all of the cities of the nations which will pass away with the destruction of this creation, and we can readily grasp that those whose who made up Babylon or Mystery Babylon as she is described in chapter seventeen would be subject to special consideration in the rendering of judgment in the day of his wrath. It is, however, more difficult to take up issues involving judgments that are destined to fall upon those who have identified themselves as believers in Christ.

The popular theology of the day does not impose much spiritual responsibility on those who profess to belong to the household of faith. Among those who identify themselves as evangelicals the broadly accepted theological view is that one having been "born again" most certainly is guaranteed an entrance into the kingdom and a passing into immediate and eternal blessing when they stand before him to be judged. There is an expectation then by those that the only differentiation between individuals will be the degree or amount of the rewards they will receive in that day. These people unfortunately have not been instructed in the whole truth as it is revealed all the way through the Holy Scriptures. This doctrine of "eternal security" has excused many, if not most of the Lord's people to take an either passive or casual attitude as concerns their walk spiritually and the outworking of their salvation as Paul has admonished all believers in his epistle to the Philippians. The Scriptures are to numerous to even begin to cite which shows and teaches each of us that a spiritual mandate to faithfulness and holiness of life has been imposed upon all who would name the name of Christ. There is no **uninterrupted** eternal security simply based on the fact of the new birth or being born of the spirit. We need to go no father than the letters to the seven churches in Asia where we are admonished over and over again by the Holy Spirit with clear and definite warning that it is to them that overcome who will be granted those blessings of inheritance in the kingdom which will be established at the time of his judgment. Please read it again seven times over it is repeated to each of the churches. The Spirit of God has spoken it seven times and then encouraged each believer that *"he that has an ear to hear let him hear what the Spirit says unto the churches."* I will not further belabor this point here but as we look at Scripture in chapter sixteen and then again in chapter twenty there is no way to avoid the fact that according to the Word of God there will be a dividing of the people of God at the judgment and it will not be merely a matter of rewards which will be distributed to them. This background was and is necessary in order to make sense of some of the Scriptures we must deal with as we go forward.

Now the Scripture immediately at hand which we have already spoken of as concerns the cities of the nations and their fall, and great Babylon come in remembrance before God is verse nineteen. *"And that great city was divided into three parts . . ."* (Rev. 16:19a). There are only two cities in view in the entirety of the Revelation. Babylon is mentioned separately in this very verse. The other city is that great city which comprises all of the people of God. Take note of the mention of the great city. The first portion of the verse states that the great city shall be divided into three parts by an act of judgment by the Lord himself which is apparent here and will become more understandably apparent as we move to chapter twenty. The prophet Zechariah comes to our assistance in understanding this matter of the dividing of the people of God first by setting apart Judah and Israel under the old covenant into two parts and then by a declaration of the prophet that the dividing shall ultimately involve a three part division.

"And I took my staff Beauty, and cut it asunder that I might break my covenant, which I had made with all of the people. And it was broken in that day: and so the poor of the flock that waited on me knew it was the word of the Lord." (Zechariah 11: 10-11). *"And took my other staff even Bands, that I might break the brother hood between Judah and Israel."* (Zechariah 11:14). It is clear in the history of Israel under the

old covenant that there was a dividing of Israel (ten northern tribes) and Judah in the south comprised of the tribe of Judah and Benjamin. This dividing was based on judgment as the northern tribes set up their false worship in Samaria and became a wicked and idolatrous people who were ultimately destroyed by the Assyrians and carried away into a captivity from which there has never been a recovery.

Judah remained to carry forth the testimony of the Lord at Jerusalem but in the entirety of her history there was only five kings which the Lord made mention of as having been faithful and true to him and in any finding acceptance. Judah to was carried into the Babylonian captivity but there remained a small discernable remnant out of Judah and there was later an opportunity after the captivity was over for some to return to Jerusalem and rebuild the city, the wall and the testimony. There was always a small discernable remnant of faithful ones under that covenant and so it continues to be also unto this present time. What we have seen in this example is that Judah originally represented that separated remnant but as their history went forward it was also tainted with rebellion and sin causing them to come under judgment. So what we have seen here is another dividing of a remnant out from a remnant. Looking at another Scripture in chapter twelve we find some more verses that more directly support and relate to the phrase under consideration in chapter sixteen and verse nine, Zechariah speaks the word of the Lord where we will specifically focus at chapter thirteen verses seven through nine where we read the following: *"Awake, O sword against my Shepard"*,(a reference to the crucifixion of Christ as is cited at Matt.26:31) *"and against the man that is my fellow, saith the Lord of hosts: smite the Shepard, and the sheep shall be scattered: and I will turn my hand upon the little ones. And it shall come to pass that in all the land, saith the Lord, two parts therein shall be cut off and die; but the third part shall be left therein.*

And I will bring the third part through the fire, and will refine them as silver is refined, and will try them as gold is tried: they shall call on my name, and I will hear them: I will say, It is my people: and they shall say, the Lord is my God." Numerous Scriptures bear out the reality that many who have begun with the Lord will not finish the course, so to speak. Even Paul at the very end of his time proclaimed that he had continued faithful and there was therefore, a crown of glory laid up for him. As we move to chapter twenty Revelation and that portion dealing with the judgment of the dead we will enlarge on this concept, which is understood by so few within the church.

Chapter Twenty-Eight

The First Resurrection and The Second Death

Chapter twenty begins with the vision of an Angel coming down out of heaven. We would say at the outset that the Angel is the Lord Jesus Christ. This is not that difficult to discern even if we had not previously laid an extensive background in previous chapters concerning the Angel's identity. Christ is God's ultimate messenger, and as we read the text we see that he possesses a great chain in his hand. And He lays hold on that old serpent the Devil and Satan and binds him a thousand years. Of course, we do not need to be too theologically astute to understand that the one who has authority and power to bind the Devil can only be Christ. The chain represents a metaphorical means of expressing the binding as we would not understand all of the spiritual issues involved in binding Satan but can relate to the explanation of binding with a chain, and thus the metaphor is used. Further we are told from the vision that a seal is set upon him that he can deceive the nations no more until the thousand years have been fulfilled. Our Lord accomplishes this special judgment at the end of days before he undertakes the great and awesome judgment of the dead.

John has yet another vision directly related to this time of final judgment wherein he sees thrones and they that sat upon them, and judgment was given unto them. Who might these be who are seated upon thrones with judgment committed unto them? *"And he that overcomes and keeps my works unto the end, to him will I give power over the nations: and he shall rule them with a rod of iron; as the vessels of potter shall they be broken".* (Rev. 2:26-27). And again: *"To them that overcome will I grant to sit with me in my throne, even as I also am sat down with my Father in his throne".* (Rev. 3:21). Clearly these are those who have been faithful and have become the bride as it were of the Lord Jesus Christ, i.e. they have overcome the world, the flesh and the devil and prevailed to receive the crown of life and are destined to reign with Christ. The narrative of the vision goes on to reveal the souls of them that were beheaded (martyred) for the witness of Jesus, for the word of God, and those that had refused to worship the beast and his image. *"And they lived and reigned with Christ one thousand years".* (Rev. 20:4).

Now it becomes clear in verse five that they were the only ones who lived for we are told that *"the rest of the dead lived not again until the thousand years sere finished. This is the first resurrection.".* (Rev. 20:5).

The Holy Spirit in this portion of John's vision concerning a "first resurrection" has raised the issue. In my study of doctrine and theological issues over many years I have never encountered a teacher or a preacher who made any mention whatsoever of a first resurrection which makes it implicit that there must be more than one resurrection. To raise a matter such as this with almost any believer would be to subject yourself to scorn and ridicule as an heretic for surely you must know that everything is finalized with God at the judgment and your white stone (good vote), or, on the contrary your condemnation is a once and forever determination i.e. you are either destined to enter the kingdom or you are condemned to hellfire and judgment forever and ever….and ever. My study of the Scriptures over the years has convinced me that this view is a serious error in doctrine and it obscures certain truths that are critical to our overall understanding of the purposes of God with mankind. We have already discussed the dividing of the city, or in another way of expressing it, the people of God being separated into three parts or portions. The testimony of Zechariah the prophet is undisputable that two of those three shall be cut off and the third will be brought through a process of spiritual purification under the hand of God and he will receive them for they remain faithful to their calling. This truth lays the foundation for understanding that there will be more than one resurrection. Many, if not most, of the people who name the name of Christ are in a state of more or less spiritual lethargy living lives that are not clearly dominated by the direction of the Holy Spirit. There are awesome and severe consequences for crucifying *"to themselves the Son of God afresh and putting him to an open shame"* (Hebrews 6:6), and thus doing *"despite unto the Spirit of grace"*. (Hebrews 10:29). The New Testament is replete with such warnings to the so called Christian, and the heretical theological position declaring that if you have been "born again" your destination is heaven's glory in spite of what the fruit of your life may reveal is a blasphemous lie. Have you ever read the parable of the sewer and understood that there are many spiritual pitfalls between a new birth and the reality of *"<u>but he that endures to the end</u>, the same shall be saved."* (Matthew 24:11). Even the apostle Paul puts this matter in perspective for himself and all that will hear him in his epistle to the Philippians in chapter three and verses eleven and twelve where he writes *"If by any means I might attain unto the resurrection of the dead: not as though I had already attained but I follow after, that I may apprehend that for which I am apprehended of Christ Jesus."* The apostle Paul did not believe that because of his conversion to Christ that he was "home free". *"I press towards the mark for the price of the high calling of God in Christ Jesus."* (Verse 14). The word used for resurrection in the passage means literally in the Greek, "the out resurrection from among the dead" according to Vine's Expository Dictionary of the New Testament. The clear testimony of all of the New Covenant is that those who overcome are described as those who are found faithful: *"And they overcame him by the blood o the Lamb and by the word of their testimony and they loved not their lives unto the death."* (Rev.12:11), and again*"...and those that are with him are called, and chosen, and faithful"*.(Rev.19:14).

Returning to John's vision we see that they who are partakers in the first resurrection *"lived and reigned with Christ a thousand years, but the rest of the dead lived not again until the thousand years were finished. This is the first resurrection. Blessed and holy is he that has part in the first resurrection: on such the second death has no power, but they shall be priests of God and of Christ and shall reign with Him a thousand years."* (Rev. 20:4-6). Now we have opened up here immense and awesome doctrinal considerations that are virtually not theologically dealt with in any place that I know of. We have now before us a "first resurrection", and "a second death", and those who <u>did not live again</u> until the thousand years were finished. It becomes clear that if there is a resurrection, which the Holy Spirit identifies as the first resurrection then it is obvious that there must be—no it is, <u>required that there is more than one resurrection</u>. Also if *the "rest of the dead lived not again until the thousand years were finished,"* the clear and definite implication is that there will be those who will live again after the thousand years.

This premise raises the necessity that we gain a better understanding of he meaning of the "second death" for it has no power over them who are blessed in the "first resurrection". There are two deaths, which are dealt with by the Scripture, both of which are the consequence of sin in the ordering of things by the Lord. The first death is physical in nature. We have been created in the image of God and as such we are tripartite i.e. we are made up of three distinct components those being a body, a soul, and a spirit. When physical death occurs the body dies as a result of trauma, sickness, etc. What happens is that the body as the temple or housing for the soul and spirit ceases to be able to continue to fulfill its function as such. Upon the occurrence if this death the soul and the spirit within are not destroyed bat are simply removed to another realm. Our purpose here is not to develop a theological explanation of the place of their departure, but we do know of a surety from the writings of Paul in the first epistle to the Corinthians that for a faithful believer *"to be absent from the body is to be present with the Lord."* The non-material elements of an unbeliever also do not cease to exist but become separated, disembodied and unable to function within the physical realm. Now then there becomes a need for an explanation of the second death, which is being referenced here in John's vision. If you are in a communing relationship with the Lord you are alive to him, and that is because the Holy Spirit is quickening your spirit. On the other hand, if you are living your life apart from a communion and relationship with Christ then you are dead while you live because the only life you are experiencing is a natural physical life which is the same as that which is experienced by all of those who do not have a relationship with Christ. The second death can thus be explained very simply as a separation from the Spirit of the Lord. So then it is not a matter of the loss of one's existence but rather the loss of one's communion with, or the separation from your source of life. This condition is expressed several places in the gospel's and Matthew in particular as having been *"cast into outer darkness where there will be weeping and gnashing of teeth."* (Cp. Matthew. 13:41-42). Only those who have been found faithful and true in their communion with Christ and who have been obedient to the Holy Spirit are destined to rule and reign with Christ through that period or ordering which is spoken of as the thousand years. All others are dead both physically (because they are disembodied spirits and souls), and they are likewise dead spiritually because they are separated from the life of the Lord. Again it is clearly implied that of those in this state there is a future remedy and the possibility of living again. Further light and commentary on the issue of the second death is found at Rev. 21:7-8 where we read: *"He that overcomes shall inherit all things, and I will be his God and he shall be my son. But the fearful and unbelieving, and the abominable and murders, and whore mongers, and sorcerers, and idolaters, and all liars, shall have their parting the lake which burns with fire and brimstone: which is the second death."* (Rev 21:7-8).

We can add somewhat to this explanation as relates to those who have suffered the consequences of the second death which state is imposed upon them because of sin. Note again that the condition of escaping the judgment of the second death (i.e. separation from the Lord) is *overcoming*.

To overcome means to prevail or to be victorious. In this portion we have placed in contrast the first resurrection (for there is clearly more than one) with the issue of the second death. We have an enemy who seeks to destroy us spiritually. He must be resisted, and we must abide (continue) in faithfulness in Christ if we are to inherit the promises.

Chapter Twenty-Nine

THE BOOK OF LIFE

Because this subject is addressed frequently through the Scriptures it obviously is of the utmost importance as we see in the conclusion at Revalation 20:15 where we read: *"And whosoever was not found written in the book if life was cast into the lake of fire.".* We are now dealing with ultimate destiny and the preceding portion of Scripture leading up to this verse is often referred to theologically as the great white throne judgment. It is in reality the judgment seat of Christ who is the final judge of all things as relates to the destiny of man whether it be blessing or cursing. We are told by the apostle Paul at II Cor, 5:10 *"For we must all appear before the judgment seat of Christ; that every one may receive the things done in the body, according to that he hath done whether it be good or bad."* To explore the truths presented in the Scripture concerning this final judgment of men (and women) personally and individually it seems to me to be of value to first trace the references to the Book of Life through the word and then return to this final portion in Revelation chapter 20.

We begin our search with Moses in Exodus at chapter thirty and verses thirty-one and thirty two. The occasion here is when Moses discovered the sin of the golden calf, which had been formed by the Israelites and became an object of worship. Reading: *"And Mores returned unto the Lord and said, Oh this people have sinned a great sin, and made them gods of gold. Yet now if thou will forgive their sin—: and if not, blot me I pray thee, out of thy book, which thou hast written. And the Lord said to Moses. Whosoever has sinned against me, him will I blot out of the book."* The Israelites were a redeemed people in that they had been delivered by the blood of the Passover lamb out of the land of Egypt and were under a mandate by virtue of that deliverance to serve the Lord. Sin then interrupted that relationship and he would visit by the Word of the Lord their sin upon them, and the consequences were declared to be a blotting out from the book, which the Lord had written for those who had sinned.

David speaks very forcefully against the enemies of the Lord in Ps. 69 making the following proclamation: *"Let their habitation be made desolate and let none live in their tents. For they persecute him who thou has smitten; and they talk to the grief of those whom thou has wounded. Add iniquity to their iniquity, and let them not come into your righteousness. Let them be blotted out of the book of the living; and not be written with the righteous"* This Psalm of David who is here speaking as a prophet in this Messianic Psalm and so we have cited verses 26 through 28. The prophet Isaiah also sees that great day of Judgment when he prophesies at Isaiah 4:3-4 saying: *"And it shall come to pass that he that is left in Zion; and he hat remains in Jerusalem shall be called holy, even everyone that is <u>written among he living</u> in Jerusalem: when the Lord shall have washed away the filth of the daughters of Zion, and shall have purged the blood of Jerusalem from the midst thereof by the spirit of judgment and by the spirit of burning".*

The Lord has a writing containg the names of those he counts among the righteous, The prophet Malachi gives further confirmation as we read at Malachi 3:16-17. *"Then they that feared the Lord spoke often one o another and the Lord hearkened, and heard it, and a book of remembrance was written before him for then that feared the Lord, and hat thought on his name. And they shall be mine, saith the Lord of hosts, in that day when I make up my jewels; and I will spare them as a man spares his own son that serves him".*

The Lord giving instruction to his apostles at Luke 10:19-20 gives them cause for rejoicing when he says to them: *"Behold I give unto you power to tread on serpents and scorpions, and over all the power of the enemy: and nothing by any means shall hurt you. Notwithstanding in this rejoice not, that the spirits are subject to you; but rather rejoice, because your names are written in heaven".* And Paul writing to the Philippians says: *"I entreat you also, true yokefellow, help those women hat labored with me in the gospel, with Clement also, and with other my fellow laborers whose names are in the book of life." (Phil. 4:3).*

And then we find a solemn warning from John as he addresses the church at Sardis: *"Remember therefore how thou has received and hold fast, and repent. If therefore, thou shall not watch, I will come to you as a thief and you shall not know what hour I come upon you. Thou has a few names in Sardis that have not defiled their garments; and they shall walk with me in white for they are worthy.* **He that overcomes shall be clothed in white raiment,** *I will not blot his name out of the book of life."* (Rev 3: 3-5).

As we approach the Scriptures dealing with the Lord's judgment upon his people we discern from the several citations of Scripture that there is a record of the saints called the book of life and those who are abiding faithful remain written down there. We further discover that we are to watch, and abide faithful in our walk and communion with Christ for we are subject *to defile our garments* or fall into some manner of sin. If one does not repent concerning sin and defilement, i. e. if we fall away from the truth then the consequences for sin unless repented of has been proclaimed; he shall be blotted from the Lamb's Book of Life. Many will not believe this important truth taught consistently through the Scriptures.

We now return to our original text in chapter twenty revealing to us that white throne of righteousness and the judgment seat of Christ. *"And I saw a great white throne and Him that sat upon it, from whose face the earth and the heavens fled away; and there was found no place for them. And I saw the dead small and great, stand before God; and the books were opened: and another book was opened, which is the book of life and the dead were judged out of the things which were written in the book, according to their works. And the sea gave up the dead, which were in it; and death and hell delivered up which were in them; and they were judged every man according to his works. And death and hell were cast into the lake of fire. This is hthe second death. And whosoever was not found written in the book of life was cast into the lake of fire."* (Rev.

20:11-15). So if is clear from the passage that all of the dead, whether small or great, shall come before His throne to be judged. It is a truth of Scripture that he died for the sins of the whole world. He made a provision for the salvation of all with the shedding of His blood and the giving up of his life in total commitment to the will of the Father. Those who have not availed themselves of this grace extended to mankind by faith will be judged according to those things recorded in the "books". The Lord has a complete record of all things, which men have committed, performed and done. Each man who is not found written in the Book of Life will be judged according to those works and deeds. People commit evil and mock the God d of glory thinking that they will not be required to give an account. What an awesome and fearful thing to then stand before Him and realize that there is a complete record of the life and nothing has been forgotten. The day of justice and judgment will come upon all men.

If one may be so blessed to find that his name is written in the Book of Life, and as we have reviewed the truths surrounding that reality, then that one will receive that gracious acceptance and blessings prepared from before the foundation of the world. "*When the Son of man shall come in his glory, and all of his holy angels with him, then shall he sit upon the throne of his glory, and before him shall be gathered all nations: and he shall separate then one from another, as a shepherd divides his sheep from his goats: and he shall set the sheep on the right hand and the goats on the left. Then shall the king say unto them on his right hand, come you blessed of my father, and inherit the kingdom prepared for you from the foundation of the world......*" ((Mathew 25:31-34).

Chapter Thirty

GOG AND MAGOG

Passing on now to a portion of chapter twenty, which takes us on beyond that awesome account of the great white throne judgment of Christ; we move to these few verses in the middle of the text of this chapter. This is another portion of Scripture, which has not been understood, and the theologians have generally placed it at another time and provided very different and confusing interpretations to make it virtually indiscernible in the context.

The content of the text here to be considered is as follows: *"And when the thousand years have expired, Satan shall be loosed out of his prison. And he shall go out to deceive the nations which are in the four quarters of he earth, Gog and Magog, to gather them together unto battle: the number of them is as the sand of the sea. And they went up in the breadth of the earth, and compassed the camp of the saints about, and the beloved city: And fire came down from out of haven from God and devoured them. And the devil that deceived them was cast into the lake of fire and brimstone, where the beast and false prophet are and shall be tormented day and night for ever and ever."* (Rev. 20:7-10).

Examining the text we see first of all that what transpires is <u>after</u> the thousand years at a juncture in God's further dealings with men, wherein Satan is loosed for a season out of his prison where he has been confined during this period by the Lord according to Rev.20:1. His activity immediately becomes to deceive and then gather by the deception those, which are identified as Gog and Magog, and to bring this multitude against the camp of the saints. Judgment comes down upon them from God and the devil is again restrained; this time being cast into the lake of fire where the beast and the false prophet were previously confined in judgment at the end of the previous age. Having then placed these events in the distant future after the thousand years (I do not know if that one thousand years is a literal or a figurative representation covering the passage of another age outside the context of what we understand as time). Whatever the truth of that may be we are truly being instructed concerning things, which reach beyond the first resurrection and the establishment of the New Jerusalem.

We will need to go back to the words of the prophet Ezekiel to begin to gain an understanding of the elements of this prophecy. The reference point there is the two chapters, which I believe, provide the details for the interpretation of these four verses in the revelation given to the prophet John.

First we would assert that this is the only other source of instruction in Scripture concerning Gog and Magog, and the Word of God provides its own commentary if we know where to go to find it. Reading several verses from Ezekiel 38 we can begin to unravel the mystery of the revelation passage. *"Son of man set thy face against Gog, the land of Magog, the prince of Mesheck and Tubal and prophesy against him, and say, Thus saith the Lord God; behold I am against thee, O Gog, the chief prince of Mesheck and Tubal: and I will turn thee back and put hooks in thy jaws, and I will bring you forth and all thine army, horses and horsemen, all of them clothed with all sorts of amour, even a great company with bucklers and shields, all of them handling swords. Persia, Ethiopia and Lydia with them; all of them with shield and helmet. Gomer and all his bands; the house of Togarmah of the north quarters, and all husbands: and many people with them. After many days thou shalt be visited; in the latter days thou shalt come into the land that is brought back from the sword, and is gathered out of many people, against the mountains of Israel which have always been waste: but it is brought forth out of the nations, and they shall dwell safely all of them . .* (verses 2-9). *"Son of man prophesy and say unto Gog. Thus says the Lord God; in that day when my people of Israel dwells safely, shall you not know it?"* (Verse 14). *"And I will call for a sword against him throughout all of my mountains says the Lord God: every man's sword shall be against his brother. And I will plead against him with pestilence and blood; and I will rain upon him and upon his bands, and upon the many people that are with him, an overflowing rain, and great hailstones, and brimstone. Thus will I magnify myself and sanctify myself; and I will be known in the eyes I many nations, and they shall know that I am the Lord."* (verses 21-23).

In contemplating a comparison of the brief passage in Revelation with chapter thirty- eight of Ezekiel we would learn several things. First Gog and Magog are a collective reference to heathen people or those who stand in opposition to the Lord. Magog was a son of Japheth in the postdiluvian era and he had a lineage or posterity. Gog makes reference to a northern region and they are here aligned with each other. Additional information is given to provide us with further confirmation that they represent collectively the heathen peoples, Togormah was likewise a son of Japheth according to the lineages given and we see Tubal to be a postdiluvian patriarch. Added in the text are the names of other heathen peoples including Persia, Ethiopia and Libya. The point is one of identification, and we see the other player in the text to be Israel. Clearly what is being outlined in the narrative is a conflict between these peoples and those which we would identify as belonging to the Lord, i.e. Israel, but remember we are within the framework of the Old Testament, and the peoples of Israel do not persevere in faithfulness to the Lord so we have come to an understanding through our previous study and examination of Scripture who Israel actually is under the new and everlasting covenant, i.e. a people of faith that are not identified by natural posterity. This point is being emphasized again here simply because the Revelation passage takes us, by the stated context completely out of the present age to a time in the distant future when Satan is loosed again after having been taken captive and bound. So, we can only conclude that the details of the conflict being given in this passage and the following chapter thirty-nine have their application outside of the conventional context of time and into a yet distant future where they will find fulfillment.

This, of course, will be considered to be a ridiculous conclusion by any that still hold to the doctrinal belief that the physical nation of Israel continues to be the "chosen people" of God unto this present time. To connect the time of application we must rely on the latter revelation in chapter twenty, and then we must conclude that this is not depicting some battle to be carried out against the current nation of Israel by some presumed army from Russia or the northern regions in relation to the geography of the area. It will be impossible to understand this context as being after the millennium if you have not seen beyond the first resurrection, and gained insights into the reality hat God's dealings with men transcend this age. Undeniably the Revelation passage takes us to a period for fulfillment when Satan is again loosed to go forth and deceive the nations. Furthermore, it becomes obvious that the text of these chapters is not dealing with a flesh and blood conventional warfare conducted on horses with swords and conventional amour. These are only the metaphors being used by he Holy Spirit so that we can make an application of what is being revealed. We see that the conflict is resolved "by *an overflowing rain, and great hailstones and brimstone,"* (fire and brimstone which comes down form heaven) as is stated in the Revelation text. The two texts are speaking of the same events, which are concluded outside of the framework of time that we are conversant with based on the sun and the moon, and the he earth, the seasons and he passing years. I believe that this understanding is important to free us from an expectation of events, which will not happen. While there are other vital truths in Ezekiel chapters thirty-nine and following which also carry us into that future millennial age for their fulfillment, we will wait and investigate those issues under a later topic.

Chapter Thirty-One

THE NEW HEAVENS AND THE NEW EARTH

If your theological persuasions have followed along the lines of dispensational pre-millennialism you should be impressed that the further you delve into eschatological considerations the greater becomes the conflict with the truths as they are revealed in the Scriptures. We have previously set forth a number of these issues with that system of theology, which cannot be reconciled with the Word of God, but when we come to this current subject the issues become blatantly irreconcilable. The reason that it is needful to again bring attention to the many theological errors of that system is simply to once again seek to awaken those who have been deceived with false doctrines with the hope that the whole content of this treatise on prophecy might result in an acceptance of vitally important spiritual truths. We need to discuss more specifically those irreconcilable issues once again in this context. Those who hold steadfastly to traditional dispensationalism believe there are two separate kingdoms, which will be manifest during the coming age. First, they must make a place for the natural posterity of Israel believing that they are the recipients of the promises made to Abraham, and they do so with the establishment of an earthly kingdom centered in earthly Jerusalem over which they believe that literally Christ will rein sitting on the throne of David for one thousand years.

A second kingdom must then be established for the New Testament church is in heaven and this is accomplished by providing them a residency in the New Jerusalem which is seen by them as being constructed with literal walls, gates, streets of gold, etc. I believe these to be metaphors. So we are to believe that these two kingdoms over which Christ reigns coexist though out the entirety of the millennium. An earthly kingdom for all of those of Jewish progeny, and a heavenly kingdom for the saints of the new covenant, and never the twain shall meet because in their view these are two entirely different covenants. What happens at the end of the coming age? Is this an eternal arrangement? How can these two separate kingdoms ever be reconciled? So then let us look at what the Scriptures have revealed.

In the consummation of the age and the final judgments of the Day of the Lord it is clear that all that is related to this present order of creation shall be destroyed and the Lord will make *"all things new"*. The present earth and heavens are to be totally destroyed and replaced with new heavens and a new earth. The apostle Peter informs us fully of this reality in chapter three of second Peter beginning at verse seven: *"But the heavens and the earth which are now by the same word are kept in store, reserved unto fire against the Day of Judgment and perdition of ungodly men. But beloved be not ignorant of this one thing, that one day is with the Lord as a thousand years, and a thousand years as one day. The Lord is not slack concerning His promise, as some men count slackness: but is longsuffering to us-ward, not willing that any should perish, but that all should come to repentance. But the day of the Lord will come as a thief in the night; in which the heavens will pass away with a great noise, and the elements shall melt with fervent heat, the earth also and the works that are therein shall be burned up. Seeing then that all of these things shall be dissolved, what manner of people ought you to be in all holy conversation and godliness, looking for and hasting unto the coming of he day of God, wherein the heavens being on fire shall be dissolved and the elements shall melt with fervent heat? Nevertheless, we, according to his promise look for new heavens and a new earth wherein dwelleth righteousness."* (II Peter 3:7-13). Where then is the earthly Jerusalem, the "holy land" and all of those who comprise and adhere to the earthly Israel? These things of which Peter writes obviously happen at the end of this age in the day of his wrath. Do we not then see the utter heresy and foolishness of dividing the kingdom into two separate entities?

What then is the truth of the matter? Blessed and holy are those who have part in the first resurrection for they shall become the priests of God and reign with Christ for a thousand years. *"And I saw a new heaven and a new earth: for the first heaven and first earth were passed away; and here was no more sea. And I saw the holy city, New Jerusalem, coming down from God out of heaven,* **prepared as a bride adorned for her husband**. *And I heard a great voice out of heaven saying, Behold the tabernacle of God is with men, and he will dwell with them, and they shall be his people, and God himself shall be with them, and be their God."* (Rev.21: 1-3). We graphically see that the former things are passed away. We further have the revelation of the New Jerusalem as the center of the new heavens and new earth. It is clear that the New Jerusalem, which is portrayed as a city, but is in truth and reality actually the church glorified. It is all of the people of God who have had part in the first resurrection. We know this for we see her personified as a bride prepared and adorned for her husband. This is consistent with the other New Testament Scriptures. *"For we are members of His body, of His flesh, and of His bones. For this cause shall a man leave his father and mother, and shall be joined unto his wife, and they two shall be one flesh.*

This is a great mystery but I speak concerning Christ and the church".(Eph. 5:30-32) And there came to John in the vision on of the seven angels, which had the seven vials and he spoke to John saying;" *Come thither and I will show you he bride, the Lamb's wife."* (Rev.21: 9).

Please remember from a previous discourse when we encounter an Angel (messenger) acting to reveal the truths of a given vision that the Angel is a manifestation of the Holy Spirit. It is the Holy Spirit, which teaches us and allows us to see anything within the realm of the kingdom revealing spiritual truths. Now the Holy Spirit is about to reveal to us *"the bride, the Lamb's wife. "And he carried me away in the Spirit to a great and high mountain, and showed me that great city, the holy Jerusalem descending out of heaven from God. Having the glory of God, and her light was like unto a stone most precious, even a jasper stone, clear as crystal, And had a wall great and high, and had twelve gates, and at the gates twelve angels, and names written thereon, which were eth names of the twelve tribes of Israel."* What is being seen here is that heavenly city made up of all of the saints and the gates or entry thereof is designated by the name of the twelve tribes of Israel. In the gathering of he elect in chapter seven of the book we saw that the whole multitude, which snood before the throne, which no man could number were first identified as being twelve thousand from each of the twelve tribes of Israel. This is not literal but represents then the whole compliment of those partaking of the glorious first resurrection referred to chapter twenty and verse four and they shall be the priests of God and reign with Christ for a thousand years. Now we are being given in metaphorically language the constituency of the holy city, the heavenly Jerusalem. First we get the twelve gates representing entry points for the twelve tribes. And after this the Spirit reveals twelve foundations and in them written the twelve apostles of the Lamb. He that talked with him then again gives John a golden reed and he is instructed to measure the city, and the gates thereof, and the walls thereof. Remember at the beginning of chapter eleven he was likewise given a reed by the Lord to measure the temple and them that worshipped therein, but those in the outer court were not to be measured as they were given *"to the Gentiles and the holy city shall they tread under foot forty and two months".* (Rev. 11:2). Now the city as being measured is complete with the full compliment of the saints as conceived by the Lord. It is his bride. The measurements as set forth speak again of the completeness and perfection of the city, and they are equal in all of their dimensions as to the length and the breadth, and the height. And *"they are all according to the measure of a man that is of the Angel."* What is meant by the measure of a man and that being the Angel (the messenger-Jesus Christ revealed in Rev.1:1? What is God's thought about the measure of a man and who is that Son of Man who established the measure? It is Christ. And what is His purpose with man insofar as that measure is concerned? It is *"Until we all come in the unity of the faith, and of the knowledge of the*

Son of God unto a perfect man, unto the measure of the stature of the fullness of Christ" (Eph. 4:13). This then is the measure being taken and revealed as a reality in the bride, the Lamb's wife. We then see a lengthy description of he components of the walls and the foundations all being expressed in terms of precious stones and valuable jewels. These are metaphors as are the streets of gold. This is God's way of helping us to understand that the city is made up of those elements (people) that are very valuable and very precious to Him. *"And they shall be mine says the Lord of hosts, in that day when I make up my jewels; and I will spare them as a man spares his own son that serves him.* (Malachi 3:17). So we then see that the description of the city is the description of the bride set forth in metaphorical terminology. He that has ears to hear let him hear and also see what the Spirit is teaching us concerning the heavenly city, the New Jerusalem. The vision continues: *"And I saw no temple therein for the Lord God and the Lamb are the temple of it; and the city had no need of the sun in it: for the glory of God did lighten it; and the Lamb is the light thereof; and the nations of them which are saved shall walk in the light of it; And the gates of it shall not be shut at all by day; for there shall be no night there. And they shall bring the honor of the nations into I; and there shall in no wise enter into it anything that defiles. Neither whatsoever works abomination, or makes a lie; but they, which are written in the Lamb's Book of Life."* (Rev. 21:22-27). The text is clear. It is the collective habitation and fellowship of the *Israel of God* in completeness and perfection. You cannot add commentary to that.

Chapter Thirty-Two

A Kingdom Of Priests

"And he showed me a pure river of water of life, clear as crystal. proceeding out of the throne of God and the Lamb. In the midst of the street of, and on either side of the river, was there the tree of life, which bares twelve manner of fruits, and yielded her fruit every month, and the leaves of the tree were for the healing of the nations. And there was no more curse: but the throne of God and the Lamb shall be in it: and his savants will serve him: and they shall see His face: And His name shall be written in their foreheads." (Rev. 22:1-4).

Because such confusion reigns in the world of the theologians and particularly where the subject matter addresses doctrinal issues of prophecy and eschatology, there is almost no light cast upon any aspect of truth after the first resurrection. A failure to discern the true spiritual nature and identity of Israel ends up with a divided kingdom in the writings and teachings of dispensationalists. Also due to a failure to see beyond the first resurrection and because there is no recognition that there is more than one resurrection, these very important considerations are either misinterpreted or generally are not dealt with at all.

What is introduced in the final chapter of the Revelation is a ministry that transcends this present age and clearly teaches us that God is not through with His dealings with man just because a time of judgment has been executed and consummated. A vast company of saints have reached the glory of resurrection into the kingdom. The purpose of this topical consideration will be an attempt to cast new light on spiritual issues that are not yet completed in the plans and purpose of the Lord, and bring some new understanding to His people as to how these matters may directly and dramatically affect them now as well as in the future.

First, it is of foundational importance that the reality of the priesthood of the true believer be addressed. It is certain from Scripture that God has purposed to call and establish a kingdom of priests. Peter is very clear in his writings. *"To whom coming as unto a living stone, disallowed indeed of men, but chosen of God, and precious. Ye also, as living stones are built up a spiritual house an holy priesthood, to offer up spiritual sacrifices, acceptable to God by Jesus Christ."* (I Peter2: 4-5). Christ himself is the great High Priest of the new and everlasting covenant who is past into the heavens to minister before the father on behalf of his people. We are called too share with him in this ministry of priesthood and that is not only for this present time, but also passes into the eternal state in resurrection, *"And from Jesus Christ, who is the faithful witness, and the first begotten of the dead, and the prince of the kings of the earth, Unto him that loved us and washed us from sins in his own blood, and made us to be kings and priests unto God and his father, to him be glory and dominion forever and ever, Amen."* (Rev. 1: 5-6). And again we read towards the end oft the book of Revelation at chapter 20:5-6. *"But the rest of the dead lived not again until he thousand years are finished. This is the first resurrection. Blessed and holy is he that hath part in the first resurrection: on such the second death hath no power, but they shall be **priests of God and of Christ**, and shall reign with him a thousand years."*

The subject of priesthood is a very relevant theme of Scripture, and we understand clearly from its place and function that it has to do with not only ministering to the Lord in worship and service but equally important is the function of ministering to others in relation to the purposes of God. Our God has set His heart upon a people who, because of their faith and responsiveness to him and his truth, become His servants. He desires to engage these servants in reaching out in ministry to others in a discipline designed and ministered to bring about perfection. *"And he that overcometh and keepeth my works unto the end, to him will I give power over the nations: and he shall rule them with a rod of iron: as the vessels of a potter they shall be broken."* (Revelation 2:26-27). The Lord has great and wonderful things in store in the age to come for those who re found to be faithful and true. As we can see even from the early verses of the book even to the end in chapter 22, there remains the very real possibility that many even multitudes of yet unbelieving people can yet find a remedy and redemption through a process of ministry, judgment and discipline. So what is our purpose and function beyond the first resurrection? Is it not to be found worthy to be the servants of the Most High? That service will be carried out in all that is encompassed in the mind of God pertaining to priesthood.

Various functions and duties will no doubt be included, but when you give thought to the things of God beyond this life and touching the kingdom of heaven, it is the highest calling to be found in His service forevermore. To attain unto the calling will require the utmost devotion and obedience during this earthly sojourn. The apostle Paul expressed it well when he wrote, *"Brethren I count not myself to have apprehended but this one thing I do, forgetting those things which are behind, and reaching forth unto those things which are before, I press toward the mark for the prize of the high calling of God in Christ Jesus."* (Philippians 3: 13-14). For it is expedient for us to lay hold of the mater of priesthood and service even now in his present time and be preparing ourselves for an even far greater ministry in the eternal kingdom. This is indeed the high calling of God in Christ Jesus. So to whom does this ministry extend? Most clearly based on the testimony of Scripture it extends to the nations. The generally accepted theological view is that the eternal destiny of the lost and those who have not been joined to Christ by faith is that they will burn in hell forever and ever.

First of all it must be understood that hell while expressed in terms of fire hell cannot literally be fire, as we understand it. The metaphor has been chosen by the Holy Spirit to express that there is an all consuming state of separation from God, which will cause in its effect on the soul and spirit of a man an intense remorse sorrow and agony. The nations shall be broken as the shivers of a potter's vessel and that is somehow affected by the operation or actions of the heavenly priesthood. That does not necessarily mean that a complete destruction takes place. Remember that we have brought forth and expounded the truth that there is more than one resurrection. Is it possible that through acts of administered judgment by the Lord and/or his servants there could exist a healing remedy and correction in the hearts of many whom we have thoroughly condemned?

There remains a tree of life bearing fruit *"and the leaves of the tree were for the healing of the nations,"* The prophet Ezekiel brings assistance to our commentary in this regard. *"And by the river upon the bank thereof, on this side and on that side, shall grow all manner of trees for meat, whose leaf shall not fade, neither shall the fruit thereof be consumed: it shall bring forth new fruit according to its months because their waters they issued out of the sanctuary: and the fruit thereof shall be for meat, and the leaf thereof shall be for medicine."* (for bruises and sores i.e. a remedy-Strong's concor.) Ezekiel 47:42. Is it not true that the mercy of the Lord endures forever? There are a vast innumerable number of souls that transcend the white throne judgment who are judged according to their works and whose names are not found written in the Book of Life. Has God condemned them all forever or does there remain the possibility of corrective judgment and the application of a potential remedy? I believe the answer to be yes.

As we have seen, Satan is bound for a thousand years (what ever that period may precisely represent) and after that he is loosed for a little season and he sponsors a great rebellion against the Lord and the company of the saints. Gog and Magog represent the heathen nations, which are deceived by him and join in the rebellion. This does not preclude the possibility or should I say the probability, that out from that vast company of lost souls there have been multitudes that have partaken of spiritual healing. As with Ezekiel chapters 38 and 39 the events spoken of in the context, it is my belief that these events happen after the millennium, and not at the end of this age. Likewise Ezekiel's prophecies also address with subject matter and issues that transpire during this period. It is needful to interject here again that the concept of the millennium (a supposed thousand year period) is a theological term. It is not a term drawn from the Scriptures but has been assumed by the reference to a "thousand years" at Revelation 20:6. This is the only place in Scripture that the designation is made and it could be used for the purpose of providing some perspective on a period yet future in which events will occur, but are not related to a framework of time as we understand it in this present world. We know that in the new havens and earth there will be no sun for the Lamb shall be the light of it. (See Rev.21: 21). We measure our days and nights and seasons by the activities of the sun and the moon, There will not be a sun in that future reality, only a Son. Because if our finite minds we cannot grasp all of the concepts of the eternal state. Because our reference point has always been in time, so the millennium is only used as a tool to help us understand that a period is involved, and we know not how long it lasts because it is in a perspective beyond time.

Our topic of consideration here in this segment is ministry in the age to come. What becomes of those who do not partake of the first resurrection? *"And death and hell were cast into the lake of fire. This is the second death."* (Revelation 20:14). Death is not annihilation. It is separation. When we die physically our souls and spirits are separated from the body and we can no longer relate to the earthly environment, we will continue to exist in some state. The second death is a separation of the inward parts of our being (soul and spirit) from the life of the Lord, hence we are spiritually dead. Our God is the God of life and His desire is to restore life and preserve life in accordance with his purposes. We would or should be exercised to at all costs avoid the second death that we might live in his presence. The following Scriptures teach us the conditions of the covenant he has made and how we may confidently enter into the kingdom as living souls.

These Prophets

The following Scriptures re cited to demonstrate that being counted worthy to be blessed in the first resurrection and to reign as priests with Christ is conditioned upon our faith, and our continuance in that unwavering steadfast faith. The goal and the prize is to enter the kingdom. *"And I say unto that many shall come from the east and the west, and shall sit down with Abraham, and Isaac, and Jacob in the kingdom of heaven. But the children of the kingdom shall be cast out onto outer darkness: there shall be weeping and gnashing of teeth."* (Matthew 8:11-12). *"The Son of man shall send forth his angels and they shall gather out of his kingdom all things that offend, and them which do iniquity, and shall cast them into a furnace of fire: there shall be wailing and gnashing of teeth. Then shall the righteous shine forth as the sun in the kingdom of their father. Who has ears to hear let him hear."* (Mattew 13:42-43). *"For other foundation can no man lay than that is laid, which is Jesus Christ. Now if any man build upon that foundation gold, solver, precious tones, wood, hay, stubble, every man's work shall be made manifest: for the day will declare it, because it shall be revealed by fire: and the fire shall try every man's work of what sort it is. If any man's work shall abide which he has built thereupon, he shall receive a reward. If any man's work shall be burned, he shall suffer loss: but he himself shall be saved: yet so as by fire. Know ye not that ye are the temple of God and that the Spirit of God dwelleth in you? If any man defiles the temple of God, him will God destroy: for the temple of God is holy which temple ye are. Let no man deceive himself. If any man among you seems to be wise in this world, let him become a fool, that he may be wise."* (I Cor. 3: 11-18)). *"For this you know that no whoremonger, or unclean person, nor covetous man, who is an idolater, have any inheritance in the kingdom of Christ and of God. Let no man deceive you with vain words: for because of these things cometh the wrath of God on the children of disobedience. Be not ye therefore partakers with them. For ye were sometimes darkness, but now are ye light in the Lord: walk as children of light."* (Ephesians 5:5-7).

"If we sin willfully after receiving a knowledge of the truth there remaineth no more sacrifice for sin, but a certain fearful looking for of judgment and fiery indignation which shall devour the adversaries. He who despised Moses' law died without mercy under two or three witnesses. Of how much sorer punishment suppose ye, shall he thought worthy: who

hath trodden under foot the Son of God, and hath counted the blood of the covenant, wherewith he was sanctified an unholy thing, and hath dome despite unto the Spirit of grace? For we know Him that has said, vengeance belongeth to me, I will recompense, saith the Lord. And again the Lord shall judge His people" (Hebrews 10:26-30). *"For Christ hath also hath once suffered for sins, the just for the unjust, that He might bring us to God, being put to death in the flesh, but quickened by the Spirit: By which also He went and preached unto the spirits in prison: which sometime were disobedient, when once the long suffering of God waited in the days of Noah, while the ark was preparing . . .* (II Peter 3: 19-20). *"For this cause was the gospel preached also to them that are dead, that they might be judged according to men in the flesh, but live according to God in the Spirit."* (II Peter 4:6). *"Wherefore he saith, when He ascended up on high, he led captivity captive, and gave gifts unto men, now that he ascended, what is it but that he also descended first into the lower parts of the earth? He that descended is the same that ascended up above all heavens, that he might fulfill all things"* (Ephesians 4: 8-10). *"And you who were sometimes alienated and enemies in your mind by wicked works, yet now hath he reconciled, in the body of his flesh through death, to present your body as unblameable and unreproveable in his sight: If you continue in the faith grounded and settled, and be not moved away from the hope of the gospel, which you have heard, and which was preached to every creature which is under heaven: wherefore I Paul am made a minister."* (Colossians 1: 21-23), and *"looking diligently lest any man fail of the grace of God: lest any root of bitterness springing up trouble you, and thereby many be defiled: lest there be any fornicator, or profane person, as Esau who for one morsel of meat sold his birthright. For you know that how afterward, when he would have inherited the blessings, he was rejected: for he found no place of repentance, though he sought it carefully with tears."* (Hebrews 12: 15-17).

Many other like Scriptures could also be cited. So why then has effort been taken to cite these Scriptures? Because there is in the Christian community at large, doctrines, which have been authored by men, which have led to the deception of multitudes of those who have been born of the Spirit. In its simple form these doctrines and teachings in application state that having been born again is equal to salvation, i.e. being "saved". Being born again is a spiritual event, which brings about regeneration. Salvation is the necessary spiritual process, which must follow and accompany this new birth. We have been admonished in the Scripture to *"work out our own salvation with fear and trembling for it is God who works within us both to will and do His good pleasure"*. This was written by the apostle Paul in his epistle to the Philippians. Will we reign with Christ and become a people who will exercise the reality of **A Kingdom o Priests**, or will we judged with the unbelievers?

Now hear the conclusion of the parable of the wedding: *"And when the king came in to see the guests, he saw there a man who had not on a wedding garment: And he sauth unto him, friend, How camest thou in hither not having a wedding garment? And he was speechless. Then said the king to the servants, bind him hand and foot and take him away, and cast him into outer darkness, there shall be weeping and gnashing of teeth, For many are called but few are chosen."* (Matthew 22: 11-14), and *"And behold, I come quickly, and my reward is with me, to give every man according as his work shall be. Blessed is he that do his commandments that they might have right to the tree of live, and may enter in through the gates into the city."* (Revelation 22:12-14). These will be the ministers and priests of God to reign with him in his kingdom administering judgment, justice, righteousness, and truth for those who have failed of the grace of God.

Remember beloved that we have established that there is more than one resurrection and it is incumbent that each one endure and persevere in faith to be blessed in the first resurrection. And so we emphasis again what Paul has warned, "If *by any means I might attain unto the resurrection* (this word in the Greek—*exanstasis*—literally the resurrection out from among the dead. (See Vine's New Testament Word Studies) of *the dead. Not as though I had already attained, either were already perfect: but I follow after, if that I may apprehend that for which also I am apprehended of Christ Jesus. Brethren, I count not myself to have apprehended: but this one thing I do, forgetting those things which are behind, and reaching forth unto those things which are before, I press towards the mark for the prize of the high calling of God in Christ Jesus."* (Philippians 3: 11-14).

Epilogue

Hopefully by the time you have reached this portion you have read the full text of the topically divided treatise, which precedes these final thoughts and considerations. Because of the nature and complexity of the various elements of the subject matter it has seemed to the writer that it would be fitting to add this rather lengthy addendum to further support the developments of the fulfillment of the prophetic Scriptures by tracking past, and current events in the secular world with a view to understanding how those events are related. These include both applications which are currently unfolding in America as well as the world at large. Many of the readers may already have some knowledge concerning the emerging **New World Order**, and if you do you are steps ahead in grasping world events as they play out in front of all of us. The coming world government, which is being orchestrated by certain groups and networks of the world's elite, is in fact a vast conspiracy, which is being carried out in concert with the god of this world, i.e. Satan. Major world events and changes are not the product of chance, but are in fact well planned and manipulated through the control of the world's monetary systems of fiat currencies as the first instance of causation, and then secondarily, the control of the geopolitical world and it's acting leaders and politicians by using the control of the monetary system as a primary tool. There are two of the basic components to the conspiracy. First with the control of the fiat money system resulting in the creation of massive national debt as well a personal debt. Then, subsequently through the control of geopolitical power bringing nations into subservience ultimately with the objective of controlling the entire world. To gain further insights into the history and operation of the fraudulent money system, which controls not only America but most of the world, the writer recommends the reading of *The Creature from Jekyll Island* by G. Edward Griffin, which will prove to be a very valuable resource in gaining an understanding of these issues. This epilogue will include a vast array of factors leading us inevitably to the formation of a one world government. Included will be examinations of the current world system viewed from the financial, historic, geopolitical, legal, religious, and even cultural developments.

Since most who will read this treatise are United States citizens; it is fitting that we should take America as an example and initial focal point of our considerations. We need to track the progressive destruction of this once great Republic, which was originally conceived and formed by men of honor who sought to lay a foundation for enduring freedom through personal responsibility with the provision of a limited republican form of government through the original organic Constitution, and subsequent Bill of Rights. What they began has been defiled, debased, and destroyed almost completely, First by the destruction of the Republic itself via the Fourteenth Amendment, which was put into place after the so-called Civil War. It was ratified by coercion and force by the corrupt central government in Washington D. C. It's effect was to destroy not only the sovereignty of the individual republic states, but also the sovereignty of citizens . . . And then through progressive steps of political, economic and legislative deterioration leading up to the Federal Reserve Act of 1913, wherein the international banking cartel gained complete monetary control of America. This gave monetary and fiscal control of the country to an international banking cartel who became the lender of last resort. The Fourteenth Amendment had previously mandated the payment of the national debt without remedy. This, in turn precipitated the subsequent bankruptcy via the Federal Reserve Act made possible the enslavement of America through the Emergency Banking Relief Act of March 9, 1933 (48 Stat.1, Public Law 89-719) and finalized by the abrogation of constitutional specie(gold and silver)with House

Joint Resolution (HJR 192). This was the complete abrogation of the gold and silver coinage standard established in the Constitution. The international bankruptcy was orchestrated and declared by the United States under the influence of the internationally controlled Federal Reserve System who became the creditor and beneficiary of all payments. Soon to pass in conjunction with this fraud was the Sixteenth Amendments requiring an income tax which is not supported by the Constitution and which was never lawfully gratified by the states. See Bill Benson's book—The Law that Never Was. This enslaved the American population to the continuing tyranny of the Federal government and monetary control.

Politically the citizens of the several states, which originally were sovereign countries prior to the addition of the Fourteenth Amendment to the Constitution implemented in July of 1868.became subjects and citizens of Washington D.C. By virtue of this unratified Amendment each individual became a United States citizen. (A concept in total contradiction to the Organic Constitution). This resulted in the progressive increase of power and federal control over the once sovereign states as well as "citizens" both politically and ultimately economically as well. The states (countries) of the American Union lost their sovereignty as free and independent states and the individual citizens also lost their sovereign status through the provisions of this contrived 14th Amendment. A new citizenship was established subjecting the people to this new jurisdiction gained neither legally, or lawfully. The war designated as the Civil War was in reality the second war of independence. A recommended reading is *The Red Amendment, L.B. Bork, 2007 edition*, which will thoroughly educate one on the subject of the destruction of the American Republic, including its cause and effect. These facts have virtually escaped the comprehension of the American people. This became a progression of ever increasing political dominance leading up to the capture of complete control of the monetary system, and the subsequent bankruptcy as we have stated above. The banking elitists in gaining control pf the monetary power then affected the seizure of gold and the issuance of Federal Reserve Notes, which are simply evidences of debt. This progressive political and economic coup has resulted in the confiscation of all of the real wealth of America via the Federal Reserve Act (1913) and the subsequent bankruptcy (1933) being placed under the control of the Federal Reserve system (an international banking cartel) and thus placing the laws and monetary policy under the control of an even greater international worldwide banking cartel, which includes the Federal Reserve, the Bank of England, Central Banks of Europe, Bank of Japan, The International Monetary Fund, The World Bank, The Bank of International Settlement et al. These international bankers have likewise stolen the real wealth of most of western civilization and much of the rest of the world with their fiat money scheme and counterfeit paper currencies, which represent debt and which have no intrinsic value. By the declared bankruptcy via the Emergency Banking Relief Act of March 9, 1933 and subsequent seizure of Constitutional specie through House Joint Resolution HJR192 of June 5, 1933. Americans have been deprived of their lawful and Constitutional status as citizens of the Republic. They have also been robbed of their financial independence and wealth through the introduction of a counterfeit currency, i.e. the dollar. represented by Federal Reserve Notes is not money, but rather the evidence of debt.

Socialism cane to America through the subsequent "New Deal" legislation, and numerous other socialistic legislative acts such as the Social Security Act, the "Great Society", Medicare, the Patriot Act, Obamacare, as well as many others, and they have progressively taken control of the land, real property rights, many personal property rights, and natural resources, as well as most of our freedoms. The citizens of this new *American Empire* cannot protest the debt for they are bound to it through the provisions of the Fourteenth Amendment, Article 4, and the sworn affirmation of their status (see your IRS 1040 form for the text of your sworn affirmation as a United States citizens). The people have now become unwittingly nothing more than **human resources** and debt slaves having lost their sovereignty and freedom. It is amazing that they are oblivious to this relity.

They are now bound to the servicing of the created debt, which is impossible to pay. The American people are now and have been for decades the debt slaves of the privately owned international Federal

Reserve System and its association with an international cartel of central banks, which has created un-payable debt through the endless printing of fiat currency and the resulting transfer of the repayment of the debt to the American people via the 14th Amendment. Through its agencies, including the International Monetary Fund, whose governing officer is the Secretary of the United States Treasury Department, and employing as its collection arm, the Internal Revenue Service (IRS) bringing the nation as a whole, and each United States citizen under the bondage of an un-playable debt and the resulting enslavement to this masterful "ponzi scheme". The admitted debt is now more than twenty-one trillion dollars increasing by multiplied millions every hour . . . And this does not include the multiplied and untold trillions in contingency and entitlement obligations, pensions, etc., which are unsustainable and in fact are also un-payable. These fraudulent "money" schemes, as Federal Reserve Notes are not money, but only evidences of debt are doomed to collapse. The Federal Reserve Act, was legislated as the brainchild of an international banking cartel, was passed by a corrupted Congress, (see *The Creature from Jekyl Island*, G. Edward Griffin), which had one goal in mind; to control by design and then to economically enslave America and ultimately the entire world. The Federal Reserve is international in scope and vast amounts of the "bailout money (TARP), the so-called stimulus packages and other legislative actions were utilized internationally by this cartel of elitist and extremely wealthy Jewish banking families. Americans have become the borrowers and debtors through this fraudulent agency and the corruption of their alleged elected representatives in Congress. Through this carefully planned and orchestrated scheme the controlling "money" powers have effectively destroyed the precepts of American freedom.

    A people under the bondage of debt, even though it has been instigated by fraud, cannot be free and the borrower will always be the servant of the lender. America is now hopelessly enslaved and has no options for its recovery apart from a total uprising of the population to overthrow this criminal operation, which controls the country. It would become necessary in the same manner, and for the some basic reasons as was undertaken in the American Revolution against the tyranny of England. This is not likely to happen, even though the seeds of revolution are in the air. The writer realizes that this course of action os not even possible until a significant number of people prepared to undertake a revolution it would not be successful. Also there are only small percentage of the people who have any real understanding of what has happened to them. If the tide of internal revolution does occur it will be at the loss of millions of lives and the final demise of the nation.

The receipt of the distribution of government "benefits" controls many, if not most. About fifty percent of Americans receive some sort of government assistance. We are even now on the course to a certain final total collapse of the economy, which is a planned event by those in control. The dollar cannot remain as the world's reserve currency and a new monetary system will come into being at the appropriate time as determined by the world planners. The implementation of a more universal international currency is the next goal of the Bank of International Settlement under Basil III. The goal of the money elite is world government, which is progressively being formed. There has occurred a recent power shift in the international monetary arena towards China. We are very likely to soon experience a worldwide currency revaluation removing the dollar as the world's reserve currency. That may even be the case by the time this book goes into publication. Currency wars are ongoing internationally and there is resistance to the dollar retaining its status. Possibly communist China could become the controlling dynasty to finalize a world government. We do not know but we will most certainly be looking at anew word currency in the not distant future.

They call it the New World Order, *Novus Ordo Seclorum* (Announcing the New Order of the Ages). Observe the seal on the back of a dollar bill depicting the occult symbol of the great pyramid of Giza and the all seeing eye of the evil one as becoming the capstone. It is in your face, and it is in fact the progressive manifestation of the fourth beast of Daniel's dream and visions, and that same beast, which being affirmed by the Apostle John as seen rising up out of the sea having seven heads and ten horns in Revelation chapter thirteen. This will be more completely realized as world events continue according to the plans of those who are controlled by the "principalities and powers" of darkness. The world government plan, agenda and system is Luciferian in cause and effect.

America has been the driving engine of this emerging new order of the ages . . . The powerful and wealthy elitists operating behind the scenes have controlled the presidents, elections, and the Congress for decades using America's influence, fiat money, and military might to do their bidding internationally in the overthrow of nations, including the Moslem nations of Iraq, Afghanistan, Libya, and Egypt, to name just a few with the dual purpose of gaining both political and monetary control and ultimately regional consolidations realizing total dominion, as is symbolized by the ten toes interpreted by Daniel the prophet in explaining Nebuchadnezzar's dream. The demise of Iran and Syria will be necessary to bring those nations under the control of the Zionist elite. We are currently observing the activities of ISIS in a terrorist attempt to overthrow Syria, but since the Russians have intervened there it will require a new initiative. Do not be deceived into thinking this is a spontaneous uprising of radical Islam to establish a caliphate. It has much more to-do with destabilizing the Middle East on behalf of Israel and its sponsors and funding comes from the United States and Zionist interests. The training and supplies for their activities involve both the CIA and the Israeli Mossad. It is a foregone conclusion that Iran is on the list of targeted nations and that either by military action initiated by Israel, the United States, or both, or through sanctions of isolation these nations must also be destabilized. A mew major war in the region is imminent for Syria and Iran must become defeated nations according to the Zionist plans.

Russia represents a very real adversary and the ongoing conflict over the Middle East and could very well be a trigger point to a third world war. A central purpose involves the preservation of Israel; and ultimately the planned destabilization and/or control of all of the Moslem nations of the Middle East. The American military power has been nothing more than a lackey servant and pawn which has been used by the Zionist banking and "money" power structure through America's corrupt and compromised presidents and Congress to enslave and control the nations. Do you believe that any of those conflicts in the Middle East have anything to do whatsoever with defending your freedom? Of course, people in the military as well as the population as a whole have been brainwashed by the controlled media into believing that they are the protectors of America's freedom, and are waging this endless "war on terrorism" in the interest of "national security" and the preservation of our "freedom.". In fact, they are only a tool of the world banking elite to assist in bringing about their preconceived world control. If you believe that America is still a free country, then you are living in the other world of a carefully created illusion. America has been taken captive financially and politically and has become a nation of debt slaves being manipulated, used and totally controlled by deception and even now we are living under all ten planks of the Communist Manifesto.

By simply reading the Communist Manifesto, and comparing it to today's political and economic realities one can easily document this proclaimed fact. Wake up America, and especially wake up Christians if you still believe we are living in "the land of the free and the home of the brave", and of you believe the theological lie that America has a God ordained purpose in the protection of Israel. You have been effectively deceived by your doctrine favoring an earthly kingdom for the "chosen people". While the politicians have sworn an oath to preserve and defend the united States Constititution, they only give lip service to it and have found loopholes to skirt around it (See Article I, Section 8, clause 17 of the Constitution), in which is made provision for another UNITED STATES, a corporation originating from Washington D.C, which operates as a legislative democracy instead of in the founders' intent in the formation of a Constitutional Republic. In this venue virtually every act of legislation that is passed is in direct opposition to the limited and delegated powers of the original tenets of the Constitution. The Constitution delegated nineteen specific and enumerated powers to the Federal government, **nothing more**. It obviously has exercised power and tyranny over virtually everything.

Other tools of the elitists in accomplishing the enslavement of the United States citizens has been the "brainwashing" through the controlled main stream media, and a carefully planned and executed "dumbing down" of the population through the public educational system, both of which are dictated by the existing de facto political system of the corporation and its international masters. Why is it that many, if not most of those graduating from high school cannot read at a fifth or sixth grade level, and have been deprived of the knowledge necessary to understand history and the legitimate function of government in a free society? America has become a nation of poorly educated as well as deceived people because the system has carefully planned, purposed and then programmed them to obey the concepts of submission to a system of collectivism conceived by the elitist government's dictates and regulations. Since knowledge is power, the people are destroyed by the absence of it; *My people are destroyed for lack of knowledge,* (Hosea 4:6), and in this truth lay the foundation for all tyranny and ultimately the coming planned world totalitarianism.

President Barak Obama was not only devoted to Islam; he was also a very far left socialist i.e. embracing Marxism, educated and mentored by Frank Marshall Davis, an avowed communist and political activist, which facts can be easily documented if you care to do the research. All of the available information points to the likelihood that he is not an American citizen. Maybe he does not need to be a citizen in conformity to the original organic Constitution because he was actually the CEO of a corporation known as the UNITED STATES. This is true also our current President Donald Trump . . . The UNITED STATES was incorporated on February 21, 1871. You do not live in a country. You are a sub corporation of a foreign owned corporation. You will note that you are addressed in all official government documents or banking transactions as an all capital letter artificial person, i.e. JOHN Q DOE. If you have any awareness of what is going on you will remember that there has been considerable debate about Obama's birth certificate issue, some of it even reaching into the controlled media outlets, so we are only reporting facts that have already been a part of public debate, and the law suits which have reached the Supreme Court. His directives and influence originated with the Zionist elitists who controlled him along with the majority of the key members of the United States Senate and House of Representatives. Many of our elected and appointed officials and representatives are bought and paid for with bribes and payoffs for 'earmarks" obtained through the corporate and special interests that operate in concert with the government, and through their lobbying efforts to bring about legislation, which is drafted for the benefit of these special interests, and the further promotion of the principles of collectivism. Obamacare (the Affordable Care Act) is a great example of socialist control of the population. If you are at all an informed citizen, you know that these things are true and can be documented. If you can get elected to Congress, to allegedly serve as a representative of the people, you will have an opportunity to retire with considerable wealth for besides their handsome salaries and perks, these people are further enriched and compensated by the corporate lobbyists, given special privileges, insider trading opportunities, and are exempt from many of the unconstitutional laws which they pass. This results in the progressive deterioration of any freedom that might still remain, while they continue to enslave the citizens with endless laws, regulations and schemes of debt and taxation, as well as, the systematic extraction of their sustenance and potential wealth. Many powerful lobbyists and special interest groups control the Washington D. C. 'swamp'. Principle among them is AIPAC. This is the American Israel Political Acton Committee, Congressman sign a pledge to support without question the actions and initiative of Israel and if you refuse to sign on you will not be reelected.

 Barak Obama with the assistance of Hillary Clinton has orchestrated the "Arab Spring", completed a war unilaterally in Libya with the assistance of NATO and overthrew Gadhafi without any Congressional approval. Other Arab nations along with Libya were once sovereign with Libya having its own monetary system backed by gold, no debt and considerable wealth, but now itis another puppet of the emerging world order, the International Monetary Fund, United Nations, et al. This was accomplished without the approval of Congress, and then accomplished through the mass murder of thousands of innocent Libyans. Wars now can be initiated unilaterally by the President with no Congressional authority. The Libyan government had to be overthrown as did the government in Iraq simply because their national monetary system was operating independent of the control of the International Monetary Fund and the international banking cartel. These actions also utilized NATO, which is nothing more than a transnational organization of the power elite to bring about preconceived geopolitical results. Have you recently taken time to read the Declaration of Independence? Are these not the actions of the powers of a dictator refusing to submit to the interests and freedoms of the American public? What has happened to the Constitutional system of checks and balances? The American public at large sits idly by, for the most part without any clue as to what is actually happening. Many of them are just waiting for their next benefit check or issue of food stamps. As a bankrupt government those checks and "benefits" will not continue forever, or even far into the future and government agencies such as the EPA and the FDA are progressively regulating away the freedoms and options for economic survival of all Americans and their ability to provide a reasonable living for their families. These draconian regulations are often carried out without the passing of any legislative authorization from the Congress; enforcing them through regulations and bureaucrats, absent of any due process of law and certainly without the consent of the people.

Why will the Federal government not enforce the immigration laws and protect the borders of the country from the invasion of multiplied millions of illegal immigrants who are streaming over our borders, which is their most basic Constitutional mandate? We are now working on amnesty to be brought about through the legislative acts of the corrupted Congress. The cost of these illegal foreign aliens to the state governments is overwhelming the states financially. They cannot pay their debts, and do not have the powers of money creation available to the Federal government through the Federal Reserve. A large contributing factor is the huge costs and expenses to the state governments in welfare support, medical, educational, and other benefits provided to these people who are here illegally, and these benefits are mandated by an out of control government. Municipal bonds will soon become worthless pieces of paper held by investors because the states, cities and municipalities are likewise becoming bankrupt and will have no ability to honor these obligations. There is a reason why the federal government will not exercise its mandate constitutionally to protect the nation's borders. It is because the plan is to regionalize America along with Canada and Mexico, destroying the sovereign borders and ultimately the sovereignty of these individual nations (see the Communist Manifesto), and will merge them into the North American Union, and thus into one region of the New World Order. The operation of fiat money has progressively destroyed the sovereignty of the states bringing them under the control of federalism and ultimately internationalism. Through this process and the financial destruction of the nation, America in union with Mexico and Canada will become one of the ten world regional governments, which also answers to the ten toes revealed in Nebuchadnezzar's image and the ten-horned beast of Daniel's and John's prophecies.

When America collapses under the burden of un-playable debt and the political and social structure breaks down completely it will be relatively easy to merge it with these countries into a union, and set up a new monetary and political system. Make no mistake the model for this revolution is contained within the plan for **international communism, Agenda 21** being orchestrated by the **United Nations**. You might want to pick up a copy of **Agenda 21** and read it, and see what the international elite have in store for you. It is being progressively planned and systematically implemented by those occult powers, which control the financial system as well as the political leaders of the majority of the world simply because of the control exercised through the fiat money system, which in reality is only worthless paper representing debt. The United Nations **Agenda 21** is the blueprint for world government based on communistic principles and ultimate total control or the world's financial and political systems. They call it "sustainable development" and it is well advanced in implementation. This will ultimately lead to the universal nark of the beast!!. This is the most colossal and far reaching fraud ever perpetrated in the history of the world. So much has been said for the progressive demise of the once free American Republic.

Looking at the larger picture internationally, it becomes clear that the **United Nations** and its various agencies provide the fundamental framework for world government. While it may seem to be behind the scenes and largely impotent this de facto communistic world body is assisting in the issues, directives and the resolutions, which are changing and molding the world into a unified whole, destroying national sovereignty and individual liberty. It has the power to shape conflicts and by resolution bring about the predetermined political and economic results desired by the international power elitists as it works in concert with the International Monetary Fund and World Bank, and ultimately the Bank of International Settlement in Basil, Switzerland. The elitists having control of these institutions, and are able to enslave nations and take control of their assets by virtue of the conditions placed on the credits and loans they receive. Again, the borrower will always be the servant of the lender. (Proverbs 22:7). Believers have been admonished by the Word of God to *owe no man anything save to love him for he that loves his brother has fulfilled the law.* (Rom. 13:8). Is it not true that the vast numbers of Americans have been enslaved by credit card debt, i.e. the creation of "money" out of nothing? This processes us ongoing, (Federal Reserve programs, QE 1, 2, and 3) and debt is the principal mode of enslavement in this international scheme to gain control of the entire world. The money is valueless international credits, unbacked by anything of substance, which really represent debt having no intrinsic worth, but at the same time being used as the sustenance for nations and the currencies of international trade. This is controlled by the Illuminati with its diverse network of associated groups including the Trilateral Commission, the Counsel on Foreign Relations, The Royal Institute for International Affairs, (Britain), the Bilderberg Group, the Skull and Bones Society (both Bush's and John Kerry), the CIA and many other organizations and secret societies. Yes, the United States CIA is a secret society contrived and performing murder, revolution, assassinations, and political unrest worldwide, as well as sponsoring and implementing insurgencies around the world through subterfuge. There are countless other known and unknown secret groups, organizations and entities sharing a common purpose and goal, and that being a one world government.

These objectives will be realized more completely as they bring about the consolidation of regional geopolitical units, which will total ten in number. The European Union, which I believe will soon become (after the collapse of the current coalition and the Euro) the "United States of Europe" due to the impending created debt crisis and the North American Union assisted by the American financial debt crises. The results will be just two of those ten regions to be subsequently joined by an African Union, a South American Union, an Asian Union, etc., until the ten toed image of Nebuchadnezzar's dream has been realized.

The precursors to these unions are being formed as regional agreements controlling commerce and trade are put in place as these predetermined geopolitical regions are yet in the process of being formed. The precursor to the North American Union is the NAFTA trade agreement brought into being during the presidential administration of Bill Clinton, and the current impending and unsolvable debt debacle the banking elite have imposed upon America. Remember there is also an overriding World Trade Agreement through the World Trade Organization (WTO). These international trade agreements deal with much more than just commerce. The eventually override the sovereignty of nations. Watch commerce, international trade agreements, inevitable changes in world currencies, and watch as these regional geopolitical and economic entities come into being for they signal the revelation and ultimate complete manifestation of the fourth beast of Daniel's prophesies, and the prophetic revelations of the Apostle John. The time is growing short as Mystery Babylon is already in active manifestation to engulf and control the entire world.

It is necessary to understand some further purposes in this quest for a unified power and enslavement of the entire world for it is always in relation to the mind and purpose of the evil one. Satan, the god of this world system, as he seeks to consolidate the world into a unified whole so that he may stand up through the agency of the Antichrist in the place of God and require worship of himself through a unified and undivided worldwide devotion. *"And all that dwell upon the earth shall worship him, whose names are not written in the book of life of the Lamb slain from the foundation of the world."* (Rev.13:8.) How will this unification come about? As the Lord removes his restraint through the power of the Holy Spirit the wicked one will then be revealed. The conflict is ultimately spiritual in nature as Lucifer strives to obtain his ascendancy over mankind. Please read the second chapter of II Thessalonians verses 1-12 for a further commentary and understanding of this concept. The Antichrist will be a Jew (again, I am mot anti-Semitic as God is not a respecter of persons) as we have previously recounted from chapter eleven of Daniel's prophecies at verses 36 and 37.

The people behind the formation of this world government are also primarily very wealthy Jewish Zionists and they engage large numbers of lackey political Gentile and economic puppets to assist them along with their own Zionist elitists to carry out much of their work in the governments and financial structures of the nations. Thy are Ashkenazi "Jews" which is an assumed identity because they have embraced Orthodox Judaism based on the Babylonian Talmud and the mystical writings of the Kabballah. They are not Jews (Sephardic) based on possessing the progeny and DNA of Abraham, Isaac and Jacob. But take note of how many of these Zionists are in the high political offices of the United States. The chairman of he Federal Reserve Board has been a Jew (Zionist) for decades. The Secretary of the Treasury (who is also the governor of the International Monetary Fund) is Jewish. These people, even if not ethnic Jews are co-conspirators and they are all Zionists promoting the Zionist agenda for world government. You must understand that they completely control America, and ultimately intend to destroy it. Also, it is a fact that these people have controlled the presidency of the United States for Society, a secret society of the occult, and so was his father George W. Bush as well as his grandfather Senator Prescott Bush. The initiation into Skull and Bones at Yale University involves lying naked in a coffin and ceremonially swearing an oath to serve Satan. George Bush is no Christian despite the fact that he was able to deceive the vast majority of Christian evangelicals that he was "born again". But please understand that it is not just because they are either Jewish or are controlled by or in support of this Jewish agenda that I state these things, for I repeat myself, I am not anti-Semitic, but recognize that a Jewish elite is behind the manipulation of world events. And while I have nothing against those who have been born Jewish per se, likewise, the Lord is not a respecter of persons. All Jews are not Zionists and all Zionists are not Jews. Large numbers of Jewish people will fall victim to this internationally orchestrated Zionist movement, which is in the hands of a relatively small number of extremely wealthy elitist Jews engaged in sorcery and the ancient rights, symbolism and religious practices of ancient Egypt, and ancient Babylon. Their guiding documents are the Protocols of the Learned Elders of Zion, the Babylonian Talmud, and the Kabbalah derived from ancient Babylon It is a revival of, or more accurately, a continuation of the same "ancient wisdom", which has never changed, and these "illuminated" ones are the sworn servants of Satan seeking to exalt him and cause him to be worshipped as god. They are also Zionists seeking as their ultimate goal the return to power and dominion of the nation and land of a "Greater Israel" believing in their deception that they are the "chosen people", the "Master Race", if you will. They claim that they have the right to hold dominion over the earth, and to do so through the power of Antichrist who they will ultimately proclaim to be their messiah. If you think that all of this is just a "conspiracy theory", I would urge you to read The Protocols of the Learned Elders of Zion, which were written over a century ago, and which contains documented proof, and through which each individual protocol explains the different elements of the Zionist plan for world government. You can find these Protocols on the Internet, as well as other places, www.freedomlaw.com, or through a web search. Their methods and belief systems are satanically inspired, deceptively conceived, and those things are kept in deep secrecy among those who are the initiates into the highest degrees of the Masonic Order (32nd degree and beyond), including the Illuminati and many other occult secret societies and organizations such as Skull and Bones, which was the Bush connection. There is a vast network of these secret societies and organizations. They have secret signs; symbols, practices and oaths, and they indeed answer to and are identified as Mystery (secretive) Babylon (pagan and occultist) as described in chapter seventeen and eighteen of the Revelation. The role of the nation of Israel is played out as a masterpiece of deception before the peoples of the earth for many have some sense that there may be a special destiny for that land and the Jewish people gathered there. These deceptions will assist in the advancement and completion of the false and counterfeit earthly Zionist movement. Obtain at major booksellers and read my other title The Israel Deception.

Zionism is the belief in the restoration of the Jews in their native land and the bringing into political and religious power, authority, dominance and control of those ethnic and national people in direct relation to the ancient land of Israel. Please study and read again the later verses of Daniel chapter eleven beginning with verse thirty-six and continuing to the end of the chapter. Yes, tiny Israel, the *"little horn"* through the Antichrist has a dramatic role to play in the unfolding of events before, and into the tribulation period. But it is not as a people, who are in the favor of or covenant relationship with the Lord, but rather those who are under the power and deception of the evil one, and which will untimely include the vast majority of all the peoples of the earth. These are hard things to be understood, and complicated by the fact that most of the Christian community has been taught that Jesus Christ is going to return to reign on the throne of David over an earthly kingdom from geographic Israel and Jerusalem for a period of one thousand years. This flies in the face of the prophets as we have previously expounded. The false and deceptive theological conclusions, which have been accepted as truth by many in the religious world, and many of those who would identify themselves as Christians, must be overcome.

The major purpose in the writing of this prophetic treatise is to clarify and bring to an understanding these vital truths, and bring them to light as we approach the end of the age. Satan, his army of demons, and the powers of darkness have deceived many—no, probably *almost* everyone. When the Antichrist rises in ascendancy the multitudes are going to wonder after him believing that he is the Christ. The Devil is the father of lies and the master of all deception. We are provided in Matthew's gospel chapter twenty- four and reading from verse twenty-three through verse twenty-eight a warning given by the words of Jesus concerning the appearance of Antichrist on the earth representing himself to be Christ.as that this will be a time of great deception for all of the peoples on the earth, including most in the religious world. We have previously established that the Church as a whole living on the earth at the time of the end will go though the three and one-half years (not seven) of great tribulation excepting the man child remnant of Revelation 12:1-5. If you have lingering doubts or questions concerning those things, which have been set forth in the prophetic portion of this treatise, I would encourage you to read again and study thoroughly certain of the appropriate topics covered in the text of this treatise, which I believe to have been clearly set forth and thoroughly supported by the Scriptures, and other documentation, and which through your concentrated attention will provide unanswered questions on these most important issues. Those of particular importance for review would include: Who is Israel? (for the purpose of understanding the covenants God has authored); Zionism (including the fallacy of so-called Christian Zionism); The Abomination of Desolation (when and how does the Antichrist manifest himself?); Daniel's Seventy Weeks (refuting and proving the fallacy of the contrived dispensational "gap" theory; The Little Horn (showing the role of political Israel at the end of the age); Measuring the Temple (detailing the testimony of the saints during the tribulation); Measuring the Temple— The Woman and the man–child (explaining how and why a faithful remnant out of the Church will escape the great tribulation); and the section covering Mystery Babylon (who is the Luciferian whore deceiving the nations and controlling the world?) These truths are vitally important if one is to stand in the evil day for each one must possess the wisdom and understanding to discern the truth and reject the lies. This wisdom will be given by the Holy Spirit to those whose hearts are faithful and undivided.

These Prophets

Barack Obama completed two terms as President of the United States. This is not a curious or unexpected outcome of the corrupt election process. He has faithfully executed his promise given before his election, i.e. the fundamental transformation of America. Obama is the selected one of the international masters and has done an exceptional job of carrying out their mandates for the planned destruction of America during the first term and even more so in the second term of his presidency. It is important that the population as a whole has the illusion of having a choice in selecting their leader and so the election process is carefully orchestrated as being a competition between competing political parties so that the election is accepted as a legitimate expression of the voice of the majority of the people. In fact both candidates from the alleged two different political parties have been pre- selected and the outcome of the election has also been predetermined. Abundant evidence of election fraud could be presented, but the fact is that the voting machines can so easily be programmed to produce a desired result. At least as concerning the electron of a president, the American people do not have any control of the outcome in spite of the fact that the illusion of "democracy" is carefully preserved. After the election it becomes clearer that many are not satisfied with the result albeit that there is nothing they can do about it. America is still largely asleep, and deceived, but notably many are awakening. It is not likely that there would ever be enough people rising up against the established system of government to completely overthrow it. Does America have the heart and will for a revolution? Only time will tell.

Barak Obama was an avowed communist and he was able to infiltrate the government with many like him to the great detriment of the people and the Constitution. Many acts which were unconstitutional were implemented by him through executive orders. These acts and actions in denial of freedom have transferred the country into a virtual communist dictatorship. Obamacare was his crowning effort of control enslaving many to the Affordable Care Act which is neither affordable nor does it provide much of effective care. It serves to enslave people through alleged medical care which then becomes another control mechanism. It is interesting that in spite of the many promises of the Republicans to repeal the legislation they failed. This is clear evidence that we in reality have a one party government which is corrupt throughout. The right of habeas corpus has been suspended in the National Defense Authorization Act passed at the end of 2011, and the implementation of police and military power has been prepared to deal with all who would stand against the emerging police state and federal tyranny.

Wars and rumors of wars will no doubt continue during the months and years ahead for Jesus himself prophesied them. We know the strife and chaos in the Middle East is an ongoing reality. There also exists the real possibility of international warfare involving the United States against Russia and/or China. These wars have strong implications for the shaping of world government. We have seen from Scripture that that last form of world dominance is in the form of regional governments and not sovereign nation states. Warfare may very well be the catalyst necessary to bring these ten regional units into existence. When we observe that phenomenon coming into place we will know of a certainty we are very near the end of this age. The signal event of the "abomination of desolation "spoken of by Daniel the prophet will inform us that the great tribulation is imminent. Then it will be three and one-half years measured to the end of the age and the coming in power of Jesus Christ, not to reign on the earth but rather to destroy it. He will not appear somewhere on the earth as his coming is in the clouds and form heaven. The Antichrist kingdom of world government is earthly. The kingdom of our Lord is heavenly so his coming is in the clouds together all who belong to him in truth. (See Matthew 24:29-31).

In conclusion we must summarize where we are at in he time of the writing and publication of this book. We have witnessed the election of Donald Trump on the numerous campaign promises to 'Make America Great Again'. He has tried to move forward on some of his campaign promises as he represented himself as an 'outsider'. He gained much support from Christian evangelicals and has experienced much resistance from the mainstream media which is totally corrupted with leftwing ideology. He has gained a certain base of popularity and is clearly a man of intelligence with ascertain degree of charisma. Whaatever positive things which could be said about him we must not be deceived . . . He is clearly demonstrating strong support of the Zionist agenda through several of his decisions . . . The designation of Jerusalem as the capitol of Israel is historic for that squares with what we covered in the closing verses of Daniel eleven. His formal rejection of the Iran nuclear deal and his general rhetoric as concerns Iran have strong Zionist overtones for Iran is the sworn enemy of Israel. On two occasions Trump has ordered missile sticks on Syria. These we based on 'lose flag' vents of alleged gas attacks by Assad on his own people. These allegations lack any substance or support in fact, but they indicate that the Trump administration is still acting in aggression against Syria. These actions are strong indications that there will be ongoing military activity in the Middle East on behalf of Israel as their objective are to establish a 'Greater Israel' and gain control of the entire region eventually dominating the entire world.

There is a great spiritual war in progress pitting the devil against the Almighty God and that "we wrestle not against flesh and blood, but against principalities, against powers, against the rulers of the darkness of this world, against spiritual wickedness in high places." (Ephesians 6:12). Antichrist will come with great subtlety appearing to be a world savior and hope for mankind. The masses of the people will be deceived by his unveiling and demonstration of the power of the dragon. The only hope of escaping his lies and deceptions will be based on ones' own faith and humility before God and a fervent commitment to the truths of the gospel of Jesus Christ. We cannot put a time frame on all of the developments of these evolving and ominous conditions, but clearly they are all in progress, and the Zionist agenda is well advanced and is most certain to come to pass based on the clear testimony of the Word of God.

*"Wherefore, beloved, seeing that you look for such things, be diligent that you may be found of Him in peace, without spot and blameless, and account that the longsuffering of our Lord is salvation: even as our beloved brother Paul also according to the wisdom given unto him has written unto you; as also in all of his epistles, speaking in them of these things; in which **are some things hard to be understood**, which they that are unlearned and unstable wrest, as they do also the other Scriptures, unto their own destruction. You, therefore beloved, knowing these things before beware lest you be led away with the error of the wicked fall from your own steadfastness, but grow in the grace and knowledge of our Lord and Savior Jesus Christ to whom be glory and honor both now and forever, Amen. (II Peter 3:14-18.).*

www.ingramcontent.com/pod-product-compliance
Ingram Content Group UK Ltd.
Pitfield, Milton Keynes, MK11 3LW, UK
UKHW022228230426
12048UKWH00016BA/1127